BIANCA'S VINEYARD

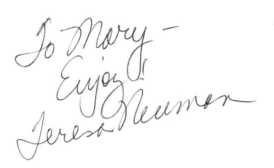

To Mary —
Enjoy it
Teresa Neuman

BIANCA'S VINEYARD

TERESA NEUMANN

ALL'S WELL HOUSE
LEBANON. OREGON

All's Well House
PO Box 2489
Lebanon, Oregon 97355
www.teresaneumann.com
www.biancasvineyard.com

ISBN: 978-0-9831210-0-8
Library of Congress Control Number: 2010916292

Cover/Book Design
Jennifer Omner, ALL Publications

To my mother-in-law, Babe.
It started with you, a true Bertozzi.

"Nowhere in all the land were there found women as beautiful as Job's daughters, and their father granted them an inheritance along with their brothers."—Job 42:15

La Famiglia
Bertozzi

Luigi & Carmela Bertozzi

Francesco	Egisto	Carilda	Alberto
Pia	Armida	Barlaam, Frediani	Augusta

Ario	Silverio	Rina	Loriana
Aladino	Violenza	Bice	Wanda
Lola		Lida	Stefano
		Bianca	

Danilo Corrotti
Renzo
Lucia

prologue

BIANCA CORROTTI MASSAGED her aching eighty-eight-year-old hip, squinted while she fumbled about for her glasses, and then read the time on her alarm clock: 3:13 a.m. She tucked her swollen feet into a pair of slippers and shuffled into her villa's cavernous entryway. Moonlight poured through tall, massive French doors and bounced off the white marble floor onto dozens of family photographs lining the ten-foot-high walls. Her throat tightened as she focused on the center frame, the one of her late husband Danilo. In his hand, he cradled a trophy awarded him by the Piaggio Company for his role in developing the Vespa motor scooter. Next to him was a portrait of their wedding. Having never thought of herself as beautiful due to a congenital hip deformity that caused her to walk with an awkward gait, she had avoided looking into the camera lens that day. Danilo, on the other hand, not in the least deterred by her handicap, had openly devoured her with his eyes.

She moved on to the oldest family photo of her collection. Taking off her glasses, she rubbed the sleep from her eyes and peered closely at the faces smiling back at her. Taken around 1920 outside the home where her mother Carilda Bertozzi had grown up, the serene facial expressions and relaxed demeanor of the Bertozzi clan were sure indicators that it was the month of October—the deliriously happy month of wine-making.

Only Uncle Egisto and his family in America were missing from the picture.

Bianca's eyes squeezed shut as she tried to remember how her mother's brother had looked the last time she had seen him. Though the heat in the foyer was oppressive, unwelcome memories sent a chill up her bent spine, so she stepped back, opened the doors leading out onto the empty Via Strettoia, and inhaled the thick night air. Across the street, directly above her, the old Bertozzi homestead was visible, its tiled roof jutting up over the top of an ancient olive grove on the lower slope of Monte di Ripa. To its right was Bianca's vineyard. The luring aroma of thousands of warm ripened grapes on the vine tingled her senses. She stole into the kitchen and switched on the light. Her sewing lay on the table where she had left it before going to bed. After pouring some Bertozzi wine into one of her grandmother's crystal glasses, Bianca sat down, picked up a needle, and began basting together long sections of fine imported silk. At first the methodical pushing-and-pulling action of the needle calmed her, but then her gnarled hands began to shake, so she took another drink and began talking out loud, pretending her mother Carilda and her husband, both long since departed, were present in the house with her.

"Why do you think he is coming here after all of these years?" she ventured, her question echoing in the empty kitchen.

From across the table, stitching away on her own invisible fabric, her mother's phantom voice replied, *"Who are you talking about, Bianca?"*

"You know, mama, Egisto's grandson from America. David. He and his wife will be here tomorrow."

Bianca couldn't bear imagining Danilo in the same room with her, so she pretended she heard him speak from the dining room. *"Why, darling,"* he said, *"you asked him to come didn't you? You've been dreaming of this day ever since your Uncle Egisto died."*

"Certemente." It was true. After Egisto had passed away in 1974 they had lost touch with the American Bertozzis. Then, seemingly out of nowhere, Egisto's grandson David contacted her, and on behalf of all the Bertozzis she had extended an invitation to Egisto's grandson to come meet his Italian family.

Her mother's omniscient voice interrupted her thoughts. *"I know what you are thinking, Bianca. You are worried some of the Bertozzis will not receive the Americans back into the family."*

Bianca lowered her sewing, her heart beating violently in her chest.

"And you are worried they will discover the secrets."

❧

I CONFESS *I am worried about the secrets. Maybe because the Americans will think less of our family or lay blame where it doesn't belong. I'll wait until tomorrow, after they've relaxed at the beach and settled in and then I'll tell David the story, from the beginning. Yes, that's what I'll do. Nonno always said I was good at explaining things, at untangling the knots in people's lives. Once they know what it was really like here during the war, how everything changed forever, Egisto's grandson will understand. Please God, let him understand.*

❧

SPEEDING TOWARD THE beach in Forte dei Marmi, David and Teresa's faces were pressed against the windows of Carlo and Lucia's silver Alpha Romero. In the front seat, Carlo spoke reverently of the Buffalo soldiers as he pointed eastward toward the marble-capped Carrara Mountains framing the Tuscan coastline. He singled out Michelangelo's Peak where the Florentine artist had hand-selected the marble for his greatest creations. Carlo used his finger to trace the infamous German Gothic Line which ran beneath it and when it became apparent the Americans had never heard of the Gothic Line and knew little of the Buffalo Soldiers, Carlo looked at his wife—Bianca's daughter, Lucia—and shook his head in disbelief. Lucia turned around in her seat and said something to David in Italian.

"Lucia says we will teach you our history," said Carlo. "It is very important for you to know." Motioning toward the west where the Ligurian Sea was coming into view, he added, "She says to tell you we are nearly there."

Lucia, still facing David, blushed and said something else. Trying to find the right words in English, Carlo said, "And she asks you, David, to forgive her if she stares at you. You look so much like your grandfather Egisto."

Arriving at the beach moments later, they were joined by legions of effusive Bertozzi cousins pressing close to get a good look at the Americans. Amidst the commotion, the throng suddenly parted, allowing a shrunken white-haired woman in a one-piece bathing suit to approach David. She stared openly at him, but directed her questions at Carlo. The name "Egisto" was heard several times. David assumed the woman was another of his cousins.

"No, she is not a relation," said Carlo. "This is Vittoria Tamagnini. Your grandfather was in love with her mother. Your grandmother, Armida, was not your grandfather's first love, you know. Your grandfather and Vittoria's mother, Marietta Tarabella, loved each other before your grandfather married Armida."

When it became apparent that David had known nothing of his grandfather's "first love," the crowd that had gathered around them fell silent.

"I'm sorry," Carlo apologized. "I thought you knew the story. Oh, it was a tragic love affair. Many in our village still talk about it today." He glanced at Vittoria, her feet planted firmly in the sand, still staring unapologetically at David. "And some," he added, "have not learned to forgive."

PART I

Ripa—Toscano—Italia

1913

Mogli e buoi dei paesi tuoi

"Wives and oxen from your own land"

chapter one

BREASTS THEY WERE, swelling orbs of life-sustaining flesh. To Egisto Bertozzi, at least, that's what the cluster of grapes he had carved on the creamy Carrara marble headstone looked like. He finished sanding them and then cupped his rough hand over the entire bunch, deciding they were as smooth as real grapes, or perhaps real breasts, would be. Glancing at the dates marking the deceased's exceptionally long, barren life—Aprile 3, 1820 to Agosto 12, 1913—an idea came to him. The Widow Pavone had died a bitter woman, her greatest dream—that of having children—never realized. He replaced the diamond sandpaper with his smallest chisel, selected a single grape in the center of the clump, and with a keen artistic eye, sculpted a soft nipple in relief. No one would ever notice the stone breast amidst her fruited companions, but Egisto, who believed there was nothing more beautiful than a nursing mother, would see the nippled grape, its marbled blue veins pulsating with life, if he ever visited the cemetery. It was the least he could do for the widow, he mused, this small, subversive act of justice.

"Are you daydreaming again, Egisto?" The voice of his brother Francesco, who was working on a separate project, startled Egisto back to reality. "You'd better snap out of it. Here comes papa!"

Francesco dropped his tools and darted through dozens of half-finished plaques and statues in the cramped makeshift studio, finally hiding behind a littered work bench where he would be able to discreetly observe all that was about to transpire. Readjusting his apron, he hissed, "A nice scandal you created for us today, brother. The whole town is talking about it. You'd better figure out a way to win Marietta back soon. If you don't, this family will never live down the shame."

Before Egisto could reply, the towering figure of Luigi Bertozzi materialized in the doorway. Golden shafts of morning sunlight streamed into the room and around his tall angular form, carrying on them the distinct sounds and aromas of late October. The smell of burning leaves and aging wine mingled with the chatter of women hanging laundry in the courtyard.

"Your mother and I met with signore Tarabella this morning, Egisto. What are you thinking?"

A loud thud at the back of the shop seemed to startle Luigi. Egisto watched as his father caught a glimpse of his eldest son spying on them from behind a half-finished statue of St. Francis. Papa leveled a stern rebuke to Francesco, who wordlessly dropped his tools and departed.

Luigi tossed a burlap-wrapped bundle of apples and olives on the desk and growled, "Your mother is consumed with grief. Still, she wants you to eat." Bending down, he dusted off a stool near Egisto and eased his lean body onto it. "Signore Tarabella tells us you refuse to marry his daughter in the Church. How is this possible?"

"You know very well how it is possible! I don't believe in religion. I don't believe in government. I'm an anarchist. This is news to you?"

"What is news to me is that you have not yet come to your senses. Surely the opportunity to marry signorina Tarabella is reason enough to abandon your idiotic ideals. Anarchy," he groused, "will be the death of us all!"

"You know I am no fool when it comes to world affairs, papa. Didn't I predict Italy would be the first to use airplanes to drop bombs in a war? Didn't I say that after the war in Turkey the Ottomans would sign a peace treaty with us? Besides," he added, "I am no different than Francesco."

"Francesco talks like an anarchist, but when it came right down to it he married in the Church didn't he? So did Alberto. Your brothers will do what they must to prosper. For them, anarchy is *capriccio*, a fad—nothing but talk." Luigi rose and approached his son. "I assumed you were like your brothers. Where does this stubbornness come from, Egisto? Your damned philosophy is ruining our lives."

"Whose life am I ruining and how?"

"You are ruining your mother's life, for one. She goes to Mass every day to offer up prayers on your behalf and how do you thank her? You throw it in her face. If you don't care about your own soul—*Lord in heaven, redeem him from his godlessness!*—you could at least show respect for the Bertozzi name. Today, we are the talk of the town!" He loosened his tie and raised both hands, stirring the air with his tightly cupped fingers as though he were conducting a Wagnerian opera. "You say you believe only in love. Well, what about family; what about duty? Men of my generation knew what duty meant. We married women selected by our families. We didn't concern ourselves with feelings. Either we fell in love with our wives eventually or we found love elsewhere."

Egisto looked beyond his father into the courtyard where the women were stuffing clothes into wicker baskets, balancing them precariously on their hips. Feeling his eyes on her, his mother turned to meet his gaze. Even from a distance, he could tell her eyes were swollen and red from crying. He felt himself drifting away, already an ocean apart from his father.

"You have waited for Marietta to come of age so you could marry her," continued Luigi, "and she has waited for you. And now, you are willing to risk our family's reputation just to protect your ego." He grabbed Egisto's shoulders. "This is all about your pride. Admit it, son."

Egisto pulled away. "What else does a man have? Marietta led me to believe she understood me, but suddenly, when it comes down to the wedding, she surrenders to tradition. Yes, my pride is wounded. She has chosen her father over me."

"And rightly so! Marietta is an obedient daughter. Her father knows what is best for her. If you knew what was best for a woman you would never have asked Marietta to marry outside of the Church."

Drawing a handkerchief out of his pocket, Luigi held it up to his face and sneezed into it before continuing. "Maybe now your anarchy seems, how do you say, *avant garde?* But mark my word, if you had eloped with Marietta without the blessings of the Church the day would have come when she would regret it . . . when the children are born and she wants them baptized, or when they are sick, and she turns to God for help."

Luigi flicked his kerchief in the air for effect. "You are young, yet you think you understand the entire scope of human nature. Do you really think you and your anarchist friends can solve all the problems of the world? Wait until everything is pulled out from under your feet and all of the brilliant philosophies in the world and all of your big-talking friends combined can not help you. You will think of God then. I guarantee it."

Stuffing the handkerchief back into his pocket, Luigi pointed his finger at Egisto. "At least Marietta has come to her senses. If you know what is good for you, and if you love your mother and me, you will swallow your pride and come to your senses as well. You must go to Marietta's father, beg his forgiveness, and agree to marry his daughter in the Church. I only pray it's not too late. Signore Tarabella is *caparbio*, a hard-headed man, just like his father and grandfather before him."

"There must be another way," replied Egisto. "I can't appear to compromise my conscience now. I would lose my self-respect. Without that I don't know what kind of husband I would be."

"There is no other way, Egisto, and time is running out. You leave for America in two weeks. If you want Marietta for your wife, you will have to compromise . . . just like Francesco and Alberto."

Leaning closer, in the event Francesco was eavesdropping, Luigi lowered his voice. "You are our chosen son, Egisto. It is you who is privileged to go to America and help support the family. How can you shame us by leaving home without a wife? It will multiply our shame!"

"It wouldn't be the end of the world. Others have gone to America without a wife."

"Such a cavalier attitude, Egisto. Do, you imagine Marietta's parents are going to relent without an apology from you or that she will run after you to America if you leave without her? Think again. I have it on good authority that signora Tarabella is looking for a replacement for you as we speak. Emilio Lucchesi, you know, has long had his eye on Marietta."

Egisto laughed inwardly at the supposed threat. Emilio Lucchesi, in his estimation, was an atonal boor, unenlightened and at least seven years older than Marietta. But, just as quickly, he doused his humor with the reality that the scandal of their broken engagement had humiliated the Tarabellas and Marietta's mother was formidable when crossed. It wasn't a stretch of the imagination to believe she probably was doing everything in her power to mitigate the damage done to their daughter's reputation.

"I'm sure your 'good authority' is none other than Marietta's mother herself," muttered Egisto.

Luigi grunted rather than admit the truth. Signora Tarabella had never tried to hide the fact that she felt her daughter should marry into money and Emilio Lucchesi, despite all else he might be, was from a wealthy Luccan family.

Egisto hardened his resolve. "If that's the way signora Tarabella wants to play the game," he said, "let her play it. We'll see what Marietta is made of. If I'm not good enough for her and she is fool enough to listen to her mother then she can have Emilio Lucchesi."

As much as Egisto was tempted to share his fears with his father, he didn't dare. How could he confess that he *was* banking on Marietta revolting against her parents' demands and eloping with him? How could he admit that he was, indeed, defending his pride, that he was frightened of the future, that he feared he might not get Marietta back, and that his excitement for a new life in America was tempered by his dread of leaving his family and friends? Such confessions would only make him look *smidollato*—spineless.

Luigi, seeming to sense Egisto's torment, framed his son's face in his hands. "Your mother cannot stop crying: Why won't Egisto marry Marietta in the Church? Will he leave for America without a wife? Will he forget about his mama and papa? Heaven forbid he marries a foreign woman and fathers strange children who don't speak Italian!"

With a firm pat on his son's cheek, Luigi formally ended the discussion. "We know we can trust you to do the right thing. Eh?"

Not uttering a word, Egisto stepped around his father and made his way through the bustling Bertozzi courtyard, past his weeping mother, and into the family vineyard, his favorite retreat. There, he found a spot shielded from a fresh tramontana wind suddenly gusting down the mountains from the north, and sat down. He slipped his hand into the inner pocket of his vest and pulled out a picture of Marietta.

He studied her lucent eyes, the color of freshly tilled earth; the contours of her oval face and high, aristocratic forehead; her wide, full-lipped smile, and the way she tilted her head so that her profile accentuated her straight, narrow nose. How had it come to this? Why had she cowered behind her father last night when he told signore Tarabella he wanted a civil ceremony rather than a wedding in the Church? Marietta had all but assured him her father would agree to a civil ceremony. She was sure, also, that once they were husband and wife, her mother would warm to him. He doubted it.

Had Marietta stood up to her father, had she stepped forward and taken Egisto's hand in hers in a show of unity rather than remain silent while her father ranted and raved, hurling insults and threats at him, they wouldn't be in this predicament. Instead, Marietta had let her mother whisk her away to another room where, he imagined, she launched a scheme to impugn his character and turn her daughter against him.

The wind, suddenly colder and stronger, whipped the top half of the photograph down over his fingers. Reluctantly, he slid it back inside his vest, the marble dust on the palms of his hands leaving a trail of grey powder on the dark wool cloth.

Apart from her most recent display of familial cowardice, he sighed, Marietta was everything he loved in a woman. In his estimation, she was sensitive, trusting, mild-tempered and beautiful. She was also intelligent, witty and artistic— traits he had thought were essential in a mate.

Standing up, he faced the wind. *Either Marietta's parents will have to yield to my convictions and let her marry me outside of the Church*, he thought, his determination wavering, *or I'm making the biggest mistake of my life.*

chapter two

FROM THE COUNTER inside the popular Cantina di Strettoia, Egisto watched as his two brothers conspired together. Their table was situated near the side entrance where the musicians were tuning up their instruments.

What should I do? he wondered.

Francesco and Alberto wanted him to get drunk with them, even though it was the last thing he wanted to do. He shivered as the damp night air blasted its way through the propped-open door. It barely made a dent in the smoke-filled tavern.

In a sweaty passion, a balding, mustachioed musician, his belly swollen with the evening's dinner special, pumped away on his concertina. His scrawny partner leaned against the bar, strumming an old beat-up mandolin with equal zest, his stained fingers plucking along so fast they were a veritable blur. Egisto stationed himself next to the open door hoping the cold air might jump-start his deflated spirit.

He debated slipping out and going back home without telling his brothers, but thought better of it. They had gone to great lengths to arrange an evening together with him and he knew they meant well. Not wanting to alienate them any more than he already had, he made his way back to the table. When he noticed Francesco had refilled his wine glass, he changed his mind yet again.

"See you two later," he said. "I'm going home."

"Fine!" growled Francesco. "Go home, Egisto, and cry in your soup!" He flipped his hand around in a gesture of disgust. "I'm tired of trying to help you when you do not even care to help yourself."

Egisto opened his mouth to reply, but could think of no response equal to the accusation. He hung his head, hesitated, and sat down, lifting his glass half-heartedly before pouring it down his throat in one long draught. Francesco slapped him on the back and poured another round. Together, the three brothers toasted each other's good looks.

Filippo Bertolli, the owner of Cantina di Strettoia, brought a bottle of fumetto to their table. "Here!" he boomed. "For you, Egisto. On the house!" The music stopped as everyone in the room turned to soberly salute yet another village son soon to depart for the New World. Filippo uncorked the bottle. Using his apron to hold it while he poured them each a shot, he sang an aria from *The Barber of Seville*. Crowning his solo with a flourish, he pinched Egisto's cheek and added, "Remember me when you get to America, okay?" He wiped a tear from his eye and set the half-empty bottle next to Francesco.

"Mille grazie, Filippo!" A burning sensation roared down Egisto's throat and exploded in his chest cavity. He grimaced, wiped his mouth, and slid his glass toward Francesco for another drink. The musicians resumed playing, only louder and with a more raucous beat. Fun-loving Alberto began to tap his fingers on the table, wagging his head in time with the music.

After swigging three shots of fumetto in a row, Egisto covered his glass as Francesco attempted to fill it again. He knew he was on the brink of total inebriation.

Stumbling over his words, Egisto thanked Francesco and Alberto. "You are good brothers! I feel better already!" As if to prove it, he threw his head back and yelled, "Bravo!" when the musicians ended their song with a particularly rousing chorus. Then, he banged his hand on the table and shouted, "I feel like dancing!"

"We need some girls for that," quipped Alberto.

"Let's set some things straight before we think about dancing," said Francesco.

Egisto was so relaxed that, thinking he might be drooling, he wiped his mouth with his coat sleeve. "Take it away, Francesco!"

Alberto burst out laughing, spitting wine all over the table and himself. His immaturity obviously irked Francesco, who glared at him disapprovingly before lashing out at Egisto. "You've been mooning around here long enough, Egisto," he said, "and in one more week you leave for America. Forget about Marietta. Everyone—but you apparently—knows it's over. Her parents have a grip on her so tight you'll never see her again. Time is running out and you need a wife."

"My life is not your business."

"Oh, but it is my business, brother. We both have our duties. As the oldest son, I must stay here and do what is required of me, while you must support the family from America. I am doing my part. I have sacrificed my dreams to do what is expected of me. You, however, get to experience the world and see things I will never be able to see. Yet, you complain. You complain about such little things! How hard is it to find a woman to marry you?"

"It's not hard, Egisto," Alberto interrupted, thumping his chest. "I did it."

Francesco rolled his eyes and continued. "Everybody

knows Italian men who go to America without a wife end up marrying someone who makes them forget about home. Pretty soon the money stops coming in because the foreign wife demands the money for herself and her family. Remember Aldo Nerucci? He married an Irish scullery maid in Boston, even though he swore he would send for Beata Domenici to come to America so they could marry. He hasn't been back to Ripa in nearly ten years He might as well have dropped off the face of the earth. Don't be stupid Egisto."

Alberto nodded in agreement. "Si, Egisto, and you're not getting any younger either."

Egisto grimaced and tried to formulate an answer, but his brain wouldn't cooperate. Through lips that felt like inflated rubber, he garbled, "What are you suggesting?"

"I'm suggesting you open your mind. Consider other options." Francesco mentioned a homely girl who had once had a crush on Egisto.

"*Che schifo!*" Egisto's mouth pursed as he pronounced the last vowel. Gross!

Alberto recommended his wife's sister.

"Another drink, per favore!" shouted Egisto.

Scowling, Francesco ordered Filippo to ignore his brother. "You've had enough!" he said, removing the drink from Egisto's hands. "Get serious, would you? Who cares who the girl is as long as you are married before you leave for America? You have nothing to lose."

Egisto stuck out his lower lip. He idolized his older brother. Even his own obsession with anarchy was a result of Francesco's dabbling fascination with it. But suddenly, he no longer felt sure of what he believed about anything.

Although he seemed contrite, Francesco reworded his last comment. "I *do* care who it is that you marry, Egisto, but I can't do anything about it. You alone have to make the decision."

"Maybe if I go to Marietta's father tomorrow and . . . "

"It's too late, Egisto. Signore Tarabella would disown Marietta before he'd let her see you again."

"But she loves me."

"*Stupido!* When will you get it through that thick head of yours that your sweet little Marietta is a *spugna*, a sponge? She has no mind of her own. Perhaps she pretended to accept your beliefs, but you saw with your own eyes what happened. The minute her father turned on you that was it. If she really loved you she would have defied her father's wishes. Face it, Egisto, you are history now."

Alberto, who had only been half-listening to the conversation, leaned forward and pointed toward the bar. "Look!"

Their heads turned in unison to see the object of his attention. Wearing a dress she had obviously outgrown, a busty woman with high burnished cheeks and a head of thick unruly hair maneuvered her way through the crowded tables. It was unusual for women to patronize taverns and Francesco took special note that no one attempted to speak to her. She ordered a drink and proceeded to a table at the far end of the room where she joined another woman and a man who appeared to be husband and wife.

"Who is she, Alberto?" Francesco asked.

"She looks like Armida Sigali, although I don't remember her looking quite so . . . mature. Her brother goes to the art school in Pietrasanta with Casanova here," added Alberto, digging his elbow into Egisto's side. "She's a seamstress or something." He lit a cigarette. "Big family, the Sigalis. Eleven kids. I think she is one of the younger ones. Funny I never noticed her before."

Without asking, Francesco grabbed the cigarette out of Alberto's hand and started smoking it. "She looks young, but she's probably about twenty-one or so, don't you think, Alberto?"

Alberto shrugged.

"Do something for me," said Francesco, removing the cigarette from his lips and pointing it toward Egisto.

"What?"

"You said you felt like dancing? Do it. I dare you. Go over there to signorina Sigali." Francesco handed the cigarette back to Alberto and reached over and grabbed Egisto's chin, turning it forcibly in her direction. "See her there? Ask her to dance. Prove to us you are willing to consider someone other than Marietta Tarabella as a wife."

"At least," continued Francesco, "it will prove you have what it takes to get a woman. Otherwise," he leaned over and whispered, "in your quest for perfection, you may never marry and produce children."

Emboldened with an abundance of wine, Egisto rose and said, "Watch me." He staggered his way through the crowd to Armida's table, bowed his head, held out his hand and introduced himself. "Signorina Sigali, I am Egisto Bertozzi, at your service."

Armida stared at him a moment before turning to search the faces of the couple sitting with her. Egisto noted that the man was expressionless, but the woman said something in her ear to which she nodded. Armida then rose, took Egisto's hand, and led him outside the cantina where their shadowy forms could be seen dancing at arm's length, hesitantly at first. Moments later, their bodies were intertwined, curling around each other like hungry vines.

Glancing over Armida's shoulder through the cantina's doors, Egisto noticed his two brothers trying to get his attention. Alberto slapped his knee, grinning at him as though he had won a bet. Francesco gave him a thumbs up, his face somber with approval. Then, they turned to each other, shook hands and poured another round of drinks.

Egisto pulled Armida farther away; away from the lighted windows and the noise, and his brothers' prying eyes. The last thing that went through his mind, before the sticky blackness of complete inebriation brought him to his knees, was that maybe his brothers were right.

chapter three

EGISTO ROLLED OVER in a futile effort to lessen the throbbing in his head, but a scraping sound, compounding his discomfort, refused to go away.

Where am I? he thought, assuming he was still at the cantina. He wondered if he had gotten into a fight and was just regaining consciousness. It had been a long time since he'd been involved in a brawl, but then it had been a long time since he'd been so emotionally charged too. Maybe someone had ribbed him about Marietta and he just snapped.

As the background noise intensified, turning into a steady slapping rhythm, his curiosity drove him to lift his head, and with great difficulty, open one eye. The room in which he found himself appeared to be spinning out of control, sending waves of nausea throughout his belly. Slowly, he raised himself to a sitting position and froze in horror at the scene before him.

He wasn't at the cantina. He was in a strange house with a strange woman, her back to him, kneading a large mass of bread dough with syncopated gusto. Panic gripped him as he reached down to button his shirt, only to realize the shirt was not his.

The woman turned. "Feeling better?"

When Egisto said nothing, she shrugged, scooped up the dough and placed it in a bowl to rise. Perspiration stained the back of her dress, even though biting drafts of cold air scuttled along the earthen floor where Egisto's bare feet peered sheepishly out of a pair of trousers he realized were also not his.

The room, which on closer inspection appeared to be the entire house, was heated by an oven that crackled and popped whenever the woman opened it to toss in several small pieces of wood. Grasping the corners of her apron, she wiped her forehead and tucked some damp ringlets at the nape of her neck back up into a loosely fashioned chignon.

She turned once again and repeated, "Feeling better?"

An unintelligible garble lodged in his throat, refusing to surface on his tongue.

She brought a plate of bread and cheese over and sat down next to him. "You need to eat. This will make you feel better."

Cautiously, he ate the proffered food. "Thank you, whoever you are."

Her face clouded. "I know you were drunk last night," she said, "but I thought surely you would remember me this morning."

"I'm sorry. I don't."

She stood up to face him. "Well, I am signorina Armida Sigali. We spent quite an evening together. It is unfortunate you remember none of it." Turning on her heels, she walked rigidly over to the oven and tossed some more wood into it.

Egisto strained to remember. Vaguely he recalled sitting in the Cantina di Strettoia with his brothers, drinking and discussing women. Other recollections flashed surreally in his mind: dancing outside the cantina with someone who smelled like deep summer, kissing the lips of someone whose response was at once both shy and eager, and caressing the satin skin of a woman whose warmth touched a dormant nerve in his flesh. Disconnected mental snapshots clawed at his muddled memory. He blushed.

"I remember only a very little," he apologized. "I must ask your forgiveness if I was in any way . . . if I was anything other than a . . . "

"A gentleman?"

Egisto noticed the rise and fall of her shoulders as she tried to compose herself. "If you're asking me if we shared the same bed," she said, "no, we didn't. We did spend the night here together, however. Just you and I. For most people, my family and yours, that would be grounds for me to demand that you marry me. If that's what I wanted."

A sense of dread permeated his question. "Is that what you want?"

"You poured your heart out to me, Egisto."

"I did?"

"Perhaps I should start at the beginning, since your memory is so poor?"

Nodding, Egisto waited.

"I was minding my own business at the cantina last night," she began, "when you suddenly appeared at my table and asked me to dance. My sister approved only if we danced outside the cantina. So we did. I must say, you did not waste any time in proclaiming your passion for me!"

"Oh yes," she continued. "You told me Marietta Tarabella turned down your offer of marriage and then you begged me to run away with you to America. You said your family would be thrilled to know you would not be leaving Italy empty-handed and that their dreams of having more grandchildren would come true because of me."

"Surely," Egisto stammered, "you realized I was drunk."

"Of course I knew you were drunk," she shot back. "How

could I not know, when you were throwing up all over yourself and me? How do you think you got here?"

"That was my next question."

"I didn't want to shame you by taking you back into the cantina, in front of everyone, covered with your own vomit. So we walked down the hill to the hot springs where I thought I could at least help you get cleaned up. You were so drunk you fell in and dragged me in with you. The water was warm, though you probably don't remember that either. It felt so good that we ended up just sitting there laughing and talking."

"After awhile," she continued, "I realized it must be getting late. I told you we'd better go back to the cantina, but when you got out of the pool you passed out. I tried to wake you up but you wouldn't budge. I ran up to find your brothers but they had already left, and so had my sister. Evidently they had looked outside for us and when they couldn't find us they assumed we had moved somewhere else. Filippo was the only one left in the cantina. Realizing what I must look like, I panicked. Filippo asked what had happened to me, but I was afraid if he knew we were together in the hot springs he would jump to the wrong conclusion, so I pretended I didn't know where you were."

Egisto shifted his weight on the couch as the story went from bad to worse.

"I hate lying," said Armida. "I told Filippo you had thrown up on me and left me alone outside and that I didn't know where you were. I told him I was too embarrassed to come back into the cantina with my dress soiled, so I went down to the springs and while I was cleaning my dress, I slipped and fell in, and then I was too embarrassed to come back to the cantina until I thought everyone but my sister had left!"

"What did he say?" asked Egisto, his voice cracking.

"He believed me. He reminded me that my sister and her husband are not the best chaperones in the world. Filippo offered to take me home, so I let him. But when I got home I couldn't sleep because I was worried you might freeze to death, so I went back and got you."

Egisto stared woodenly at her. "How did you get me here?"

"I took our mule. When I found you, I thought you were dead. I finally roused you enough to get you to climb on the back of our mule, and then you passed out again.

I didn't know what to do. I thought of taking you back to your house on Monte di Ripa. I thought I would just knock on the door and leave you there, but I was afraid someone might see me."

She stuck out her chin. "You're not the only one who has a reputation to safe-guard you know. So I brought you to my grandfather's *fattoria*, and here we are."

Egisto didn't quite understand.

"I couldn't take you back to my house. What would my brothers say?"

"Your brothers?"

"Don't worry. I left a note at home telling them where I would be. Since my grandparents died, I come up here during the winter to keep the place warm and dry. It's old and needs a lot of work, but when my father returns from America he says he will tear it down and rebuild. It has potential, don't you think?"

Egisto looked around at the crumbling walls and cob-webbed ceiling and didn't reply. Armida, taking his quiet appraisal as disapproval, pressed ahead. "So, everything you told me last night was a lie then," she said.

"I remember nothing you claim I said. I told you, I was

drunk. It's true that Marietta refused to marry me, or shall I say her father refused to let her marry me. Surely you know why. There are no secrets in Ripa."

"Everyone knows your families arranged the marriage and she refused your offer because you wouldn't get married in the Church." She shrugged her shoulders. "What's new? Parents arrange marriages all the time. It's a business transaction."

She went into the kitchen, removed her apron and hung it on a nail. "It's also not news that you are an anarchist, Egisto. Just find someone who will marry you outside of the Church. It can't be that difficult."

Sunlight began to creep through the only window in the house.

"I have to get out of here before someone sees me," said Egisto, his voice somewhere between desperation and genuine remorse. "I'm sorry, Armida. I promise I'll make it up to you someday." No sooner were the words out of his mouth than he was struck squarely in the chest with a vegetable brush.

"I don't want your sympathy," she screamed, groping about for another object to hurl at him. "Get out!"

Egisto tried to approach her. "Please Armida, be reasonable! If someone sees me leaving here, it's you they'll be talking about too. We've got to do this right for both our sakes."

Biting her lip, Armida finally conceded. "I put your clothes outside because they smelled like sulfur. They're probably still wet. I'll hand them in to you and you can get dressed while I wait outside. When it's clear, I'll knock on the door twice and you can come out."

"Fair enough." Egisto picked up the vegetable brush and handed it back to her. "I *am* sorry, Armida."

Without responding, she slipped out the door and passed his clothes in to him. Moments later, after she knocked twice, Egisto stepped outside. Armida looked up and down the deserted lane.

"If I were you, I'd get going," she said.

Egisto hesitated. He felt the responsibility of his actions weighing heavily on him. Despite his belief that men and women should be equal, he looked at Armida, her shoulders set square as she waited for him to leave, and understood the reality of the ingrained double standards that existed between men and women. She would be the one who would pay the heaviest price for his foolishness if their evening together became public. He wanted to hug Armida, or reach out and stroke her arm; some tangible sign to let her know he appreciated what she had done for him. Instead, convinced she would misinterpret any physical demonstration of gratitude as a display of affection, he turned and walked away from her, shoulders humped, his damp clothes clinging to his aching muscles.

Behind him, he heard Armida slam the door shut. It was a sound he feared he would hear many times before the day was over. It was—he shivered just thinking about it—the sound of finality.

chapter four

LOOKING FOR SOMEWHERE to waste time, Egisto found the art school open. He conducted an inventory of his studio there, placing the tools he could take to America with him in a box. About 10:00 a.m. he left the studio to meander through the statuary on display in the school's courtyard. He spent about an hour and a half studying other students' techniques and taking mental measurements of form and design hoping it would distract him from his problems. When that didn't work, he walked to the Café Rivolti, ate a leisurely lunch, and then braced himself for the inevitable confrontation with his family before beginning the final leg of his journey home. He didn't bother side-stepping the puddles along the via della Chiusa. He simply sloshed right through them, the displaced water splashing up his trousers and into his shoes. Brittle yellowed leaves swirled in a mad dervish over his head as he passed beneath a giant chestnut tree he used to climb when he was a little boy. One lodged itself in his hair. Absently, he removed it, flinging it aside.

Stopping to catch his breath, he caught sight of his home fading in and out of the fog swirling along the flanks of Monte di Ripa. He turned right, onto the narrow path leading up the hill, and heard a steady hammering coming from the studio. Francesco, he realized, must still be working. Francesco's wife Pia was, no doubt, helping his mother and sister prepare dinner. Egisto was certain he could smell pheasant—fresh from the hunter's bag—stewing in the kitchen. Faintly, he discerned three figures moving about in their vineyard and detected the voices of Luigi, Alberto, and Carilda's husband Barlaam. They would be mulching the vines, a task they had always done together.

Without warning, a pain unlike any he had ever experienced shot through his torso. He clutched his chest, falling back against the stone wall abutting the mountain path. The Bertozzi villa with its blue-shuttered windows, massive doors and timbered trellises, the studio he shared with Francesco, the courtyard where everyone gathered when they made wine, the olive orchard and the vineyard—none of it, he realized, would ever be his. This must be how Carilda feels, he thought. With no right of inheritance, his sister, like him, would ultimately be a spectator rather than an inhabitant of what once was the most precious piece of real estate on earth.

Few immigrants from Tuscany to the New World ever came back, with or without Italian wives. Occasionally, one would return for a visit, but such extravagance at the expense of the family in Italy who desperately needed the income from America, was rare. Egisto would have to become a rich man to afford it. The thought of perhaps never taking part in another *Festa del Vino*, the annual contests and festivities held every September in celebration of the local region's vintners and winemaking history, made him sick. It had been one of the highlights of his childhood.

Indeed, he had first proclaimed his love to Marietta three years ago at one of the *Festa's* booths where she was helping her parents display their wine. He had created a diversion, and when her parents left her alone for a few moments he nervously placed in her palm a marble cameo he had carved with her profile engraved on it, along with the words *Semper Aternumque Te Amabo*, "I will love you always and forever," in Latin. Remembering that day—the way her stained lips curved into a smile when she saw the cameo and then kissed it, holding it up to Egisto's lips for a kiss before she hid it away so her parents couldn't see it—caused his heart to race.

What a fool he was!

But, the thought of never walking into his childhood home to eat his mother's food, of never harvesting grapes with his father, never working with Francesco, never joking with Alberto, never teasing Carilda or playing with his nieces and nephews again? Those thoughts paralyzed him. Grinding his teeth, he willed his fears into submission. The pain subsided. Steadying himself, he resumed his climb.

Rounding the corner, he saw Carilda pacing back and forth at the bottom of the vineyard. He approached her quietly, listening to her humming a lullaby to a bundle she cradled in her arms.

"Carilda?"

"Egisto!"

Carilda threw one arm over her brother's shoulder. Nestled between them he felt Bianca. She was swaddled in a white, hand-knit blanket, and the odor of cigarette smoke clinging to the fibers of his coat was in such stark contrast to her fragrance—the essence of fresh raindrops on roses—that he cringed.

If there were a heaven, it would smell like babies, he thought. Softly, he asked, "How is she?"

"She cried all night, poor thing, but mama stayed up with me and this morning her fever broke. She's been sleeping in my arms ever since. The minute I try to put her down, she wakes up and fusses. You know how babies are."

He mumbled something about knowing very little of babies.

On an impulse, Carilda thrust Bianca into Egisto's unsuspecting arms, pulling his coat lapels out away from his chest and then readjusting them to cover her daughter's tiny body.

"There," she teased. "You shall learn." More soberly, she added, "Follow me."

Egisto shifted the baby awkwardly in his arms and followed his sister from the vineyard to the herb garden. With a long pointed stick, she poked through rows of plants, many with silvery—almost black—leaves and shoots, until her digging produced some scraggly looking onion and garlic bulbs. She brushed them off and placed them in a knit bag attached to her wrist.

"The stew needs more flavor," she explained, spying out any last vestiges of basil. She found some, but the early, unseasonably hard freezes of the last few nights had rendered the herb unusable. Egisto watched as her eyes roamed beyond the garden's borders for any *finocchio selvatico*, a type of wild-growing fennel she particularly loved to use in her cooking. Waiting patiently, he peeked into his overcoat at his niece every now and then, rocking clumsily in the involuntary motion peculiar to men unaccustomed to holding babies. The sweet warmth of Bianca's body next to his still-pounding heart gave him an indescribable sense of peace.

Returning to him, Carilda suddenly demanded, "Where have you been, Egisto? What happened last night?"

"Nothing."

"Nothing? Egisto, the whole town knows what happened!"

Egisto held Bianca tightly, imagining she could prevent his heart from racing out of control again.

"Mama is beside herself," said Carilda.

"Mama is always beside herself," he grumbled.

"Yes, well, this time she has every right to be. We were all worried sick about you, Egisto! When Francesco and Alberto came home last night without you, papa was in a panic. He demanded to know what was going on and was furious when they told him." She made the sign of the cross over herself. "It was terrible."

"I suppose they'll be glad to see me then," he quipped. "I got drunk, that's all."

"If only that *were* all that happened to you! Papa made Francesco and Alberto go with him in the middle of the night to find you, and when they couldn't, they began waking people up, asking them if they had seen you. Guilio Manzini told them he woke up around midnight because of a commotion in the field behind his stables. When he and his son went to see what was going on, they caught a glimpse of you and a woman laughing and splashing each other in his hot spring. Signore Manzini chalked it up to—he told papa—a young man's fancy, adding that Marietta Tarabella may not be so forgiving! Of course, papa knew who the woman was. That much, at least, Francesco had told him."

Carilda drew closer, whispering as though the fog itself were recording their conversation. "They asked Guilio for permission to go through his field to the hot spring, but you weren't there. Papa insisted on going to the Sigalis'. It must have been three o'clock in the morning. Armida's brother told papa she had left a note saying she was at her grandfather's farm."

Carilda crossed herself again. "If Francesco hadn't intervened, Armida's brother would have taken his gun and gone with them! Francesco apologized for alarming him and assured him they only wondered if Armida might know what happened to Egisto and that if anything was amiss they would let him know. Alberto told me they found your clothes hanging outside Armida's house. Francesco told papa it would be pointless to confront you because you would have been too drunk to know what was going on and anyway, they did not want to create a scene. Papa was so ashamed, he came back home and hasn't spoken to anyone since."

She stopped and sighed. Noting Egisto's pained expression, she stroked his cheek gently. "Why did this have to happen now, of all times? What were you thinking?"

Egisto swallowed hard before mouthing the question, "Marietta?"

"She knows."

Carilda reached into Egisto's overcoat and retrieved Bianca, kissing her on the forehead and folding her securely beneath her own heavy shawl again. "Word travels fast," she said. "Evidently, someone saw you leaving the Sigali farmhouse around dawn."

"So, this could give signore Tarabella ammunition to push Emilio Lucchesi on to Marietta, even though I know Marietta would never accept a proposal from him."

"I heard last night that Marietta already refused to consider Emilio, but there's more: signore Tarabella sent word to us this morning that he was sending Marietta to Rome on the afternoon train to stay with family there for awhile. The rumor is they'll be looking for a husband for her there."

Egisto blanched. "Papa was right; this has been all about

my pride. What a fool I've been! Compromising my beliefs would be a small price to pay to have Marietta as my wife. She would listen to you, Carilda. Maybe you could write her; tell her it's all a terrible mistake. Nothing happened last night. I swear it."

Carilda placed her hand under her brother's elbow and began leading him toward the house. "I talked to her this morning, as soon as we received signore Tarabella's message. Marietta may be the sweetest person in the world, but even she is not immune to jealousy. Now she is angry and I can't say that I blame her. She never wants to see you again, and although it is possible she may someday change her mind, I am afraid it will not be anytime soon. Accident or not, Egisto, it looks like you will be going to America alone.

❦

I was too young, of course, to remember Uncle Egisto before he left for America, but mama told me about his troubles. Told me how distraught and tormented he was after that night; how worried he was that he had sealed his fate with Marietta Tarabella and that there might not be any going back because of it. Mama said many prayers for Egisto after that. She told me that she prayed God would give Egisto the wife he needed—the woman he deserved.

❦

As the approaching lights of Rome became visible through the streaked windows of the Roma Coach Express, Marietta Tarabella's tear-swollen eyes stared back at their own reflection. Her thick, knotted, chestnut hair hung loosely down her back. She hadn't taken the time to pin it up, let alone comb it. The condescending touch of her mother's hand resting on hers did little to comfort her.

"I told you this would happen, Marietta," her mother chided. "If Egisto Bertozzi has no respect for the Church, then he has no respect for women. You are better off without him, believe me. You deserve better."

"Maybe so." Marietta, miserable, brushed her mother's hand away. She leaned closer to the window and created a layer of steam with her hot breath in which she traced her initials alongside Egisto's. Immediately, she crossed them out. *How could he do this to me? I will never forgive him. Never!*

She conjured up several mental scenes to match the wild rumors that had swept through Ripa before they left: Egisto and Armida dancing shamelessly together at the cantina in front of everyone, Egisto and Armida bathing together, naked no less, in Guilio Manzini's hot spring, Egisto and Armida making love all night in the empty Sigali farmhouse. Though she didn't know Armida Sigali, she was clearly without scruples. The woman had to be extremely attractive, lamented Marietta—remarkable in some way—to snare Egisto, who had just weeks ago sworn that no other woman could hold a candle to her.

Having never known rejection, having never experienced even a hint of jealously in her entire life, Marietta felt her abdomen convulse as though her body was trying to disgorge any remnant of love or trust left in her. Dry-heaving, she covered her mouth with her sweater. Her mother quickly retrieved a small blanket from the overhead compartment and held it out for Marietta to use, but Marietta lashed out with one arm and shoved it away.

"I don't need it, mama. Leave me alone!"

"Fine. I'll go and freshen up. You should freshen up too, Marietta. *Come sei conciato!* You look a sight."

A well-dressed businessman sitting opposite them raised his hat politely to signora Tarabella as she excused herself, but then proceeded to ogle Marietta in her mother's absence.

Marietta stiffened and curled her upper lip as if to say, *You are despicable, like all men.* Turning away from him, she stared again at her reflection in the window. Moments later, the train began to slow down on its approach to the Roma Ostiense railway station.

Face it, she told herself, completely spent from hours of internal wrestling. *Even though you'll never really know if the rumors are true or not, it doesn't matter. You still love him. You always will. There will never be anyone for you but Egisto Bertozzi.*

When her mother returned, the businessman nodded at her as though he had done her a favor by protecting her daughter while she was gone. In response, signora Tarabella flashed him an alluring smile. Then she turned to her daughter.

"I thought I told you to freshen up," she scolded. "We're almost there." She tugged at her Marietta's elbow until Marietta turned to look at her.

"*Mi dispiace,* mama. I'm sorry. I just don't care how I look right now."

"Well, you'd better care," her mother replied, reaching out to adjust some of Marietta's errant curls. "I might as well tell you now that my sister—your zia Felica—has agreed not only to host us for a month in her villa but also to help us find a suitable husband for you."

As the train came shuddering to a halt, signora Tarabella paused and looked sideways at the businessman, busy gathering up his belongings. "And there's no better place to find a rich man than in Rome."

chapter five

EGISTO WALKED THE two miles from Francesco's house in Querceta, near Ripa, to the seaside town of Forte dei Marmi where he nervously began searching the crowded streets and alleys. Finally, craning his neck above the hordes of pedestrians milling about via Carducci, he saw what he'd been looking for. He arched his hands around his mouth like a megaphone and called out, "Wait! Stop! I leave tomorrow for America!"

Armida Sigali, wearing the same dress she had worn at the cantina with a faded blue sweater tied around her shoulders, was lugging a basket of mending under one arm. Because she was easily within hearing distance, Egisto guessed she was trying to embarrass him into leaving her alone. Undaunted, he weaved in and out of the crowd to keep up with her.

When he got close enough to stretch out his hand and touch her, he blurted, "Will you marry me?"

Armida stopped so abruptly that a fisherman, walking between her and Egisto and carrying a bulging net of mackerel and reef mullet, crashed into her. In turn, Egisto fell onto both of them. "Sorry!" he sputtered, stopping to help pick up the escaped fish scuttling along the sidewalk.

"Never mind," the old man muttered, tipping his tattered, dingy cap in Armida's direction. "It looks like I'm the one in the way."

Egisto wiped his hands along the lower part of his coat and looked at Armida as if to say, *Well?*

She sized him up with a look of contempt and continued on her way without saying a word. A primitive impulse propelled Egisto forward. Elbowing his way through shoppers and street vendors, he sprinted after her.

"Armida," he shouted. "Come back!"

Armida picked up her pace and disappeared around a corner. Spotting her maneuver, Egisto rounded the same corner. He caught her hiding in the shadow of an empty shop's recessed doorway. Before she could bolt from him, he threw himself in front of her, stretching his arms spread-eagle over the abandoned entry to prevent her from escaping.

"Please," he said, panting hard. "Marry me."

"You're drunk."

"I've never been more sober."

"You made a fool of me once. It won't happen again." She tried to push past him, but he wouldn't budge. "Get out of my way."

"Not until we talk," he insisted.

She turned her face away from him.

"I don't blame you for hating me, Armida. What I did was stupid . . . and selfish. I wish I could go back and change what happened, but I can't."

She tightened her grip on the clothes basket, wedging it between them.

"When I asked you to marry me the other night I *was* drunk, but I'm not drunk now. I've had time to think and I've finally come to a decision."

"Lucky me," she spat. "What happened? Did Marietta Tarabella refuse you a second time?"

Egisto's face hardened. He inched closer to her and with exaggerated candor declared, "There *was* no second time."

A man walked by slowly, one eyebrow raised as though trying to decide whether to intervene or not. Egisto waited until the man moved on, then he repositioned himself in the doorway, bracing one leg against the door jamb so Armida would have to climb over it, or under it, to leave.

Assuming an exaggerated air of boredom, she ignored him.

His voice returned to a more even, reasoned tone. "The truth is, I've given up on ever marrying Marietta. Her father heard about what happened with you and me that night at the cantina. He sent her to Rome with her mother to find a husband." He paused, before adding, "A rich one, apparently."

Armida's mouth turned down at the corners. "And that's my fault?"

"Oh, no! I take all of the blame."

"Your apology does me little good now." She pushed him with her basket. "Now, if you don't mind . . ."

"What will it take for you to say 'yes' to me, Armida?"

"To a proposal of marriage? Honesty."

"I'm being honest."

"Really? Such a sudden change. I don't believe you."

Egisto ran his fingers through his hair. "It may seem sudden to you," he said, "but it actually took me a long time to make up my mind."

"Make up your mind about what? Marietta?"

"Well, yes, but also just marriage in general. After everything that's happened, I didn't know what to do. Didn't know if I should just go to America by myself . . ." His voice trailed off.

"And?"

"I decided I didn't want to go to America alone. It will be hard enough trying to learn a new language and adapt to a different culture without having to worry about finding the right woman to settle down with. Besides, there won't be time. I start working as soon as I get there."

"Why me?"

"Why not?" he rejoined. "I recall you suggesting I view marriage as a business proposition."

Armida measured her response. "Fair enough. Is it the only reason you want to marry me?"

He looked into her eyes. "I owe it to you."

"That you do," she bristled. "I've been the talk of the town this week, thanks to you."

"I really am sorry, Armida."

"What about Marietta? Do you still love her?"

"Have you ever been rejected by someone you love?"

Put off by the question, Armida put her lips together and rolled her tongue over her teeth and along the inside of her mouth.

"Well, if you have," said Egisto, "you know that I don't know what I feel anymore. What's love if it isn't reciprocated?"

She shifted her basket to her other hip, reluctantly smiling at his sincerity.

Egisto pressed ahead. "You said the other night that it shouldn't be that difficult to find someone to marry outside of the Church. Well, you have no idea. It's impossible, really. Would you marry me outside the Church?"

"I haven't said I'd marry you at all."

"*If* you would marry me, would you do it in a civil ceremony?"

"Yes."

"You are a rare woman, signorina Sigali!"

"I'm a desperate woman. Marriage is the only recourse I have for a better life."

"And I'm a desperate man. Apparently, marrying an Italian woman is the only recourse I have to gain my family's approval."

"Really, Egisto, don't talk to me about desperation. What do you know of poverty and struggle? Your family may not be wealthy enough for the Tarabellas, but they have more money than most people in Ripa. My mother died when I was eight, and my father may as well be dead. He went to America to support us from there and we haven't heard from him since. Nothing; no checks, no letters. I have ten brothers and sisters and two of them are *insano*." Armida quickly lifted a hand and swept it over her forehead to emphasize the word "crazy."

"My older brothers," she continued, "were lucky. They, at least, received an education. With my mother dead and my father gone, there is barely enough money left for my younger brothers to go to school. There is nothing left for me or my sisters. Imagine my life, Egisto! I've spent most of it being a slave to my family."

"So, you see," she concluded. "I have nothing, and therefore, I have nothing to lose. What I do have, I've had to fight for. It means little to me if I am married in the Church or outside of the Church, as long as I can change my life."

When Egisto didn't respond immediately, she—mistaking his silence for a change of heart—blurted, "And don't think you're the first man who's ever asked me to marry him. There were others, but I refused them because they couldn't give me the kind of life I need. I may be poor, but I'm not stupid, and if you think I'm not good enough for you, I don't care, because I'm willing to wait until the right man comes along."

Egisto's eyes narrowed, as if by doing so he might be able to block out the entire world and catch a glimpse of himself in her. "We're not so different from each other, Armida," he said. "We're both desperate and both of us have to make decisions based on what's reasonable, not necessarily on what may be . . . natural to us. My offer still stands."

"Your offer leaves me no time to think, let alone prepare."

"If you accepted my offer, how much time would you need?"

"Don't be ridiculous. It's impossible."

"What would you have to do to get ready?"

"I don't know," she stuttered. "Pack, tell my brothers and sisters I'm leaving . . . "

Egisto pressed ahead before she could finish. "I spoke with the mayor today. He said he can perform a marriage in the court house as late as seven o'clock this evening. I'll be there at seven. If you are there, then we will marry. If not, then I will know your answer is 'no' and I will go to America alone."

He reached into his pocket, pulled out some bills and several twenty-lira coins and forced them into her hand. "Here, take these to buy whatever you need—clothes, luggage. It's not a bribe. If your answer is 'no' . . . well, consider it restitution for the grief I have caused you."

Measuring each word, he added slowly, "If it makes any difference to you, I find you very attractive." His face turned red. "And I admire your courage and strength. Your self-confidence is remarkable, Armida. I don't know that Marietta could have handled all the challenges of immigrating to America, but I believe you have what it will take."

Then, he straightened and lowered his leg from the door jamb so Armida could leave. Unable to tell what she was thinking, he deduced he would be standing alone at the court house come 7:00 that evening.

chapter six

"Mama, please open the door!" pleaded Carilda. "You will regret it the rest of your life if you don't."

Carmela Bertozzi, feeling all the weight of her fifty-eight years, rocked unresponsively in her chair. She looked weary: weary of raising children who never paid heed to her warnings, weary of worrying, weary of praying for her sons only to endure their godless, ideological nonsense, weary of dashed hopes and unrewarded labors.

"Really, mama, what would you have had him do?"

"He should have married Marietta in the Church," Carmela snapped.

The Bertozzi women had slaved in the kitchen all day preparing a surprise family feast for Egisto's last day. When 3:00 arrived and Egisto wasn't home they sent Francesco out to find him. After Francesco returned empty-handed, news came to them by way of a neighbor that Egisto had been sighted around 7:00 with a strange woman at the magistrate's office. It was now almost 8:00 and they were all sick with speculation.

Egisto knocked again, shouting, "Please, mama, I leave tomorrow. I may never see you again."

Luigi stood near the door, awaiting a signal from his wife. The village priest had cautioned him to be patient with Carmela. Without betraying the confessional, he had hinted—in so many words—that she blamed herself for Egisto's problems.

"She knows her foul temper puts a wedge between her and her family sometimes," the priest had told him. "And America is a long way from a mother's heart."

Still, everyone in the room knew Carmela would make Luigi's life intolerable for him if he opened the door without her approval. He didn't budge.

"We can't keep the food warm much longer," Francesco's wife, Pia, ventured.

Carmela fingered her rosary beads. The clacking noise they made when rubbed together matched the ticking of the clock on the fireplace mantle. When the knocking ceased and several moments passed without any calls of supplication, she relented, nodding at her husband to open the door.

Egisto stepped inside, turned, and drew Armida in behind him. Wearing a brown serge skirt, soft linen blouse, and a dark wool jacket, she stood awkwardly on display before them. Her small feet boasted a pair of stylish new shoes and she carried a handsome leather valise that Egisto offered to take from her.

Egisto placed his free hand on the small of her back and introduced her. "This is Armida Sigali. My wife. We were married an hour ago in a civil ceremony at the courthouse."

His announcement sucked the air out of the room. No one moved.

Luigi spoke first. "Son, why didn't you tell us? Are we so insignificant that we could not be a part of the most important day of your life?"

Carmela stopped rocking and sat rigidly in her chair, holding her apron up to her mouth in a failed attempt to conceal a sob. Francesco and Alberto stood next to their wives and children, looking thankful that they weren't in Egisto's shoes, but Carilda approached Armida and embraced her.

"Welcome to our family, Armida." she said. "You're just in time for supper." Then, she turned to Egisto and fell on him, her head buried in his chest. Unable to control himself any longer, Egisto began to weep. Moments later, Carilda stepped away, giving room for Luigi, Francesco and Alberto to surround Egisto with their arms interlocked, a heaving circle of Bertozzi strength gone limp.

When they finally tore themselves away from each other, Carilda announced it was time to eat. She ushered the newlyweds to the table, giving Egisto the seat of honor, and gathered up all the children to take their places around them. Then, putting Bianca on her hip, she and Pia served up the first of many courses. Carmela refused to join them. She sat quietly by herself, looking haggard and spent, sulking, while everyone else but Armida talked and laughed and reminisced.

It was after midnight when Luigi finally rose from the table and toasted Egisto. "Our last drink together, our last meal together, our last evening together with you, Egisto."

With glasses raised, everyone nodded in somber acknowledgement as he added, his voice cracking, "But, our hearts will never say good-bye. May you never forget us, your family, and may you always remember us with joy and longing. Salute!"

Ten goblets clinked in accord and when the last of the wine washed over the thick tongues of the Bertozzi clan, they bid each other good night. Carilda led the newlyweds upstairs to her bedroom, insisting they sleep in her bed on their honeymoon night. On the dresser, she had placed fresh linens, candles and fragrant oils.

Armida offered to help, but Carilda refused, reminding her that as a new bride she must not lift a finger.

"This is a special time for you, Armida," she said. "Your honeymoon should be memorable. When Barlaam and I were married, my mother and aunts made sure I didn't have to cook or clean for an entire week!"

Sitting on a small chaise near the bed, Egisto motioned for Armida to come sit next to him. Not looking at each other, they waited while Carilda made up the bed.

Beads of sweat pooled beneath Egisto's collar, staining his shirt. It had taken all of his resolve and every ounce of fortitude within him to carry off this day. He could only imagine how Armida felt. Loosening his tie, he told himself the worst was over, that his parents and brothers would be satisfied knowing he would be taking a wife with him to America.

He was shocked when he felt Armida's hand on his knee. He took it and squeezed it, stealing a glance at her as he did. Her eyes told him what he, himself, had feared. They were two strangers suddenly, inextricably, thrust into an intimate relationship that was supposed to last the rest of their lives . . . and it terrified them. Egisto forced a smile and gently rubbed her fingers.

Lighting the last candle and pulling the window curtains tightly shut, Carilda finally excused herself and for the second time in their lives Egisto and Armida found themselves alone together. In the flickering candlelight, they rose from the couch.

Armida faced Egisto, her expression soft, but earnest, no longer that of a cornered animal. "Well," she said, "Here we are again."

"Under completely different circumstances."

Armida smiled as though she were about to laugh. "This

time there's no running away in the morning."

Egisto wasn't sure what she meant. Was she teasing him, or was she implying she felt some kind of personal victory in having married him?

Surreally, he watched as she began to unbutton her blouse while at the same time locking eyes with him. Her eyes; he hadn't remembered them being so riveting, so . . . consuming. She placed her hands on his collar and began to unknot his tie. Her breath was hot on his fingers as he fumbled to help her. Burning pulses, raw and uncontrollable, unlike anything he had ever felt before—even with Marietta—seeped into his flesh. His senses exploded.

"There's—something—about—you—" he panted, between kisses, between peeling off his shirt and helping her undress.

"I'm different from everyone else," she whispered, her lips brushing his. "I know."

DOMINATING THE EASTERN horizon above Monte di Ripa, Michelangelo's famed marbled peak had just captured the first meloned rays of dawn when the stationmaster announced the northbound train to Paris via Genova would be arriving at the Massa Centrale train depot any moment.

Egisto double-checked his tickets. From Paris they would switch trains, go north to Le Havre on the English Channel, and then board the steamer *La France* for their transatlantic voyage to New York. Trying to juggle a plethora of emotions, Egisto suddenly wondered how his new wife would handle the crossing, since she was terrified of water.

"Every time I'm near water I feel like I can't breathe," she had told him last night, as they lay awake after making love, talking about their voyage.

He had laughed at her. "I would never have guessed it."

"Why?"

"Remember Manzini's hot spring?"

"That was only four feet deep. I'm afraid of deep water; water that I can't see the bottom of."

"Why?"

"I can't swim."

"Well, you have nothing to worry about," he had assured her, amused. Kissing her shoulder, he'd added, "I'll see to it that you don't drown on the way to America, and when we get there, and get settled in, maybe I'll find a pool or a lake and teach you how to swim."

"I think I'll pass, thank you."

They had drifted off to sleep then, her velvety smooth back cradled against his chest, his hand resting on her hip. But, this morning, at the break of dawn, when they woke up and looked at each other, it was as though it had all been a dream. Egisto noticed that Armida, pulling the sheets up over her breasts, waited until he got up and pulled on his pants before she got out of bed. Rushing to get out of the house in time, they had stolen hurried, anxious looks at each other—embarrassed and self-conscious—as though they couldn't get out of the bedroom, out of the house, and away from all the reminders of their impromptu wedding fast enough.

The truth was, Egisto realized, despite being married, despite their intense lovemaking, they both knew they were strangers to each other. The unknown gulf between them was as vast as the Atlantic they were about to cross. Yet now, standing on the boarding platform waiting for the train, he noticed that Armida appeared calm and self-assured.

Is she mercurial by nature, he mused, *or does she just feel as unsettled as I do?* She was also, he realized with a jolt, unnervingly lovely—stunning, actually—in a new dress and matching waistcoat that showcased her small waist.

His reflections were shattered when the station's loud-speakers blared out the train's arrival. "*Attenzione!* All passengers travelling northbound to Genova, the train will arrive in less than five minutes. Please have all carry-on luggage on the platform with you, ready to board."

Egisto took a deep breath and glanced at his father and two brothers who had accompanied them there, having left their wives and children asleep at home. They looked as tense as he felt. When they heard the train whistle and a moment later saw it approaching them from the south, Francesco lit a cigarette, his hand trembling. The usually smiling Alberto frowned and dipped his head down on the shoulder of his jacket as though wiping something off his cheek. Then, the train arrived, shuddering to a stop, and as the doors opened and passengers began boarding, the brothers shared a final, wordless embrace.

Luigi grasped the back of Egisto's neck with both hands and kissed him brusquely. "I feel like someone is cutting off my arm, the pain is so real," he whispered in his ear. "I will miss you, son, more than you'll ever know."

Egisto held on to both of his father's elbows for as long as he dared. "I will write, papa, and send money as soon as I get my first pay-check. Thank you for everything; thank you for my education, for . . ."

Luigi patted him on the shoulders. "You don't have to thank me, Egisto. What you're doing, going to America to work to help support the family . . . that is all a father could ask for."

Lastly, Luigi turned to Armida. He kissed her once on each cheek and said, his voice cracking, "I am glad Egisto found you. Be good to him."

Less than five minutes later, as the engine picked up steam and the train pulled away, snaking upland through sleeping vineyards, fallow fields dotted with stone and stucco farmhouses, and stretches of white sand beaches, Egisto watched his entire past recede slowly into obscurity.

His future, standing shoulder-to-shoulder with him, slipped her arm through his. "It will be all right, Egisto," she said. "We will make a new life for ourselves in America."

He stroked her hand and nodded. Deep down inside, amidst all the excitement and change and uneasiness, he found himself wondering what Marietta was doing at that moment.

❧

My sister Rina, who was three or four at the time, told me she can still recall bits and pieces of Uncle Egisto's last night in Italy with our family. She remembers mama crying for days afterwards and nonna complaining that she worried so much about him she couldn't get a decent night's sleep. And Rina says even now—she's ninety-three—she can't forget how beautiful Armida looked that night, so young and sure and full of life.

The fact is, things were never the same after Uncle Egisto left for America. That's what mama said anyway. She said nonno, though he always regretted losing the opportunity to have family ties with the Tarabellas, was proud Egisto did the honorable thing by marrying Armida . . . considering all the rumors going around about them at the time.

It's odd. Before mama died, she asked me if there was ever a time before the war, before the troubles began, that I guessed what the outcome of Egisto marrying Armida would be. I told her I did. I knew when I read between the lines of Uncle Egisto's letters.

"I thought so, Bianca," she told me. "You always could see what others can't."

❧

PART II

St. Paul, Minnesota

1923–1930

Fra il dire e il fare c'è di mezzo il mare

"An ocean lies between what is said and what is done"

chapter seven

THE MODEST, CREAM-COLORED, two-bedroom bungalow at 1044 Margaret Street was slowly regaining a semblance of normalcy. All day, since early in the morning, small delivery trucks stuffed with furniture, bicycles, clothing, and miscellaneous household items had lumbered up to the house depositing a haphazard array of accumulated treasures. A steady stream of bantering, interrupted by an occasional curse, had accompanied the comings and goings of a seemingly endless parade of old neighbors and friends.

Standing on the front porch, a bit dazed, in the center of all the commotion, Armida accepted a large pan of lasagna bolognese and two loaves of homemade pugliese bread from her closest friend, Julia Barghini.

"Grazie, Julia," she said, speaking Italian. "You really didn't need to do this."

"There's no way my lasagna can compete with yours, Armida, but the important thing is you won't have to cook tonight."

Armida kissed Julia on the cheek. "I appreciate it." Turning to her son and daughter, playing kickball in the driveway with the Barghini kids, Armida called out, "Silverio! Violenza! *Venire qui!* Come here!"

Silverio bounded up the porch steps, out of breath. "What, mama?"

"Armida thrust the pan of lasagna into his hands. "Parli italiano! Speak Italian to me. You know I can't understand English. Take this into the kitchen for me and set it near the oven." She handed the bread to her daughter. "Here, Violenza. Put these loaves of bread where your brother tells you."

"They're growing up so fast," noted Julia, watching Armida's children disappear into the house. "I can't believe Violenza will be starting school soon. It seems like just yesterday you were nursing her."

"Actually, Julia, I'm almost looking forward to some time away from her. She's been a difficult child; nothing like Silverio."

"Violenza has a mind of her own, that's for sure," replied Julia. "Like her mother."

"What do you mean?"

"I'm only teasing, Armida. But you have to admit, compared to most women born and raised in Italy you're fairly independent-minded."

"Are you saying I'm not a good wife or mother?"

"Of course not!"

Armida nodded. "I'm just tired, I guess. All this moving has taken it out of me."

"That's why I brought you a meal." Julia touched her arm. "I'm concerned for you, *mia amica*. You're working too hard."

"Once things get back to normal, I'll be fine," she replied, waving away Julia's concern. "I'll have plenty of time to rest when Violenza starts school."

Julia shook her head. "When Violenza starts school, you'll find out how much you miss her. It can be lonely when the kids aren't home, believe me."

WITH HER BACK to Egisto, Armida leaned over the kitchen sink and began scrubbing off the baked-on residue in Julia's empty lasagna pan with the force of a human jackhammer. "Are the children in bed?" she asked.

"Yes. I read them some stories and tucked them in already." Egisto sounded euphoric. "They are so happy to be in our new house."

After a pause, Armida said, "You're doing it again."

"What?"

"Staring at me."

"I like looking at you."

She set the dishcloth down and began rinsing the pan. "You study me like I'm one of your projects at Drake Marble Company."

Egisto startled her by coming up from behind and placing the palms of his hands on either side of her waist. He moved them, slowly and deliberately down until they formed parentheses around her hips.

"What are you doing?" she asked, playfully.

"I'm studying the contours of your body." He kissed the nape of her neck, lifted his hands from her hips, and stroked her back from top to bottom, his stonemason's fingers relishing the curvature of her spine. They lingered low, near her tailbone. "I'm exploring all of your ridges and hollows . . . my very own Venus de Milo."

"Not now, Egisto. I'm too tired."

"Come outside with me," he pleaded, taking the pan from her and setting it in the dish drain. "You're working too hard. Here, let me show you what I did."

Reluctantly, Armida let him lead her into their backyard. There, in the gathering dusk beneath a spreading maple, she saw two wooden chairs flanking an overturned crate. On top of the crate were several lit candles, a bottle of wine, and two glasses. He led her to the makeshift table and pulled the chair out for her.

For well over an hour, they recalled scenes from the past ten years of their life, particularly the difficulties of making do for so long in their cramped rental on Stryker Avenue in Little Italy. Armida tipped her glass toward their new home and noted that it was not for nothing, after all, that she had endured such frigid Minnesota winters and strange American customs, all without the benefit of speaking a word of English.

"You cannot avoid learning English forever," cautioned Egisto. "Soon, the children will be speaking it all the time. You will regret not understanding them."

She frowned. *I have devoted my life to my family. I have given one hundred percent of myself to them. What more do they want? If my children are ashamed of me because I don't speak English, there's nothing I can do about it.*

Egisto quickly changed the subject, expressing his delight that eight-year-old Silverio and six-year-old Violenza would now be going to Sibley Elementary School, and later, Harding High School. But Armida, fixated on his earlier comment and convinced he had judged her unfairly, tuned him out. *Why had he prefaced his pride in their children with her handicap; her failing?* Blood rushed to her face. She was thankful for the cover of deepening twilight that hid her embarrassment, anger and shame from her husband.

As Egisto continued talking about their children, she realized there was no one she could talk to about the fracture lines developing just below the surface of her life. She had ignored them at first, but lately she had felt them deepening, as though a seismic event—even a small one—would cause them to rupture. Egisto always complimented her on her strength and solidity, her ability to tackle any problem that came her way. If he knew the truth, knew that fear of rejection and failure dogged her every day, robbing her of her sleep and peace of mind, he might not admire her so much. Even Julia could never possibly understand to what extent her fears had begun to control her thoughts.

She poured herself another glass of wine, held it to her nose, and swished the ruddy liquid around, before drinking it. Egisto's voice had faded into the background of her thoughts. *Well, I know this much,* she concluded to herself, *I won't be condemned to life as an outsider in my own family just because they expect me to learn a new language. No, I will insist Violenza and Silverio speak Italian at all times in our home. Egisto too. They can speak English with their friends, but they won't speak it around me.*

Egisto must have sensed her disconnectedness because he switched topics again. This time, he tried to engage her in the conversation by talking about Italy, peppering his sentences with long sighs and clicks of his tongue when he spoke of his family. But his wistfulness only accentuated the fact that she was alienated from her own family there, and his pride in being able to help his father and brothers financially reminded her that her own family only wrote when they needed money. Ironic, she thought, given that Egisto was homesick for Italy and she was not, that it was Egisto bent on learning English and becoming Americanized, and not her.

That's my life in a nutshell, she thought. *Everyone has expectations of me, but no one asks, or cares, what I want. People have only ever wanted me for what they could get from me.*

She began to feel the effect of the wine on her exhausted mind. What was she thinking? She was better off than most immigrants she knew. They owned their first home. They were moving up in the world. Her daughter was going to get an education; something she could only have dreamed of getting in Italy.

She leaned across the table, her glass raised. "I know I haven't been myself lately," she apologized. "I'm just tired, I guess. But you're right, Egisto. Life in America *is* good."

Egisto raised his glass to her. "And it's only going to get better. Salute!"

Armida set her glass down, got up from her seat, walked around the overturned crate, and dropped into her husband's lap. Sighing, she wrapped her arms around him, her face muzzling his neck. Egisto placed his glass on the table and crossed one leg over the other to make a sort of pocket for her hips to settle into. He played with her hair for awhile and then toyed with the hem of her skirt, lifting it above her knees, before using his index finger to trace invisible designs on her legs.

"Someday, I *will* sculpt you," he said. "You will be my masterpiece."

"Don't tease me."

"I'm not," he whispered. "Life with you has been good, Armida, and it will only get better. I promise."

A FEW DAYS later, the first day of school completely ambushed Armida's desire for an orderly life. Having stayed up most of the night sewing a new skirt and blouse for Violenza, she woke up with a screaming headache. After breakfast, she walked through the living room, ignoring several boxes still waiting to be unpacked, to check on Violenza, who was sitting on her bed, dressed in her new clothes but not yet ready for school.

"Violenza! I told you to comb your hair!"

"I did."

"You did not."

Armida went into the bathroom, got a hairbrush, and came back into the bedroom. Sitting down on the bed, she said, "Turn around and let me brush it."

"Oh, mama!"

"Turn around, I said. Now!"

"Ouch!" Violenza pulled away. "You're hurting me!"

Armida rapped her daughter's head with the brush. "Sit still until I'm finished!"

"Can't you call me 'Babe' like papa does? I hate Violenza. And Siv hates his name too. No one calls him Silverio."

"No, I won't call you Babe! It's not your name. You and your brother can tell your friends that it's too bad if they don't like the names I gave you."

With renewed zeal, she resumed attacking her fidgety daughter's mass of curls. "When I was your age, Violenza, I let my mother dress me, brush my hair, *and* correct my grammar, all without a whisper. Be thankful you have a mother to brush your hair!"

Egisto peeked into the room. "What's this I hear about school friends?"

"Babbo!" Violenza leaped off the bed and ran into his arms.

Siv appeared a moment later, his hair combed, his shoes on, and his books tucked under his arm. "Come on, Babe. If you don't hurry, we'll be late."

Armida threw the brush onto the bed. "Her name's not Babe!" Letting out a groan, she fell back against the headboard, and put her head between her hands.

"Your mother's right," said Egisto, addressing Siv and

Babe. "Your friends can call you what they like, but here, at home, please use the names you were given. It will make your mother happy."

Armida felt him glance at her as she massaged the tender area along the base of her inner eyebrows with her thumbs, and heard him order Siv to the kitchen to get a glass of water for her.

Sitting down on the bed next to her, Egisto asked, "Does your head still hurt?"

Armida nodded.

Turning to Babe, he said, "Bambina, you must not give your mama cause to worry. Do you understand?"

"Capito, babbo."

He nodded in Armida's direction. "I think mama will be very lonely today without you here."

Babe appeared to weigh what her father said against how her mother had been speaking to her. Not appearing entirely convinced of her father's assessment of the situation, she walked over to Armida, took her hand in hers and said, "I'm sorry you'll be all by yourself today, mama, but I have to go to school now that I am six. Don't worry. We're just a couple of blocks away. We'll be back for lunch before you know it."

Armida offered her cheek for Violenza to kiss and then proceeded to fuss over her, fastening the top button of her wool cardigan and smoothing the collar of her crisp, new white blouse over it.

"Egisto," she said, "I think I should walk the children to school today."

Babe groaned and stamped her foot.

"I walked to school last year all by myself," said Siv, coming back into the room with a glass of water. He handed it to his mother. "It's no big deal."

"But, it's a new school and a new neighborhood," Armida replied. "What if . . ."

Egisto glanced at his watch. "I will be late if I don't leave now. Mama, I insist you allow me the honor of escorting our children to the end of the street where I will catch the trolley to Drake. Deal?"

"Deal!" Siv and Babe squealed. Together, they raced out to the front porch to wait for him.

Alone with Armida, Egisto took the empty glass from her, set it on the dresser and pulled her close to him. Rubbing his nose against hers, he said softly, "Remember what we said when we first realized we would be able to buy our own home?"

Armida blushed.

He breathed in her ear, "I say we start tonight on getting a new little bambino to keep you company. Maybe that will help your headache, no?" He kissed her fingertips and touched them to her lips. Then with a wide grin, he tipped his hat to her, and went out to the porch calling, "*Andiamo*. Let's go!"

ARMIDA REMEMBERED WHAT Julia had said a few weeks earlier; that the house would feel empty when both the children were in school. Her stomach lurched at the unexpected truth of it. Not quite sure how she was going to make it through the long and lonely day, other than bank on the hope of her husband's parting promise, she resolved, despite her throbbing headache, to make the most of her free time.

She went into the kitchen, hoping to distract herself from melancholy thoughts by organizing the pantry and cupboards and unpacking the last unopened boxes still lining the wall. Instead, she was put out by the dismal drip-drip-drip of the sink's leaky faucet. It echoed throughout the kitchen like an excruciating chorus of teardrops, reminding her she was alone. Desperate, she dug out the recipe box Julia had given her years ago as a birthday gift and searched for something special to make Silverio and Violenza for lunch; something that would demonstrate to them that she was still a signifi-cant, irreplaceable figure in the Bertozzi household. Some-thing that would convince them, and her, that her life still had value.

chapter eight

"WHERE ARE THE bay leaves?" Armida opened a box marked "Spices" and rummaged through it. She needed some for the pot of *minestra di castagne*—chestnut soup—she had decided to make. With leftover fried bread, it would be the perfect meal to serve Silverio and Violenza when they came home for lunch their first day of school.

Finding the leaves in a waxed-paper bag, she tossed three of them into the kettle of soup simmering on the stove and hung her apron on a hook near the pantry door. She debated what to do next. It was only 11:00 and the children wouldn't be home for another hour. The pain in her head had subsided, but the dripping faucet was driving her crazy, so she left the kitchen and wandered through the house in search of something else to keep her busy. It was pointless. She was beginning to feel as though she was adrift, anchorless in a sterile domestic sea, when she heard hushed voices piercing the silence.

Armida Sigali is stupid; she can't speak English.

Her children will be smarter than her.

She will be an embarrassment to them.

She listened intently. They sounded as though they were coming from the kitchen, in sync with the dripping faucet, but she was too afraid to go there and check.

Armida Sigali is all washed up. Her children don't need her anymore.

Armida Sigali is barren; she'll never get pregnant again.

No one loves her.

No one cares.

Covering her ears, she flew into Egisto's study and slammed the door shut behind her. "Stop it!" she cried over and over, shaking so badly she nearly collapsed to her knees. "Stop it!"

It wasn't the first time she had heard voices taunting her, telling her she was unloved, but never had they lasted more than a few fleeting seconds. This time, she leaned against Egisto's study door for perhaps ten minutes, trembling, willing the voices away. Gradually they ceased. Her emotions were frayed and since she had only been averaging about four hours of sleep a night for over a year now, she told herself the voices were, most likely, simply a result of being tired and overworked. Or perhaps, she thought, breathing a guarded sigh of relief, it was simply some strange result of the headache she'd had earlier that morning.

Eventually, she talked herself into following the streams of dappled sunlight, dancing into the study through the room's only window, to Egisto's desk. She plopped down in his chair, put her arms behind her head and stretched her legs out beneath the desk, willing her limbs to relax. Little did it matter to her, at that moment, that Egisto might consider it an invasion of his privacy for her to be in his study, sitting at his desk.

What luxury, she thought, closing her eyes, her breath finally steady again, *to bask uninterrupted in this warm, sunlit room!* Tentatively, she lowered one hand and placed it on her stomach, daring to smile at the prospect of becoming pregnant again. She felt the relative coolness of the chair's rich, oiled leather through her dress, beneath her thighs, and the reminder—the promise—of skin-on-skin contact with Egisto later that night made her feel deliciously alive. She day-dreamed for awhile and then, feeling guilty she wasn't being productive, she retracted her legs from underneath the desk and sat up straight.

She froze. *When I open the study door, will I hear the voices again?*

Not ready to venture out of the study yet, she opened one of the desk drawers and began fingering through the files. It was nothing but bills. She opened a different drawer and discovered a metal cigar box stuffed with old pictures of Egisto's family, but they were a painful reminder to her that she had no pictures of her own family, or of her own childhood. She sighed in self-pity and put them back. But, as she leaned back away from the desk, her sweater caught on the center drawer knob and pulled it open, revealing a bulging manila envelope amidst an assortment of office supplies. Curious, she pulled it out, and without thinking twice, she emptied its contents onto the desk.

They were letters from Egisto's family in Italy. Nothing unusual; she had read them all when they were first delivered. Just as she was ready to put them back in the envelope, her eyes fell on an unusually thick letter stuck to another in front of it. Deftly, she separated them.

How strange, she thought, inspecting it closely. *This is a letter from Egisto addressed to Francesco, but never sent.* Opening it, she pulled out two letters. The first read:

Dearest brother:

Because it is impossible for me to contact Marietta any other way, I send this to you, and you only, in strictest *confidence. I know I can trust you to make sure she receives the enclosed letter. All is well here. Armida will be giving birth soon and I know that life will never be the same.*

—Egisto

Armida unfolded the second letter. A photo of Egisto with Marietta from long ago fell out.

Marietta, my True Bride:

Life without you has been unbearable, yet I have no one to blame but myself. I have been the greatest of fools and if it were possible, I would move heaven and earth to reverse this fate that has separated us . . .

Armida dropped the letter. She felt the tectonic plates of her world slip and crash. The floor beneath her feet convulsed violently. A million tiny voices rose up from the molecules vibrating around her, gathering together into a deafening roar, like the sound of a freight train before a twister, or the grinding, hellish howl that precedes a massive earthquake.

Betrayed!

Rejected!

Unloved!

Worthless!

She clawed at her belly as she imagined her womb splitting open into a gaping black abyss. In slow motion, she watched herself fall into it, tumbling downward, her mouth open in silent terror. Drowning in nothingness, she gasped for air, grabbing on to anything to prevent her being sucked into oblivion. She heard herself scream for help, but no one was there to save her.

She was alone. All alone, except for the voices.

BABE YELLED ACROSS the back yard fence at her neighbor and newest friend, Marcelle. "I'll meet you after lunch and we can walk back to school together, okay?"

Marcelle waved back as Siv grabbed his sister's hand and yanked her up the kitchen steps. As the screen door slammed behind them Siv mumbled, "Maybe she doesn't want to meet you after lunch, Babe. Maybe Marcelle has other friends, did you ever think of that?"

"You're just jealous Siv, because no one's invited you to walk to school with them."

He ignored her, sniffing, "Something smells like it's burning." He walked over to the stove, and picking up a spoon on the counter, he stirred the bubbling soup, scraping the bottom of the pot where the contents had begun to burn.

"Mama!" yelled Babe.

Bewildered, they went from room to room looking for their mother and found her in the room they least expected; their father's study. Still sitting in the desk chair, she looked like a rag doll. One arm dangled loosely over the arm of the chair while the other, resting on her breast, held a piece of paper.

Siv shook her loose arm. "We're home, mama."

When there was no response, Babe whispered, "Maybe she's sick."

"Maybe."

"Let's call papa at work."

"Papa's not at Drake today, remember? He's working at

some church, but I don't remember which one. I'm scared, Babe. Something's wrong."

"Well, we've got to do *something*!" Heading down the hallway, Babe called out over her shoulder, "I'm going to go over to Marcelle's house and tell her mother we need help. I'm hungry!"

chapter nine

EGISTO TURNED THE corner of Margaret Street with great anticipation. Scores of men returning from work filed past him on their way to their own homes, eager to settle down to dinner and a relaxing evening with their families. After supper, he and Armida would taste what was left of last year's wine, compare it with a bottle Duke Barghini had given them, and decide which tasted better. The result would determine which farmer they would buy grapes from this year. Egisto was thankful Minnesota's prohibition laws allowed them to make their own wine, otherwise, he wasn't sure he could survive. A block from home, he spotted Silverio and Violenza sitting on the steps of their front porch. He removed his hat and waved it at them.

"Babbo!" Babe ran into his arms, burying her face in his neck.

Siv looked as though he had seen a ghost. Alarmed, Egisto asked them, "What's wrong?"

"It's mama," Babe cried. "She won't talk to us. Something's wrong. "

Egisto unlocked Babe's arms from around his neck and rushed into the house. Mrs. Sprunk, the mother of Babe's friend and neighbor, was bussing dishes from the dining room table. Having never met before, they awkwardly introduced themselves to each other.

"Mr. Bertozzi," she said hurriedly, "I'm so sorry to tell you, your wife seems to be ill. Your children asked me to come over this afternoon to check on her. I found her . . . " She groped for the right word, looking at Babe and Siv clinging to their father " . . . incapacitated."

"I brought some food over," she continued. "Your children already ate, but your wife refused to eat anything I offered her. I put a plate for you near the stove to heat up whenever you're hungry. If there's anything else I can do, Mr. Bertozzi, I'm right next door." With a sad shrug, she excused herself and left.

Wordlessly, Silverio and Violenza led their father to his study door, let go of his hands, and ran back outside. Armida was still sitting in his desk chair. Her feet were propped on the edge of the seat, her arms encircling her legs, and her face was buried between her knees.

"Armida?" Egisto touched the crown of her head.

Without lifting her head, she recoiled and said nothing. He saw a paper lying on the floor beneath the chair and stooped down to pick it up. It was the letter he had written to Marietta long ago.

"My God," he groaned.

As he stared at the letter, Armida came roaring back to life. She leaped out of the chair and began slapping him; battering his head, his shoulders, his arms. "Marietta is your only *true* love?" she shrieked. "I am nothing but a consolation prize to you?"

In an attempt to restrain her, he grabbed her wrists. "Listen to me! I wrote it a long time ago. I was confused. I was homesick and afraid of all the changes that were happening. You know that when we married it was more of an agreement between us at first. It took time for us to . . . to really fall in love with each other."

"Speak for yourself! I loved you from the beginning!" Armida went limp.

"Doesn't the fact that I never sent the letter tell you anything? I didn't send it to Marietta because I realized I didn't love her. I love *you*, Armida."

"Really? Then why did you keep it? So you could send it to her later? So you could read it and fantasize about her?"

Egisto loosened his grip on Armida's wrists, but didn't let go completely. "I don't know. Maybe I was afraid you would discover me trying to destroy it, or figured you would never find it. I don't know. It was so long ago, I can't remember what I was thinking. Marietta means nothing to me, Armida. I swear it!"

"It took you years to tell me you loved me, yet while you were married to me you told Marietta you loved her. How can you expect me to ever trust you again?" Armida stopped crying and stiffened. She yanked her wrists away from him. "I am nothing but a cook and housekeeper to you and your children! That's all you care about."

"That's not true, and you know it, Armida."

As they argued, Babe and Siv sat cringing on the porch swing. They had never heard their mother cry or their father raise his voice. Almost an hour later, they heard the back door slam. When it grew silent, they got up and peeked into the living room window. They saw their father, armed with a pillow and blanket, making a bed on the couch. Their mother was nowhere in sight.

"Where's mama?" they asked, entering the house.

Egisto sat down on the couch and drew them into his arms. "I'm not sure where she went. She wouldn't tell me."

chapter ten

THE CANDLE-LIT BISTRO tables gracing the front of Yarusso's Café beckoned to Armida and Julia Barghini as they walked by on their way home from Mound's Theatre. Rudolph Valentino, cast as a Russian Robin Hood in his new film *The Eagle*, had captivated their imaginations for the better part of the afternoon. Some pasta and a glass of wine, watered down to legal limits, in St. Paul's most popular Italian restaurant, seemed a fitting end to the day.

They selected a table and sat down. "It's so nice to get out with you again like this," Julia said, smiling at Armida. "It seems like ages since we've seen each other. We're just going to have to make more of an effort to get together now that we're not neighbors anymore."

Tony Yarusso, the proprietor, savoring a Marlboro on the front step of his café, noticed the two women eyeing his menu. Slicking back his hair, he darted toward them, insisting they be seated at a table closest to the corner of 7th and Payne where they could best view the carnival atmosphere of Little Italy.

He smiled at them through tarnished, misaligned teeth and muttered a salutation in Italian before producing a chewed-up pencil from behind his ear to take their order. His long white apron flapped carelessly in the autumn breeze. Good-naturedly, he teased the two women for being out without their husbands.

Julia sniffed. "What husband could compete with Valentino?"

Tony had to concede that Valentino had revolutionized the Italian male image. Pretending to sulk, he disappeared with their order.

"I swear," confided Julia, leaning forward, "Valentino gets more handsome the older he gets."

Armida blushed at her friend's honesty. Julia was a saucy, second-generation Italian-American, far more uninhibited than herself. Her hair was cut in the short new bob that was all the rage and her hemlines—flirting dangerously about the vicinity of her kneecaps—were astonishingly short.

Tony returned with their drinks, striking a comedic pose in an attempt to make them laugh. A long section of burned tobacco hung precariously from the Marlboro still drooping from his thin lips as he lingered over their table.

Julia reached up, pulled the cigarette from his mouth and smashed it into an ashtray. "I don't care to have your ashes in my wine. Sorry Tony. Valentino you're not."

Thrusting his nose in the air and flinging his apron over his shoulder like a Roman centurion, he raised his finger to the sky and retorted, "And you, my discriminating friend, are no leading lady!"

With a friendly slap on the arm, Julia dismissed him.

"What did you say to him?" asked Armida in Italian.

Julia remembered that Armida spoke no English. "I was just joking with him. I told him he was no match for Valentino. You know Tony. He thinks he's a ladies' man."

"Is he?"

"Is he what? "

"Is he a ladies' man, or does he just pretend that he is? After all, he's married."

"Well," Julia hedged, wary of Armida's sudden mood swing. "Tony's a good guy. He's just funny, that's all."

Armida stared petulantly at Tony as he brought them their meals. He ignored her, directing his comments to Julia, assuring her that she would love his *spaghetti cacio e pepe.*

After he excused himself again, Armida demanded, "*Now* what did he say?"

"He wants us to enjoy our meal."

"I don't like him."

"Why?"

"He admires you, but he acts like I don't exist because I'm . . . " Armida looked looking down at her belly where her dress was stretched thin. "Because I'm fat."

"Don't be ridiculous. You're not fat."

"*Allora,* ever since I found Marietta's letter it seems like all I do is sleep and eat."

"It sounds to me like you're depressed, although, honestly, by now I would have thought you'd be over it." Hesitating, Julia added, "You've got to start trusting people again, Armida."

"Would you, if you were me?"

"I don't know. I've tried to put myself in your situation, but I'm not you. I've been given many second chances in my life, so I try to give others a second chance."

"That's easy for you to say."

"Yes it is, but you know you can trust me, Armida. I've always been honest with you and I promise I'll be here for you, no matter what."

Armida forced a smile and thanked her. "That's important to me. You're the only person in America who likes me."

Julia's eyebrows shot up. "You're husband and children like you."

"My children love their father. They hate me."

"You're wrong. Oh, sure, children can be thankless little creatures when they get older. Sometimes I feel like my kids don't like me, but I know they do. They love me, and your children love you."

Armida shook her head. "It's not the same, and it's not my imagination. You're a good mother and I'm not. I yell at Silverio and Violenza—especially Violenza—all the time. You have no idea." Playing with her food, she added, "If I felt loved or appreciated—if I at least had some peace—maybe I wouldn't be this way."

"But you *are* appreciated. You must believe that, Armida! As far as peace goes, I know you don't want to hear this, but you won't have any peace until you forgive Egisto."

Armida, offended, made a move to leave, but Julia caught her hand and firmly instructed her to sit back down. "Listen to me. Egisto has sworn to you that there has never been another woman since he married you. Isn't that enough?"

"No."

"What in the world will it take for you to believe him?"

"Nothing. It's hopeless."

"Nothing is hopeless."

"You don't know what it feels like to be second-best, Julia; to know that you were not your husband's first choice for a wife. And you *certainly* don't know what it's like to live in a foreign country where you don't understand anything anyone is saying to you. People look at me like I'm crazy when I try to talk with them. They think I'm an idiot." Tears threatened to spill over Armida's lower lashes.

"You were born here, Julia," she continued. "You're an

American. You can't imagine what it is like to know your children are ashamed of you because you are not American like them. Egisto denies it, but I see the shame in his eyes when his friends ask him why I have not learned English. I feel like an outsider here. A prisoner! At least in Italy I would feel I belonged."

"Not only that," she concluded, brushing away her tears, "but a day doesn't go by that I don't wonder what my life would be like had I refused Egisto's offer of marriage. I'm sure *he* regrets the day."

Julia shook her head. "Egisto has told Duke and me many times how important you are to him. He loves you."

"I am only important to him because I am the mother of his children. Deep inside, he loves Marietta. I know it." Noticing some people were beginning to stare at her, Armida lowered her voice. "The truth is, Egisto and I are no longer close. I can't bear to share my bed with him and the longer it goes on the less respect I have for him; the less I care about him or anything else. As a matter of fact, if divorce were an option, I'd divorce him today."

"What about Silverio and Violenza?" Julia asked in disbelief.

Armida wiped her mouth with a napkin. "They are in school all day and spend most of their free time with their friends. Last year I thought I would die of loneliness when Violenza started school, but now I am resigned to it. They tolerate me, and I am learning to tolerate them in return."

After several minutes of silence, Julia put her silverware down and pushed her plate away. "I don't know how else to ask you this," she said, "but as your friend, here it is. Duke says Egisto told him you hear voices that tell you . . . all sorts of things. Is that true?"

"Yes."

"And?"

"They used to scare me. Now, I believe what they tell me."

Julia stared at Armida as though seeing her for the first time. Picking up her purse, she stuttered, "I have to use the ladies room. I'll be right back."

When she returned, Armida was gone.

The sun was beginning to set behind an ominous bank of clouds, casting eerie, sludge-colored shadows along the length of 7th Street. The street lights sputtered to life as Tony began moving tables and chairs back inside the café in anticipation of the approaching storm. Soon, a rough Saturday night crowd would be prowling the streets in search of speakeasies, easy women, and bootleg whiskey.

After glancing up and down the street, Julia asked Tony, "Did you see where Armida went?"

"Yeah," he drawled, pointing across the street, toward a park that followed the banks of the river. "She went that way."

DUKE BARGHINI AND Egisto tallied the scores from their last game of Briscola. At Duke's suggestion, they had volunteered to stay home so their wives could have an afternoon to themselves and they had made the most of it. Normal house rules were ignored, doors left wide open, shoes and clothes left wherever they had been tossed, plates of half-eaten food strewn across counters and tables. Their combined brood of energetic children, except for Duke's thumb-sucking toddler, could be heard playing bocce outdoors, even though it was almost too dark to see. Despite the fact that the air was oppressively hot and muggy, more like July than September, no one noticed the telltale signs of a severe Midwest thunderstorm sneaking up on them. The two men had exhausted the topic of politics and were beginning to discuss how they would tease their wives about seeing *The Eagle*, when Julia burst through the front door. She was soaked with sweat and out of breath.

"Armida disappeared," she cried. "I can't find her anywhere!"

While Duke tried to calm her down, Egisto called Siv and Babe into the house.

"We went to Yarusso's Café after the movie and while we were there, Armida said some things that really worried me," explained Julia, glancing sideways at Egisto. "I went to the bathroom and when I came back to our table she was gone. Tony saw her walk toward the river. It was getting dark, so I walked along the riverbank trail calling for her, but she was nowhere in sight. Then, I went back to Yarusso's and used their phone to call your house, Egisto, but she didn't answer, so I came straight home."

The baby, sensing his mother's anxiety, began to wail. Duke handed him to Julia who instinctively pressed him close to her breast, stroking his damp forehead with her shaking hands and shushing him as she rocked back and forth.

"Where do you think she is, Egisto?" she asked. "I'm terrified for her!"

Egisto stood awkwardly in front of his friends, fingering the rim of his felt hat.

"This isn't the first time she's done this, I'm afraid. She will just get up and leave at all hours of the day or night. If I ask her where she's going or where she's been, she threatens to leave and not come back. She tells me it's none of my business what she does and says if she doesn't get away she'll go crazy. What can I do?"

With a spine-tingling crack, the storm that had been brewing exploded. Thunder rattled the Barghini house down to its very foundations. Refusing Duke's admonition to stay until the storm passed, Egisto ordered Siv and Babe to cover their heads before racing out of the house to catch the evening tram back to Margaret Street. From the safety of their doorway, the Barghinis watched the three disappear down their driveway and into the storm.

Duke drew his wife and baby protectively toward him. Moments later, Julia looked up at him and said, "Armida is not only still depressed, Duke, she's also insanely jealous and insecure. And paranoid. She admitted she hears voices."

Setting the baby down, she began cleaning up the kitchen. "When I was talking with Armida tonight I felt like there was something building inside of her that wanted to destroy her and everyone around her . . . even me." She shuddered before asking, "What would you do, Duke, if I was like that?"

"If you ever even remotely started acting like Armida Bertozzi, he smiled, I'd have you committed."

"Don't kid around like that."

"Well, I'm only partly kidding." He piled some dirty dishes into the sink. "I can't believe you don't see it. Armida's crazy."

"I'll admit she's mentally fragile right now. But crazy?"

With Julia back in control of the kitchen, Duke hung back and grabbed a half-eaten apple from one of the plates. "I can say it because I can see it and you can't. You're too close to her, Julia. You're a woman—and her friend—so you make excuses for things you know aren't right because you want to protect her."

Julia rolled up her sleeves and began washing dishes. "She's not insane."

Duke leaned against the counter, thoughtfully devouring his apple. "Anyone who hears voices, screams curses at their spouse in public and gets so angry they walk out on their family and goes God-knows-where for hours . . . I'm sorry, but there's something wrong with that."

"Come on," he added, noticing Julia flinch. "Admit that there's something seriously wrong with Armida! Egisto's only told us a little of what's really going on. I'm sure we don't even know the half of it."

"All right. Armida's emotionally unstable. She's not normal; I'll admit that. But, she used to be." Julia stopped washing the dishes to look directly at Duke. "I want the old Armida back."

"So do I, if only for Egisto's sake."

"And the children's sake."

"Yes, and the children."

Julia lifted her chin. "Duke, would you really have me committed if I was like her?"

"Aw, honey." Duke tossed what was left of the apple into the trash can and swept his wife into his arms. "I was just kidding. You *are* kind of crazy, but it's a good crazy; the kind that drives me wild." He growled, taking an imaginary bite out of her neck before adding seriously, "I wasn't kidding about Armida, though. I don't know how Egisto puts up with her. I guarantee, if she doesn't change she'll end up in St. Peter's."

chapter eleven

"Your mom is really scary," Marcelle declared, as she and Babe began their ascent up Margaret Street on their way to the Hippodrome Skate Rink. An arctic wind coated the blades of the leather Strauss speed skates that hung around their necks with a thin film of ice. They walked closer together to keep warm. Babe, now ten years old, had grown accustomed to candid comments by sympathetic friends. Neighborhood bullies called her mother a zombie. Marcelle was more kind.

"I like your dad a lot," Marcelle added, not wanting to hurt Babe's feelings. "Everyone does. But your mom? She's so mean to you. How can you stand it?"

Babe pulled her wool cap down over her numb ears. "I don't know. She's just my mom."

The surprise force of a firmly packed snowball, landing squarely on the back of Babe's head, stopped them both in their tracks.

"Hey, wop! Froggie! Better watch where yer walkin'—ya might just end up on the wrong side o' the street!" The threat echoed off the houses and was followed by a round of exaggerated grunts and snickers.

Spotting the perpetrators, Marcelle screamed, "Sean Dempsey! Foley! Kelly! I'm going to tell my dad on you!"

Babe seized Marcelle's arm and escorted her around the

backside of a Model T Ford parked nearby. "Don't waste your breath, Marcelle! I've got an idea."

With a devilish grin, she pointed to a pile of frozen horse droppings behind the car and while Sean and his gang continued to hurl insults their way, Babe and Marcelle started molding snow around them.

"What are ya doin' behind that car, girlies?" Sean shouted. "Peein' like the wops in the old country?" He and his friends doubled over with laughter.

"Yeah," Jack Kelly boomed. "Maybe they need their mommies to come change their nappies!"

Patrick Foley shouted, "Hey—isn't the wop's mom crazy? Better call a shrink and take her away before it spreads!" Sean and Jack howled convulsively at Patrick's crude imitation of Armida.

Methodically placing their secret weapons on the runner of the car that shielded them from the boys, Babe yelled out, "We're making calzones!"

"But, Babe," said Marcelle, "they don't know what calzones are."

"Well, they're about to find out now, aren't they?" retorted Babe.

Just as they finished molding their last snowball, Babe's brother, Siv, called to them from the end of the block. He was with a ruddy-cheeked boy. Together, they approached Babe and Marcelle with great curiosity.

"What are you two doing?" they shouted.

"Sshh!" Both girls put their fingers to their lips and pointed over the hood of the car toward the house across the street where Sean and his gang were still hooting and hollering. Babe motioned Siv and his friend over to them.

Stealthily, they maneuvered their way to the Model T and

knelt down next to the girls. Siv introduced his new friend who had just moved close to them on Margaret Street. His name was Dick. He was almost ten years old—like Siv— and he looked as German as his last name: Neumann. Dick wagged his thumb at the sniggering boys across the street.

"Those guys givin' you a hard time?"

"Yes!" said the girls in unison.

"Hmm." He peeked over the hood of the car to get a better look at the threat before kneeling down again.

"What makes you think you can throw those things that far?" he asked, pointing to the misshapen balls aligned on the running board.

Babe reached discreetly behind her and before Dick knew what hit him, he had a face-full of snow. "That's how I know," she proclaimed. "I'm not helpless."

Rising cautiously to her feet with one of the missiles cupped eagerly in her hands, she muttered, " . . . and no one calls me a wop!" Throwing the snowball, she yelled, "Take that, you Irish scum!"

Sean, caught with his mouth wide open in the middle of a jeer, reeled backward from the impact. Tasting the undeniable flavor of horse manure, he shook his head in disbelief, wiped his mouth, and exploded into a Celtic rage that thrust him out into the middle of the street where he immediately found himself the unprotected target of an all-out assault.

"Hey," shouted Dick, slapping Babe on the back. "You got him right in the kisser!"

Sean's friends searched desperately for some manure on their side of the street, but none was to be found. The girls had stumbled across Margaret Street's mother lode, and with Siv and Dick at their side, they drove the bullies back. When their stash of snowballs was exhausted, they threw up their hands in victory, danced a jig, and made faces at their opponents across enemy lines.

As the hooligans skulked off, Dick yelled, "Beat it, ya bums! That'll teach ya to mess with wops, Dempsey!"

"Yeah!" shouted Babe, her adrenaline surging. "No one messes with me or mine!"

When Babe turned, she saw Dick give her a nod of approval. Then, he turned to Siv and said, "Swell sister you got there, Siv. I like her spunk."

"I HEARD YOU two had an interesting day today," said Egisto, his head buried in an Italian newspaper recently sent to him by his brother Francesco.

Siv and Babe, their faces still bright red from an invigorating afternoon of ice-skating, waited respectfully until he finished reading. Neatly folding the paper and placing it next to his coffee, their father crossed his arms.

"Well?" he asked.

Wide-eyed, they responded innocently, "What?"

"What? Sean Dempsey's mother paid us a visit this afternoon, that's what."

They both squirmed. Babe blurted, "Sean asked for it, papa!"

"I'm sure he did. Need I ask whose idea it was to create such an . . . innovative . . . method of retaliation?"

They hung their heads.

"Siv, it was honorable of you to help your sister. But next time, play by the rules. Go to your room. I'll talk to you later. I want to talk to Babe now . . . alone."

Siv looked relieved. "Yes, babbo." Casting a quick glance over his shoulder at Babe, he disappeared down the hallway.

"Your mother's upset," said Egisto.

"Isn't she always?" countered Babe.

"That's enough, Violenza!"

"Well, it's true."

"True or not, the fact remains that she's extraordinarily upset today. I could hear Mrs. Dempsey all the way in my study when she showed up at the back door this afternoon. Your mother was completely unprepared. Do you know why Mrs. Dempsey came, Violenza?"

"I can guess."

"Please do."

Babe sniffed, "Poor Sean smelled like road apples, I suppose."

Egisto stood up, his hands clasped loosely behind his back. "You suppose correctly. His clothes, according to his mother, are ruined."

"What a *lie!*" said Babe, indignantly. "Since when does a little manure ruin clothes? Doesn't his mother know how to do laundry? It's his *pride* that's ruined, pa!"

"No doubt. Nevertheless," he continued, "Mrs. Dempsey insists on reparation. By the time I came to your mother's aid, Mrs. Dempsey was whipped into a frenzy."

Egisto paused, his mind wandering away for a moment with another, greater concern.

Slowly, he added, "You will work to help pay for his damaged clothing."

Babe gasped.

He turned his back to her. "I will pay you to . . . " His shoulders collapsed, sagging under an unseen weight. He couldn't finish his sentence.

While she watched her father struggle to regain his composure, Babe took herself to task. *Now I've gone and hurt him,* she thought bitterly. *If only I wasn't so headstrong. Trouble seems to follow me everywhere I go.*

"I'm sorry, babbo!" she blurted, fighting back tears. "I'll try really hard not to be a problem to you anymore."

Egisto straightened, turned, and looked intently at his daughter. "You have *never* been a problem, Violenza, and you never will be." He bent down and stroked her cheek tenderly. "I don't know what I'd do without you."

"Mama hates me," she sobbed, wrapping her arms around his waist. "It's all my fault! I don't know what to do."

"Oh, bambina." Egisto consoled her, rubbing her back in little clockwise circles. "Your mother loves you. She doesn't know how to show it, that's all. She's angry with me because of something I did long ago. I'm trying to make things right but, well . . . I'm trying. Anything that is wrong in this house is my fault and no one else's."

"No, babbo! You're everything that's right!"

"Now, now. That's enough." He held her at arm's length. "We need to watch your mother very carefully. She is not well, and to be honest, I am afraid for her." Egisto's face darkened. "Even though she couldn't understand a word Mrs. Dempsey said, your mother took it very personally. I hope it's not—what do the Americans say?—"the straw that breaks the camel's back."

Returning to matters at hand, Egisto abruptly changed the subject. "Has your mother let you cook anything yet?"

"No, are you kidding? She's let me watch her cook, but she likes to do everything herself."

Egisto glanced down the hall at the closed bedroom door. "Well," he said presciently, "that may change soon. I need to speak with your brother now. Don't think I have forgotten this Dempsey business!" He pinched her cheek.

"Go peek in at your mother," he continued, "and if she's asleep, do you think you could cook up some dinner for your old babbo?"

"Sure!" Babe raced down the hall and quietly opened her parents' bedroom door.

Armida lay in a fetal position, babbling gibberish. Glancing around the room to see who her mother might be talking to, and seeing no one, Babe walked up to the bed and addressed her.

"Mama? Who are you talking to?"

Armida looked through her daughter and laughed a laugh so chilling it sent Babe racing out the door.

THAT NIGHT, VIOLENZA made *patata rifatte*. She recalled the recipe from memory, from the times she had stood at her mother's elbow, observing what she was doing. It was nerve-racking at first; finding the appropriate cookware, gathering all the ingredients, setting the table. Her father offered to help if she needed it, but he was keeping a vigil near her mother, watching to make sure she didn't leave, that she didn't hurt herself, monitoring her ravings . . .

Besides, thought Babe, *I need to show babbo I can do this by myself.*

The garlic, basil, sage, onions and tomatoes simmering in the pan smelled so good, it emboldened her. She was *cooking*—by herself! She tossed some chopped pancetta and left-over deboned pork ribs into the pan and added a few dashes of salt and pepper to taste. Finally, she sliced some day old bread and toasted it.

"Babbo! Siv! It's time to eat," she called out.

Siv rushed to the table and sat down. He tucked his napkin into his collar. "This looks great, sis!"

Egisto followed a few minutes later, pale, his mouth set in a grim line as if saying, *your mother is worse.* Worry rolled off him like hot, sticky sweat. He sat down next to Siv and looked at the single place setting on the other side of the table.

"It smells delicious, Violenza. Where is your mother's plate?" he asked.

"I set the table for three."

"I want the table always set for four. No matter what."

"Yes, babbo."

From that time forth, Babe always set the table for four, even when her mother wasn't there; even though she knew life in the little cream-colored house on Margaret Street would never be the same.

chapter twelve

1929 WAS THE year the stock market crashed, casting America into a quagmire of gloomy despair. Despite the fact that Egisto's job was secure, it was also the year Armida Sigali Bertozzi lost her will to live, flinging herself into the bowels of an open sewer pit where three unsuspecting construction workers, taking their lunch break nearby, sprang to action and rescued her—kicking and screaming—from what would have otherwise been an early grave.

Several weeks later, Siv and Babe watched in horror as their blank-faced mother clumsily tried to stab herself with a pair of kitchen shears. Increasingly irrational, Armida's behavior fluctuated unpredictably. At best she was detached and vacant. At worst she was malicious, malevolent and despotic.

In desperation, Egisto took Armida to Dr. Ludwig Meyers, a psychiatrist whose practice was on the top floor of the Plummer Building in Minneapolis. After he examined Armida, the doctor called Egisto into his office.

"Mr. Bertozzi," he said, motioning for him to sit in the chair next to his desk. "My examination reveals that a variety of factors contributed to your wife's current mental state. To begin with, she experienced abandonment at a young age due to her mother's early death, and then she suffered neglect as a result of her father's alcoholism. It appears that a life of severe poverty contributed to gross insecurity and a growing fear of failure. Then, separation anxiety and feelings of guilt and remorse regarding the untimely death of one of her sisters compounded her mental distress."

"More recent developments," he continued, "have exacerbated her condition. She insists you harbor feelings for another woman. Whether this is true or not is none of my business. What is relevant to our current situation is that she believes it to be so and that belief has pushed her over a psychological edge."

Egisto stared past the doctor, out the enormous window behind his desk at the sleek new Foshay Tower finished just months before the crash on Wall Street. The financier who had built the landmark structure—touted as the tallest building west of the Mississippi—was now bankrupt. Egisto looked at the skyscraper, the strength and beauty that belied its financial collapse, and saw the sham that his marriage had become.

In the background of his thoughts he heard the doctor still reading from his notes. "I found Armida to be quarrelsome, delusional, alternately grandiose and paranoid, consistently incoherent and, in general, suffering from acute melancholia and severe mania." He stopped and looked directly at Egisto. "I am sorry to tell you that your wife is acutely—and quite possibly chronically—insane."

Egisto jerked as though he'd taken a step off the top story of the Foshay Tower and was hurtling downward to the street below.

The doctor waited a moment for the diagnosis to sink in. "My conclusions," he continued, "are based upon Armida's behavior. Granted, there could be physiological reasons contributing to her psychosis. She complains of fatigue and weight gain, and I did notice a slight thickening in her neck, suggesting the possibility of a goiter, although it may be too early to tell. If that were the case, an adjustment in your wife's iodine levels would be in order. It's a fairly new development in endocrinology, but doctors believe there's a link between iodine intake and hypo- or hyper-thyroid disease."

Dr. Meyers closed his file. "However, because you and your children show no indication of iodine deficiency, it's highly doubtful that it is a contributing factor in this case. Your wife's physical symptoms, I'm convinced, are rooted in her mind."

"At this point, Mr. Bertozzi," he intoned, "considering Armida is a threat to herself and your children, I recommend she be committed to St. Peter's State Hospital for the Insane. There's no guarantee she'll be cured there, but St. Peter's is the best facility for the insane in the state of Minnesota. They have a large, professional staff and they offer the most modern, up-to-date treatments available. It is a fine facility and, I assure you, she will receive good care there."

Egisto gripped the arms of his chair while Dr. Meyers pointed out that if finances were an issue, Armida could be committed as a ward of the state at no direct cost to the family. One need only sign a paper relinquishing all spousal rights, he explained, thus giving the hospital the sole power to treat and release her, although it must be understood that wards of the state were rarely released from the institution once they were committed.

The doctor sighed, his voice resigned. "My experience in this field has shown that families of patients who are wards of the state are ultimately relieved that they can go about their lives again, unburdened by problem children, parents, or spouses."

Noticing Egisto's shocked expression, he added, "I'll be brutally honest with you, Mr. Bertozzi. With your wife at St. Peters, eventually your life will return to normal. Better to do it now than wait until someone is hurt or she is removed forcibly from your home. What do you want to do?"

Egisto waited several moments before replying. "I will consider it," he said finally, "but Armida will never be a ward of the state."

"That's fine, but I suggest you make a decision soon."

IN JANUARY OF 1930, Egisto packed a single suitcase for his wife, in which he tucked some photos of the children, and made preparations to accompany her on a train destined for St. Peter's Hospital.

Silverio and Violenza, secretly relieved at the prospect of domestic normalcy, feigned concern—for their father's sake—as Egisto escorted their mother from the house. Armida ignored Siv and Babe bidding her farewell, not bothering to look back at them as she climbed into the waiting taxi.

Hours later, as the departing train steamed along stretches of frozen river banks cloaked in birch and pine forests, Egisto couldn't help but recall the last time he and Armida had taken such a long train ride together. They had been newlyweds then, on their way to the New World, and that titillating sense of freshness in their marriage had permeated their relationship right up until the day she had found The Letter. Naturally, at first, it took awhile for them to become completely used to each other, and there had been times—like when he wrote the letter to Marietta—that he had entertained second thoughts about his decision to ask Armida to marry him. But through the confusion and adjustments in those early years of marriage, he had hungered for her unlike any woman he'd ever known. He had been amazed at how well she bore herself with her pregnancies, and with the household finances when times were lean, and he'd been proud of her skills as a homemaker. She had been a wonderful wife and a loving mother; wonderful, that is, until Violenza's birth. It was only then, he had to admit in retrospect, that he had begun to notice subtle changes in her.

Now, the reality of their present circumstances made his stomach turn. Armida, to the contrary, appeared overjoyed. Acting like a schoolgirl on her first visit to the Big City, she excitedly played with her hair, her ear lobes, and the buttons, collar and hem of her dress.

If Egisto had any reservations about his wife's ability to comprehend the severity of her illness, he was forced to concede that she apparently had been rescued from the brink of total insanity by the mere change in scenery and growing distance from home. The marked change in her personality as they neared the hospital both baffled and galled him. Obviously, her hatred for everything associated with him was complete.

Egisto studied several other couples on the train. Funny, he thought, how you can guess just by looking at spouses if they belong together; if they're happy. He wondered what people thought of him, sitting stoically next to his skittish wife.

There's an average couple, they might think. *Well-matched too. Same age; same nationality.* But a prophet among them would see the truth: *A stonemason and a siren . . . how strange.*

And they would be right, thought Egisto. *I am a quiet,*

simple man; an artist who dreams with his hands. I am locked in stone, yet I am married to a woman whose passions can never be contained. How can it be? How can it last?

Indeed, Armida had begged him for a divorce before they left for St. Peter's. He replayed the scene in his mind. They were sitting at the kitchen table, where he had just served her lunch. The children were out skating with their friends.

"Give me a divorce, Egisto."

"No."

"I don't love you," she had said. "Why won't you let me go?"

Because I'm terrified of failure, of the permanency of the decision, he had thought. *Because our children need you. Because I need you. Because I miss the smell of your hair in my face in the morning and the touch of your skin at night. Because I want back the woman I married.*

Out loud, he answered, "Because I love you, Armida."

When she raged at him that he was keeping her a prisoner against her will in their home and that she would run away and never let him find her if he didn't give in to her demands, he agreed to at least set the process in motion on the condition she would stay and never attempt suicide again. But, to himself, he had thought: *I will contact a lawyer. Anything to pacify her for awhile. But I will never go through with it.*

Now, here he was, on the verge of committing his wife to a mental institution, not knowing if he would ever have her back again. Out of nowhere, Marietta Tarabella's face flashed before him. Though he felt guilty doing so, he imagined what his life would have been like had he married her instead. Marietta was tame compared to Armida. There certainly wouldn't have been the highs and lows—the fire in their lovemaking or even the passionate disagreements they'd had when the children were asleep—that had made his life with Armida so alive. Marietta would have kept her emotions under control and she would have capitulated to Egisto's every desire.

Life with Marietta would have been peaceful, he concluded. *But it would have been predictable. It would have been boring. And I wouldn't have Siv and Babe. Even with Armida as distant and hateful as she is right now, I know it's not the real her. I want the real Armida back.*

Glancing at his wife, Egisto choked on a prayer, desiccated by his own hypocrisy. *Please God, I want her back.*

By THE TIME they pulled into Kasota Junction, finally arriving on the doorsteps of St. Peter's Hospital for the Insane, wild horses couldn't have kept Armida from completely surrendering herself to a future within its confines. She acted as though the gates of St. Peter's were the veritable Gates of Heaven.

Dr. George Freeman, St. Peter's superintendent, graciously gave Egisto a tour of the facility while staff admitted Armida. The spacious grounds, with groves of naked hardwoods dotting the undulating landscape, had a soothing, anesthetic effect. The view alone was healing, thought Egisto. He buoyed himself with the belief that surely, in such a peaceful atmosphere, his wife would find herself again.

The main hall, an impressive brick structure, was connected to other buildings by a network of breezeways. Dr. Freeman pointed out the Hospital for the Tuberculous Insane and the Detention Asylum for the Criminally and Dangerously Insane, noting that they would be off-limits to patients like Armida, who would be interred in the women's ward of the institution proper. Proudly, the doctor also pointed out the garden plots, barn, wood shop and sewing

rooms that cooperative patients would be allowed to uti-
lize as part of their rehabilitation when weather permitted.
Egisto was impressed with the dignified superintendent, the
cleanliness of the hospital, the orderliness of the surroundings and the professionalism of the staff. The fears that had
previously prevented Egisto from pursuing medical intervention for his wife fled as he witnessed first-hand the modern
amenities St. Peter's Hospital offered.

When Armida's admission was complete, Egisto tried to
hold her hands as he said "good-bye," but she pushed him
away.

"I'll be back as soon as I can," he promised, undeterred.
"And Silverio and Violenza will write every week."

Armida, preoccupied with sizing up her new surroundings, muttered, "I don't care."

His shoulders slumped, his eyes stinging, Egisto turned
and left, thankful that their children weren't there to see his
misery and their mother's joy. *I must do whatever it takes,* he
thought, *to soften this blow to Violenza and Silverio; to shield
them from this sickness.*

chapter thirteen

"YOU'RE GOING TO miss my piano recital this afternoon," wailed Violenza.

"I'm so sorry, bambina! I forgot about your recital. But I've made arrangements to see your mother today. You understand, don't you?"

Babe studied her father's face, the new worry lines that had crept along the edges of his mouth and imbedded themselves across his forehead. His eyes, excruciatingly kind, were either not capable of seeing the things she saw, or were unwilling to.

Mama could care less if he comes to see her or not, she thought. *Life has been so much better around here since she's been gone. When is he going to just let her go?*

She turned from him, unable to look into his eyes any longer, unable to contemplate hurting him any more than he had been. "I understand, papa. Don't worry. There'll be another recital next month."

DR. FREEMAN ADJUSTED his round, gold-rimmed glasses. Hunched over an open file, he stared at it for at least five minutes before leaning back into his chair. Folding his delicate, almost feminine-looking hands ceremoniously across the top of his chest, he finally looked up at Egisto, sitting patiently opposite him and said. "I understand you've come to visit your wife again?"

"That is correct." Egisto's thick Tuscan accent sounded almost crude to his own ears, compared to the doctor's perfectly enunciated English.

"I understand you want to be informed of her current condition. I am afraid you will not find Armida much changed, Mr. Bertozzi. It has been less than one month since she was entrusted to our care. It will take much more time before we hope to see any improvement, if there is to be any improvement at all."

"Yes, I understand."

The doctor peered quizzically over his bifocals. "May I ask then, sir, why you are intent on visiting your wife every week? Most spouses wait until they have been notified of improvements before visiting."

"I was told that as an out-patient, my wife would be at my disposal to visit any time."

"Who told you this?"

"My lawyer."

"I see." Dr. Freeman pressed his chin into his tightly interlocked hands. "You are obviously well-educated, Mr. Bertozzi," he continued. "Surely you realize that although your wife is undergoing the most advanced therapy available, time is crucial to her complete rehabilitation. We started new treatments this week and it will take awhile for us to measure the effects. I understand that it is a sacrifice for you to make the trip here to St. Peter's, but if you were to see your wife today, it might appear to you that she has regressed, even though in reality, regression must come before we see progress. Armida will improve with time. You have my word."

"Now," he said, reaching for the telephone, "may I call a taxi for you?"

"Perhaps I am not as well-educated as you, doctor, but I did my homework before coming here, so I know what these 'advanced' therapies are that you speak of. I have also consulted many knowledgeable people on the subject. I assure you I will not be shocked. Has my wife been issued a straitjacket?"

"Camisole," corrected the doctor. He hesitated before placing the phone receiver back on its hook. "We prefer to call them camisoles. And yes, we were induced to place your wife in a *camisole* this week. It is standard procedure for all of our patients who demonstrate violent behavior here. Has your research led you to study the benefits of crib confinement?"

"Has she been confined to a crib?"

"Unfortunately, yes. Of course, we use it only as a final resort."

"She tried to kill herself again."

"Yes, I am afraid so."

"How?"

Reopening Armida's file, Dr. Freeman scanned her records, sniffing and daubing his nose with a scarlet monogrammed handkerchief. "Blasted cold. Ah, here it is. Nurse Jensen writes that your wife became extremely irate her second day here." He sneezed into his hankie and apologized before adding, "You realize that no one here speaks Italian, so, unfortunately, we can only guess at some of this."

"Go on."

"Evidently, Armida threatened to run away. She was given

some laudanum to calm her. The following day, she broke into our medicine cabinet and tried to kill herself by drinking an entire bottle of it." The doctor glanced at Egisto. "We keep our medications very closely guarded. The fact that your wife was clever enough to steal the medicine indicated to us the depth and severity of her psychosis."

Egisto's lowered his head.

"Nurse Jenson's professional intervention saved your wife's life, Mr. Bertozzi. It was at that point she was fitted with a camisole. Now, let's see." The doctor cleared his throat and returned to Armida's records, using his index finger to find what he was looking for.

"Two days ago," he continued, "your wife—still wearing a camisole of course—was allowed to go outside with some other patients to a supervised area to enjoy some fresh air. She somehow slipped away and was later discovered in the men's ward of the hospital. I assure you again, Mr. Bertozzi, this was not due to negligence on our part, but rather your wife's cunning nature. Among other things, she was begging one of our male patients to kill her . . . "

Dr. Freeman stiffened, and then as though he was having second thoughts, he put all of the papers back into Armida's file and closed it. "I am truly sorry to have to tell you these things, Mr. Bertozzi, but I'm afraid you've forced the issue."

Egisto stood. "Thank you for your time, doctor. I did not mean to disrupt your work. I would like to see my wife now."

"If you insist." Dr. Freeman rose and escorted him into the foyer, calling a nurse to accompany Egisto to the women's ward.

Mary Donnery, a talkative young woman, appeared. Dr. Freeman forewarned Egisto that Armida had not been eating well and had lost considerable weight. Then, he handed the nurse a key and returned to his office. She led Egisto through a maze of red brick corridors and up two flights of stairs to the maximum security crib room. As they walked, she told Egisto that Armida, though difficult, was a sight better than some of the other patients. The language barrier was a problem though, she confessed, unlocking the door to the ward. Then she took Egisto into a wide room lined with black and grey metal cribs. The odor of bleach failed to mask the underlying stench of urine; it wretched through the air, strangulating, eye-burningly rancid. Rusted buckets lined the aisles between the cribs, half-full of water capped with a thin layer of ice.

Nurse Donnery, noting the pained expression on Egisto's face, assured him the leaks in the roof were recent. "St. Peter's keeps growing, you know," she said apologetically. "It's hard to keep up with all the repairs. We do our best, but the economy isn't the greatest now, is it?"

Egisto tried to focus on Mary's lips as she spoke to him, wishing the sound of her voice would drown out the moans and heckling that were erupting around them.

"*Nurse! Nurse! Get me out of here!*"

"*Over here, nurse! I'll pay you to unlock my cage!*"

"*I'll give you anything nurse. Please! Just set me free!!*"

Mary was oblivious to it all, Egisto realized, as he watched her stop to cover one shivering woman with a blanket and stroke the brow of another babbling patient. Some patients cowered when they saw him, their faces reflecting unfathomable fear and dread at his closeness.

Suddenly, a chill went up his spine. He could *feel* his wife's presence behind him.

Miss Donnery peeked over his shoulder, smiled and spun him around. "Armida!" she announced. "Look who's come to see you!"

Armida could not believe her eyes. Her hands were so tightly secured beneath her camisole with wide rubber straps, she had to flip herself around like a fish in order to wipe the mucus from her eyes on the sheet of the crib just to be sure she wasn't hallucinating. She stared in disbelief as Nurse Donnery cheerfully tried various keys on her ring to unlock the grated steel lid atop her crib. Shaking uncontrollably in anticipation, Armida thrashed her feet and pounded her forehead against the rails.

What month is it? she wondered. *What year? Am I back in Italy?*

"Aiuto, Egisto!" she screamed. *Help me!*

It was more than Egisto could bear. When Nurse Donnery finally unlocked the lid, he elbowed her out of the way, shoved it open, lifted his wife up from the crib and carried her out of the ward. He collapsed on the landing at the top of the stairwell, Armida nuzzling him madly, like a starving puppy. Egisto immediately undid the bands around her wrists, but her arms continued to flap about frantically as though she were drowning. His soothing caresses and reassuring voice eventually calmed her and gradually the claustrophobic, sucking noises coming from deep within her throat receded.

"Get her out of this thing!" Egisto shouted to the nurse.

"Yes sir." Rushing toward them, Mary positioned herself on a lower step and unfastened the back of Armida's straitjacket. "Dr. Freeman instructed me to do whatever you asked."

Armida, meanwhile, allowed herself to be transported to another time and place. She didn't feel Mary's fingers unlacing her camisole; she didn't even notice when Egisto helped pull it gently off of her, tossing it down the stairs. She simply lay like a newborn babe on his chest, her hair a mass of dark, damp ringlets, her skin moist and hot. Before she faded into a twilight of sleep, she smiled at Egisto. "You promised me another baby. Remember? I'm still waiting."

EGISTO WOULD HAVE taken Armida home with him that day had Dr. Freeman not issued dire warnings of the consequences of immediately removing her from St. Peter's.

He was convinced she was still suicidal and a danger to their children. Her confinement in the crib had been necessary at the time, he insisted, but if Mr. Bertozzi refused to allow them to use such disciplinary measures, they could treat his wife with a variety of medications.

"Of course, I never say 'never,'" the supervisor said, "but, unless you leave your wife in our care for at least two years, she will make no progress. Even then, my personal opinion is that if she leaves this facility, she may appear subdued for a short time, but eventually she would revert to her current psychotic state and need to be re-admitted. In my entire career, I have yet to see someone completely, permanently cured of insanity."

"Consider your children, Mr. Bertozzi," he pleaded. "Would bringing their mother back under the assumption she was improved, only to put them through the same anguish again, be fair to them?"

Dr. Freeman stifled another sneeze beneath his crumpled handkerchief and concluded sagely, "I think not. You must come to terms with your own feelings about your wife and the viability of your marriage to her. Spare yourself and your children. Leave her with us."

"Italians do not abandon their sick," Egisto replied, "even if it is a mental sickness. The only reason she is here is that I hoped she could be helped. I am willing to leave her here for perhaps two or three months, at the most, on the condition I can continue to visit her every week—and only if you promise she will never again wear a straitjacket and never again be placed in a crib. Perhaps that is good therapy for others, but not for my Armida."

Egisto extended his hand to the doctor. "Two months. I will give you two more months under those conditions and then I will return and take my wife home. I will assume the consequences of her behavior. Thank you, Dr. Freeman, for your time and patience. I know you are doing your best."

chapter fourteen

Less than four months later, the same week the apple trees bloomed along Margaret Street's narrow verge, Armida returned home. She stepped out of the taxi before Egisto could open the door for her and shook off his hand when he tried to help with her luggage. Turning, she caught Babe and Siv staring at her from the shadows of their front porch. She approached the house indifferently. Egisto, close behind her, covertly signaled their children to welcome her home.

Siv put his arm around Babe. Together they stepped into the light at the top of the steps to greet her. When Armida reached them, she paused to touch the top of Siv's head. Wrapping one of his curls around her finger she said his name, "Siv." Babe reached out to hug her mother, but Armida ignored her completely and with nothing more to say, disappeared into the house.

And so, the spring—and summer—of 1930 passed.

Babe was thankful for Julia Barghini, flitting back and forth between households, helping as much as possible whenever Babe needed it. *I don't know what I'd do without Julia,* she thought. *She brings us meals when I can't cook and visits mama when we're not home.*

Babe had to admit her mother did make feeble attempts at establishing a veneer of normalcy in their home. She even cooked sometimes, when she wasn't sleeping or staring off into space on the front porch. On Babe's thirteenth birthday, Armida actually mustered the energy to bake a cake and make a card for her. Still, the fact remained that with the exception of the family cat, and sometimes Siv, no one in their household received any noticeable attention from her.

Maybe I'm being naïve, Babe mused one day, looking back at the months since her mother had returned home, *but it's been a relatively good summer with mama here. I don't feel the burden of cooking all the meals and doing all the laundry like I did when she was at St. Peter's. I stay out of her way and she stays out of mine. Maybe she's getting better after all.*

As soon as she thought it, though, she scolded herself for allowing hope to crawl back into her heart. She'd been disappointed too many times.

On September 15, 1930, two weeks after Babe and Siv started school and only five months after being released from St. Peter's Hospital for the Insane, Armida, without warning, again threatened suicide if she were not granted a divorce. She also began displaying greater favoritism toward Siv, saying things to him like, "Silverio, I wish you were my only child," or "Silverio, wouldn't you be happy if just you and I could live together?"

This time Egisto capitulated. With no delusions of reconciliation and his greatest fear being the possibility that Armida would make good on a vow to go back to Italy—taking Siv, but not Babe, with her—he called his attorney.

Divorce papers drawn up almost a year earlier were activated as Egisto began the arduous task of contacting his closest friends to serve as witnesses in the divorce proceedings. His fears were not without warrant. Armida, her internment at St. Peter's having soured what little positive perspective on America she may have had, decided that nothing could induce her to stay there any longer. A sudden, inexplicable and obsessive yearning for Italy possessed her.

Julia disputed her homesickness. "What makes you think there's anything for you in Italy, Armida? You haven't seen or heard from your family in years."

"My father wrote me a letter."

"I don't believe it."

When Armida produced a shiny new postcard from Tuscany with a hastily scratched note written by one of her brothers detailing the return of her father to Ripa and his failing health, Julia was forced to reconsider. Fingering the card thoughtfully she ventured, "The reason your family wants you back, Armida, is so you will help take care of your father. That's fine, but don't they realize you have a family of your own here that needs you?"

"My family in Italy is as much family to me as my family here."

After Julia left, Egisto applied the same truth to bear on his wife with no results. "Suddenly, your father needs you? After ignoring you all of these years?"

"Yes."

"What about us?"

"I'm not asking to go back forever, Egisto."

"For how long, then?"

"I don't know. What does it matter if we're divorced?"

"It is our children that matter, Armida. That's all I can allow myself to care about anymore."

"So, I don't care about our children? Go ahead and say it, Egisto. You think I am a monster just because I need to go home to Ripa and take care of my father."

"That's not why you want to go back, Armida. Stop lying

to yourself. If you cared about Siv and Babe, you wouldn't abandon them like this, and for God's sake you wouldn't be threatening to kill yourself every time things don't go your way."

"If you won't let me have custody of my own children, what's the point?"

"You don't want your children."

"I want Siv."

"How do you think that would make Babe feel?"

"Babe loves you. She's afraid of me."

"You're afraid of Babe because you can't control her."

"I *hate* you!" Armida snarled. "You think you know everything, but you know nothing about real life. You know nothing about love, or women; you know nothing about me. If you did, you'd be spending more time with me than your precious sculptures. The truth is, you bore me to tears, Egisto. I want to get as far away from you and the memories of this life as I can."

"I won't give you a divorce if you go to Italy. You can think what you want about me, but the fact is, your children need you here much more than your father needs you. You have brothers and sisters there to take care of him."

"I will kill myself if you don't let me go. I swear it."

"Kill yourself? Good God, Armida, Italy will kill you if you go back. Mark my words, Europe is ripe for another war. Mussolini will bring Italy down with him when the time comes."

"Then I choose death in Italy. I don't care. I won't stay here and nothing will change my mind."

"Fine! But you'll go alone."

"I want Siv with me."

"No!"

"I *will* kill myself if you don't let Siv come with me."

"Stop it."

"I can't go by myself."

"If you go, Armida, you will go by yourself."

"Please, Egisto!"

"Never! I'd be insane to let him go with you."

"How can you deny a mother her son?" she whined, wringing her hands. "I'll die without him; it will all be your fault!"

Egisto's chest constricted, much like it had the day he had faced his family in Ripa after having spent the night with Armida before their wedding. This time, however, instead of being fueled by fear, the burning sensation rising from his gut was spawned by a rage he had never before experienced. His eyes twitched. His knees trembled. He recalled the humiliations heaped on him by her countless public displays of madness and her veiled attempts to emasculate him. His hands shook uncontrollably as he envisioned them grasping his wife's neck, silencing her prattling lunacy once and for all.

"Go to Italy then, and good riddance, you poor excuse for a mother. I hope you never come back." Lowering his voice to just above a whisper, he said, "Do you think Siv would actually want to go with you? He's ashamed of you. Look at yourself; you're pathetic. You're . . . *crazy.*"

Armida stood and faced him. "Just for that, I'll see to it you never see either of our children again."

Egisto lifted his hand to slap her, a lifetime of self-control crushed by a tidal wave of vindication. "If you so much as touch a hair on their heads . . ."

A sharp thud in the hallway caused him to pause, his hand frozen in mid-air. Through the half-opened door, Egisto saw Silverio staring at them.

"It's ok, papa. I won't go with her. Just let her go wherever she wants."

Armida crooned as though she had won a wrestling match. "Go ahead and hit me, Egisto. Let your son see what kind of a man you really are."

Egisto lowered his hand.

"Not man enough?" she taunted him.

"You're not worth the effort to prove to you what kind of man I am."

Armida yanked Siv into the room, squeezing his arm as she ranted, "See how your father talks to me, Silverio? Men are all the same; your father is no different, although he thinks he is better than most. He has you duped into thinking he loves you. The truth is, your father doesn't love anyone but himself and his little Marietta Tarabella." She shoved Siv between herself and Egisto. "Tell him Egisto! Tell him the truth!"

Struggling to maintain his composure, Egisto said, "Silverio, find your sister and tell her I want you both to take the trolley to Barghini's. I'll call Julia in awhile."

Siv didn't move.

"Tell him, Egisto!" Armida shrieked. "You can't love our children because they're mine and not Marietta's."

"*Now*, Siv."

"Yes, papa." Siv slid out from beneath his mother's grasp, stumbled, and raced outside to fetch Babe.

Armida fell on Egisto like a rabid animal, screaming profanities while she clawed at his face. Breaking free of her,

Egisto threw her down onto the couch. A trickle of blood stained his lip and chin. He wiped it off with the back of his sleeve and said, "I'll give you a divorce. You can go to Italy, but the children stay here."

"Fine," said Armida, triumphant. "The sooner the better."

PART III

1931–1941

Me ne frego

"I do not give a damn."—Fascist slogan

chapter fifteen

1931

"If I get any mail, leave it on the table, Argene. And don't wait up for me. I may be late getting home if the Carditis stay after their meeting."

"Si, Armida." Argene acknowledged her sister's departure by waving her little finger off the needle she was intently attempting to thread.

Armida Sigali, having dropped two dress sizes, was feeling twenty years younger and thoroughly intoxicated with the early March morning. Had it only been six months ago that she had arrived? Before bounding down the steps of her veranda, she bent over to marvel at the buds on the tea rose she had planted in an old cast-iron urn last fall, shortly after her return to Tuscany.

"Astonishing," she murmured to herself, placing her hand on her flat belly and smiling. Spring was a good omen; a sign that her life was, indeed, starting over.

Circling around to the back of the house, she inhaled the oxygen rich air as though she were a drowning woman just saved from the deep. She shook the dew off her new forest-green Bianchi bicycle, and walked it out onto the bustling via Seravezza. As she coasted down the street, the owner of a local profumeria called out to her from the doorway, "Signora, you will freeze today!"

"No," retorted Armida, tossing her head. "I am warm, thank you."

They have no idea what winter can be like, thought Armida. Late February in Versilia was like late April in Minnesota. She shuddered at the remembrance of last winter: the frozen lakes, rivers and skies; the bleak, monotonous landscape; the shadow of death that leadened her spirit each year. It just wasn't natural for her, a Tuscan-bred girl, to live in that kind of environment. Even the unusual amount of rain that had fallen in Ripa upon her return last fall hadn't bothered her. She far preferred the verdant hills, the brilliant rainbows and the fresh, brisk air that the winter rains produced to the bone-chilling, brutal winter storms that had left her incapacitated in Minnesota.

She stopped at the bank to pay a bill and withdraw some cash. The gap-toothed teller forced a smile. "How are you this morning, Armida? And your sister, Argene? Is everything going well?"

"Everyone is fine. Thank you for asking."

While counting out the cash Armida requested, the clerk punctuated her tally with barbed comments. "*One, two, three*: Poor Argene! She and your other sister, Iole, have been, well, you know . . ." She shot a sympathetic look at Armida. "*Four, five, six*: Let's just say they would both still be in the mental hospital if you hadn't come back to help! *Seven, eight, nine*: Too bad. They could be attractive and get themselves husbands if they tried hard enough, because they're not really crazy. Are they?"

You know they are, thought Armida, her mouth twitching.

Out loud, she said, "They're very eccentric . . . and happy as they are."

The teller continued to gush as though she had two sets of lungs. "*Ten, eleven, twelve*: Oh, well. That's life. I don't blame you for only having Argene live in your house with you. Iole is older and far more . . . eccentric. She is better off staying at your father's house, even though she must be a great burden to him. At least the rest of your family is somewhat normal, eh?"

One glance at Armida's narrowed eyes and the cashier spoke even faster. "*Thirteen, fourteen, fifteen*: Such a terrible family life you must have all had when you were young. No mother, and your father gone all of those years. So many mouths to feed and no money! *Sixteen, seventeen, eighteen*: And who can ever forget your father's second wife! Thank God she didn't live long, eh? My mother still tells me stories about the old witch. Of course, who am I to say? It was after you left, so only your brothers and sisters would really know about that. *Nineteen, twenty lire*: There you go!" Out of breath, she placed the crisp bills neatly in a small white envelope and handed it to Armida, who turned abruptly on her heels and left.

"Anyway," the teller called out after her. "You have really fixed up that house you bought. It must be nice to have a rich husband in America. Ciao, Armida."

Slipping the money envelope into her purse, Armida proceeded directly to Polacci's panetteria to purchase some treats for the Carditi children.

"Buon giorno, Armida," said signore Polacci from behind the counter. "It has been months since I have seen you."

"Buon giorno." Armida pointed to some fresh biscuits.

"I'll take six of those. I'll also have two loaves of schiacciata, and . . . that castagnaccio. When did you bake it?"

"It just came out of the oven, signora. It's still warm. Shall I wrap everything for you?"

"Grazie."

While signore Polacci shook out a neatly folded paper sack, he asked, "How is Giuseppe?"

"My father is doing much better, thank you."

"You were an angel to return and nurse him back to health. Now that he is better and you have your sister Argene settled into the house you bought, you will probably go back to America to your family? Six months is a long time for a mother to be away from her children."

"My father still needs me here. So does Argene. My children are old enough to take care of themselves. After all, I was much younger than my daughter when my mother died and left us to fend for ourselves."

"I remember." He handed her the neatly wrapped biscotti and began the delicate process of transferring, with his enormous, gnarled hands, the moist chestnut cake into a dainty cardboard box. "But, you had many brothers and sisters to help each other, no?"

Armida shoved one hand beneath her armpit and began studying the fingernails on her other hand.

"People still talk about you and Egisto," continued the baker. "Such a sudden marriage. It took everyone by surprise. Now look at you. You are back home, living in a house many of us could never afford to live in, and you have a new job as nanny and cook to the Carditis. Perhaps now your own children can come here?"

Dropping her hand down onto the gleaming marble counter top, Armida rapped her fingers on it, replying acidly,

"Egisto likes it in America. So do my children."

The well-meaning old man slowly measured out a length of twine, cut it with some scissors and carefully tied it around the bulging box. "Luigi Bertozzi was in the other day. You know that his son, Francesco—Egisto's brother—recently opened up his own marble business?"

"No."

"Oh, yes. It is on via Marina in Querceta. He is a very gifted sculptor, but it is impossible for anyone to open a business like that without help. Luigi says Egisto's success in America has helped the family very much. They are proud of him."

Armida glanced at her watch.

"Your niece, Bianca Frediani—Carilda and Barlaam's daughter—was with Luigi when he came in," he continued. "She is a devoted granddaughter, and such a pretty girl; even with her limp. All of the Frediani girls are pretty, don't you think?"

"I wouldn't know."

"Signora!" The cake, finally wrapped and half-raised toward her, froze in his hands. "Do you mean to say you have been here six months and have not yet seen your husband's family?"

Reaching over the counter to retrieve the cake by force, Armida demanded that he put her bread in a sack and give her the bill so she could leave.

"They do not know you are here?" he asked incredulously.

"I have better things to do than waste my morning gossiping with you, signore. Hurry up before I make my purchases somewhere else."

"How is it possible in Ripa for such news to not reach them? Now that you are working, surely you can't hide your presence much longer. You are fortunate I did not mention you to Luigi. The next time I see him, I cannot promise that I will not say something."

He slid the two flat loaves of bread into individual sacks and twisted the ends shut. "Personally, I don't care what problem it is that keeps you from the Bertozzis, but you can't avoid them forever. They will find out that you are here." He waited a moment for her to respond, and when she said nothing, he added, "That will be one lira, signora."

Armida slapped a coin on top of the register and stormed out of Polacci's panetteria. As the door closed behind her, Armida heard him call out, "Say hello to the Carditis for me."

Signore Polacci had ruined her day.

How dare he threaten me! Armida zipped around unharried pedestrians, sputtering Fiats, and scores of equally distracted bicyclists. *How dare he imply I am an unfit mother!*

She had certainly miscalculated human nature's penchant for dredging up the past and the past was precisely what she had banked on escaping. Egisto had warned her he could not keep their divorce secret for long. His most recent letters informed her that he would be writing Francesco to tell him. How foolish she was to think that the Bertozzis wouldn't eventually discover she was back in Ripa.

What made me think I could come back here and blend in as though I had never left?

Nearing Forte dei Marmi, she dismounted, forced to walk through a maze of new road construction. A huge portrait of Mussolini, like the smaller replicas hung next to the Madonna in every home in Italy, beamed down at her from the freshly painted wall of the headquarters of the local squadristri. Beneath his larger-than-life portrait were the words, "We shall succeed because we shall work." A surge of pride raced through Armida as she was reminded of the glory of being a part of Italy's second Renaissance. She pitied the Italians in America who could only read about the great advancements their nation was making.

Well, let Egisto tell his brother! she groused to herself, mounting her bike again and speeding down the last few streets leading to the Carditis' villa. *I don't owe the Bertozzis anything. I let their son off easy. I could have demanded alimony but all I wanted was enough money to come back and start a new life for myself. One thousand dollars to an Italian might as well be a million lire. Idiots. Little do they know it was a drop in the bucket for Egisto. He just wanted to wash his hands of me. As for Silverio and Violenza . . . well, if anyone asks, I'll tell them Egisto refused to let me bring them here with me because he doesn't trust Mussolini. And that is the truth!*

The Carditis' villa, enclosed within an eight-foot-high stone and stucco wall, came into view. She peddled furiously to reach the wrought-iron gate before the clock in the town square struck 9:00. It was her first week on the job and she didn't want to make a bad impression.

She unlocked the giant gate, followed the palm-lined drive around to the back of the house, parked her bike near the kitchen door, smoothed her hair, took the bread, biscotti and cake out of the bicycle's wicker basket, and paused to catch her breath.

I'll have to respond to Egisto's letters soon. Maybe if I ask him not to tell his family about me yet, I'll have time to address some of these rumors going around about me before they get back to the Carditis. They can never know the truth about me. If they found out . . .

BRUNO CARDITI WAS a rich man whose wealth was directly proportionate to his allegiance to Benito Mussolini and his Fasci di Combattimento. Handsome as he was charming, Bruno was also a brutal man. His naïve wife, Chiara, had never been on the receiving end of his legendary brutality, nor had their three spoiled sons: Arturo, Paolo, and Alessandro. Far from it; they were the primary beneficiaries of Bruno's boot-licking antics in the Duce's court in Rome. Other beneficiaries, primarily lusty nubile females, occasionally suffered his savage outbursts, but only when they stupidly attempted to sabotage his marriage.

Like Italy's little square-jawed dictator—who, along with his mistress, Claretta Petacci, flaunted their illicit relationship before the world—Bruno Carditi fancied his own importance, as Versilia's Chief Minister of Fascist Youth, reason enough to live above the law. Those closest to Bruno Carditi, desperate for his approval, defended him, saying:

"He's an honest, hardworking man."

"A true patriot."

"A decent man, incapable of violence."

"A good husband and a wonderful father."

But, those outside of signore Carditi's inner circle knew a different man, a man whose ferocity was so unpredictable, they crossed the street when they saw him approaching. A man so feared, no one dared to criticize him, even in the privacy of their homes. His spies, it was said, were everywhere.

Chiara Carditi, a self-absorbed, middle-aged, illiterate woman of peasant stock, likewise fancied herself a neuvo-aristocrat, but lacked the grace or brains to carry it off. Her goal in life was to enjoy the perks of living in the shadow of her husband. A pushover when it came to abdicating labor-intensive responsibilities, signora Carditi gave Armida free rein with the three Carditi sons, who eyed their new governess with suspicion and ill intent.

"But, Chiara!" Armida had heard one of signora Carditi's friends ask her one day. "What do you know about this Armida Sigali?"

Hovering near the dining room door as she prepared to serve the women a mid-day snack of bruschetta and cheese, Armida froze.

"*Boh!*" replied Chiara. "The woman cooks better than both our mamas put together. She makes the best *pasta tordellata* I have ever had and her *gnocchi di patate* is divine. One taste of her *tiramisu,* and that is all you would need to know about her."

"What about your children? I would never hire someone who my children don't adore."

"Have you ever known anyone my children have liked?"

"Does she have a degree?"

"Really, how many women in Italy have an education?"

"But she could be a thief, an imposter! Has she been married? Does she have children of her own?"

At that point, Armida had burst into the room with their appetizers, ending their conversation.

She would later find out that the Carditis had deduced, after she told them she had "worked" in America for a few years, that her experience in another country simply meant she was well-traveled and self-sufficient. She was also flattered to discover—from one of Bruno's drunken underlings—that it was her attractive appearance and superior attitude that had landed her the enviable position in the Carditi household.

The three boys in Armida's charge worshiped their father. As a Wolf Cub in the *Sons of the She Wolf,* the youngest division of Fascist Youth, six-year-old Alessandro followed in the footsteps of his ten-year-old brother Paolo—a proud member of the prestigious *Balilla Regiment*. In turn, Paolo followed in the footsteps his fifteen-year-old brother Arturo, recently promoted to the elite *Avanguardista*—The Advance Guards. Unlike his older brothers, the darkly handsome Alessandro—Armida's favorite—was quiet and reserved. His still waters ran deep.

Over his family, Bruno's iron fist reigned supreme. As long as his authority was never questioned or challenged, happiness and domestic contentment were the rule of the day. An easy and convenient arrangement for all concerned, he rarely had to flex his blackshirt-clad muscles within the confines of his home. One deadly look from his hooded eyes usually sufficed. One dared not venture beyond that.

Armida, of course, hadn't yet tasted signore Carditi's black soul. She only saw Bruno's charismatic smile, Alessandro's deceivingly cherubic face, and a monthly paycheck that most Italians would give their front teeth to have.

What more could she ask for?

chapter sixteen

1932

"Bianca, tell your mother you're coming with me to Caf-aggio. I have an errand to run for nonna and she won't let me rest until I get it done. We'll ride our bikes, okay?"

Always looking for an opportunity to spend time with her grandfather, Bianca shouted, "Mama, I'm leaving with nonno!"

"Not now," Carilda scolded from inside the house. "I told nonna we would all come up and help plant her garden this afternoon, *after* you finish taking down the laundry."

Crestfallen, Bianca puckered her lips and threw some clothespins in a basket at her feet. Her grandfather, sup-pressing a smile, whispered covertly, "I'll talk to her."

Luigi had changed little since Egisto moved to America. Tall and refined, the only significant alteration in his sev-enty-five-year-old appearance was a stunning, thick shock of snow-white hair, which stood straight up from the top of his head like a hedgehog. A white moustache, equally prolific, protruded wildly from his upper lip. The permanent crin-kles etching the outer rims of his eyes, along with two deep vertical creases, running from beneath his cheekbone to the top of his jaw, could easily be mistaken as the markings of a dry disciplinarian—that is, until Luigi laughed, in which case the creases receded, revealing the seasoned dimples they really were.

Rising to the challenge at hand, he sprinted up the stairs into the Fredianis' home. "Come now, Carilda. I won't keep her long."

"Papa, you know very well mama needs our help this afternoon!"

Outlined against the dining room window as she bent over her sewing, Carilda's profile caused an unexpected tide of sentiment to rush over Luigi. His only daughter, Carilda, was the pride of his life. He was struck by her simple, otherworldly beauty, as though Carmela had just given birth to her and he was seeing her for the very first time.

Feeling his paternal intensity, she turned. "What are you looking at?"

Luigi, caught in the act, shuffled his feet clumsily before begging supplication. "You have four daughters. You can't spare one of them for your old babbo?"

"That's right, papa. I have *four* daughters. Why must it always be Bianca who goes with you?"

"Lida is too young still, Rina has a suitor, and Bice gets bored easily. I'm too old to keep up with her."

"You have grandsons. What about Francesco's boys?"

"They have to help their father with the business."

"Alberto's girls?"

"Their mother keeps them so busy, they don't have time for me."

"I see," she chided him. "You're feeling sorry for yourself because your grandchildren are growing up and Bianca is the only one left who still has the time and inclination to indulge you. She is not a child anymore, papa. Someday soon she will have a boyfriend too, you know. You might as well get used to it."

Leveling her gaze at him she added, "Besides, it wouldn't be fair to her sisters. They would resent having to help me work while Bianca is off with you."

"Helping *me* isn't work? What do you think we'll be doing?"

She laughed out loud. "I know exactly what you'll be doing! She will come back home with a pocket full of candy and a head full of tales."

"If it's Barlaam you're worried about, Carilda, I'll be sure she's back before he gets home from work."

"My husband," she corrected him, "spoils the girls almost as much as you, and as you *well* know, he takes your side in these matters, anyway. It's not Barlaam I'm worried about."

"Let me have Bianca for the afternoon and I promise I will come by tomorrow and help Barlaam on the house. You'd like that wouldn't you?"

Carilda sighed, glancing around the unfinished home she and her husband had started building eight years ago. "Yes, papa, Barlaam would appreciate that."

She set her mending down with a cluck of her tongue and giving in to her father's bribes, she surrendered. "Get along— the both of you. Go!"

Overjoyed, Luigi embraced his daughter with a peck on her cheek, assuring her that he would have Bianca home before dinner. As an afterthought, he asked Carilda to tell nonna that he would be home by dinner also. Carmela, he reminded her, was formidable when vexed. Carilda gave her word, recalling the many times her mother had brought judgment to bear on her father for infractions far less serious.

Following Luigi outside, Carilda stood on the balcony, watching the two conspirators as they grabbed their bicycles and sped off down via Strettoia. In unison, they looked up as they turned the corner to see her waving merrily—both arms raised—her hands opening and closing in a light-hearted farewell.

"Ciao papa! Ciao Bianca! Don't forget—be back before supper!"

IT WAS A glorious day for a bike ride. Luigi and Bianca conjured up countless ways to wile away the early March afternoon, justifying each stop they made with clever excuses in the event they were interrogated upon their return.

One such diversion was a visit to signore Ferruccio, an ailing friend of Luigi's. Ferruccio had invited Luigi to take some cuttings from some old grape vines he insisted yielded some of the best wine in all of Versilia. This was serious business, for both the proud owner who wanted to dazzle his friend, and Luigi, who refused to be dazzled. It required a lengthy discourse on the history of the particular grape, inspecting the plant itself extensively for signs of vitality and/or disease, and finally, setting up a table and three chairs beneath the grape arbor to drink some of last year's elixirs—a solemn ceremony that lasted the better part of an hour.

Bianca, a silent but rapt participant, soaked up the dance of the dueling vintners like a raisin in a bowl of warm, sweet milk. In the end, Luigi, pulling out his pocket knife and reverently slicing into some selected stems, helped the triumphant Ferruccio take cuttings, wrap them in damp cloths, and place them carefully in burlap bags bound with twine.

As they prepared to depart, their bikes laden with the tender saplings, Luigi vowed to his friend that when, not if, they celebrated their eighty-fifth birthdays, they would toast each other with wine harvested from these vines and he would judge for himself how good it was. Walking behind Luigi and Bianca to the end of the avenue, Ferruccio countered by wagering five lire that come 1941, Luigi Bertozzi would be singing Ferruccio's praises. The two cyclists waved good-bye and setting out in traffic, they turned to see Ferruccio waving his cap in a final dare, shouting out after them, "And if on our birthday you *don't* admit my grapes produce the best wine in Versilia, my friend, I will personally dig up all the vines you are taking today and give them to someone who knows great wine when they taste it!"

Then it was on to Francesco's marble shop in Querceta. This was the weekly errand that Carmela pressed her husband into doing, come fair weather or foul. Francesco, by default—as the eldest son and a businessman—was the Bertozzi family scribe. Neither Luigi nor Carmela could read or write, so it was through Francesco that Egisto's weekly letters were received and sent. As Luigi and Bianca coasted up to the Bertozzi Marble Company on 71 via Marina, they saw Francesco, sleeves rolled up, polishing statues in the courtyard.

"Ahh, papa!" Francesco laughed, guiding them through the iron gate into the courtyard. "Bianca! What a beautiful day, eh?"

Drawn to her uncle's gregarious spirit, Bianca hugged him with all the strength her thin arms could muster. "Zio Francesco!"

"You get prettier every time I see you, bambina!"

Blushing, she asked if she could poke around the shop to look at his newest creations.

"Of *course*, my pet!" he gushed, "Ario and Aladino are in

there somewhere. Ario! Aladino!" he shouted. "Your cousin Bianca is here!"

Watching her disappear into the statuary, he remarked, "You know, papa, that girl, despite her limp, is growing into a beautiful woman."

"Bianca's heart compensates for her bad hip."

"I don't know about Bianca's heart, but there is *something* extraordinary about her." He pulled an envelope out from beneath his apron. "No doubt this is what you've come here for."

Retrieving a pair of round spectacles from his sweater pocket, Luigi took the letter and inspected it thoughtfully. He found American stamps and postmarks fascinating. "A check came with it?" he asked.

"Of course."

"How much?"

"The same as always. I've already deposited it in the bank. I will do the math and bring over your share, and Alberto's, on Sunday when we come for dinner."

"Bene." Luigi removed his glasses, tucking them back into his pocket along with the letter, and waited expectantly for Francesco's customary interpretation.

"The news from America this week is not all good," ventured Francesco nervously. "Egisto and the children are fine. He is still working on the statue of St. Matthew for the cathedral in St. Paul. In his letter he described again the Cathedral. It is patterned after St. Peter's in Rome! Silverio is dating a girl named Ruth, and Violenza has been accepted at the university in Minneapolis. It is Armida that is not well."

Francesco gauged his father's mood before dropping the bomb. "They are divorced."

"Divorced?!"

"Si. Divorced."

"It is not possible! He never mentioned any problems before. You must have misread the letter."

"It is perfectly clear in his letter, papa. They are divorced. Egisto says Armida changed very much and did not want to stay in America any longer."

"What are you saying?"

"Armida now lives here in Ripa."

Luigi staggered backwards. Fearing his father might actually faint, Francesco quickly glanced about for a place where he could sit down, but Luigi seized his arm, and leaning on his son for support, asked dumbly, "Did you say she is here—in *Ripa?*"

"Si, with her family perhaps. Egisto did not say."

"What kind of mother abandons her children? Poor Silverio and Violenza! What possessed her! Oh, I wish I could talk with Egisto!"

"What good would it do, papa? What's done is done. It could be worse."

Luigi let go of his son. He eased himself down onto a flat, half-finished headstone. "Egisto must do something."

"You're not suggesting Egisto should move back here to save his marriage, are you? What would happen to us?" Francesco swept his hand across the courtyard and the marble shop. "No, he has a good job in America. Armida insisted on the divorce. It is final. That is what Egisto says."

Luigi hung his head. "The shame of it! Carmela always believed Egisto would come to his senses and return to the Church. But now? Divorce?" He put his hand to his forehead. "How am I going to tell your mother?"

"Do you want me to tell her?"

"No."

Digging into his apron pocket, Francesco pulled out a thin Viceroy cigarette and offered it to his father, who turned his nose up at it.

"Francesco, are you sure you told me *everything* in the letter?"

"Everything. It was a short letter as you can see."

Luigi stared up at the mountains for a moment, noticing the angle of the sun. It was getting late. "Bianca! Come, it's time to go!" he yelled.

At his command, Francesco's sons chased Bianca, laughing, out of the statuary. Meanwhile, Luigi agonized over the revelation. *How am I going to tell Carmela? What if she finds out before I do? It will kill her!*

"Will you be all right, papa?" asked Francesco.

"I just need some time to think."

Francesco and his sons escorted Luigi and Bianca to the gate and then watched as they skirted around the east-bound traffic on via Marina; Bianca with her head held high, and Luigi with his shoulders drooped sadly over the handle bars.

"What's wrong with nonno?" Ario asked. "He looks sick."

Francesco placed the Viceroy on his lower lip and lit it. "Nonno *is* sick, son," he murmured. "In the worst way. He is sick in his heart."

chapter seventeen

"Do we have time to stop somewhere for something to drink?" Luigi masked his fatigue by shouting at his grand-daughter more loudly than usual, as though the volume of his voice would compensate for his flagging energy.

"Sure, nonno." Bianca squinted at the sun. "It's probably only five or six o'clock. Where do you want to go?"

"You pick."

"Caffé Rivolti?"

"Caffé Rivolti it is." Luigi turned right and pulled up alongside the crowded sidewalk in front of the café.

Bianca had been too flushed with excitement to notice the change in her grandfather's behavior until they parked their bikes against a lamppost plastered with flyers adorned with images of Mussolini, or *fascio*, the "bundle of sticks" emblem of Italy's Fascist party.

Luigi scowled. "Bianca, what do these posters say?"

"You know I can't read very well, nonno."

"You read well enough. Tell me what they say."

Intently, she studied one glossy poster featuring a radiant, pregnant woman holding an infant. "This one says, '*Women! Attention! It is the Battle for Births! It is Your Duty to Give Italy Children. Every Woman who has Five Children or More Serves Her Country as a Soldier.*'"

"And this one?" asked Luigi, pointing to a flyer next to it

showcasing a young boy in a crisp uniform saluting a portrait of Mussolini.

"It says, '*War is to the Male what Childbearing is to the Female. You Are Never Too Young to Serve Your Country. Join the Fascist Youth Today.*'"

Luigi turned his back on Bianca and spit into the street before entering the café. She followed behind, standing silently next to him as he ordered a cavernous glass of Chianti from a moon-faced man tending the counter.

"What would you like, Bianca?" asked Luigi.

"I'll have a soda please."

Luigi slipped some coins into the bartender's outstretched hand, and armed with their drinks and a small basket of bread, they went back outdoors where he selected the only empty table near the edge of the sidewalk. He arched his eyebrows in a silent "*Is this okay?*" When Bianca nodded her approval, he pulled a chair around so that she could sit close to him.

"Grazie, nonno."

"Prego, bambina."

Luigi savored his wine, inhaling its smooth, citrusy bouquet before taking a sip. Resting his free arm on the back of Bianca's chair, he said, "Bianca, if you could be anything, what would you be?"

"A mother," she replied, without hesitation.

"Why?" He nodded toward the propaganda-plastered lamppost. "Because the Duce requires it? Do you think it is your *duty* to marry and bear children, Bianca?"

"No. I just can't think of anything else that would be as fulfilling."

"What if you married and had children and discovered it wasn't fulfilling. What then?"

"I would make it fulfilling."

"Ah, I believe you would."

"Why are you asking me so many questions, nonno?"

Luigi removed his arm from behind Bianca and pulled Egisto's letter out of his pocket. "Read this to me," he asked, handing her the envelope. "Per favore."

Bianca wrinkled her nose. "Not again!"

"You can do it, Bianca. Just take your time."

"Didn't zio Francesco already read this letter to you?"

"Francesco tells me what Egisto's letters say. He doesn't read them to me word for word. There is a difference."

Bianca unfolded the letter, making little surrending sighs as she did, and then, painstakingly, she began to read aloud, her mouth close to her grandfather's ear. It was much as Francesco had said, until the very end.

"Francesco, my brother, give papa and mama our love and tell them I hope they will be kind to Armida when they see her. She has taken the money I gave her in the divorce settlement and bought a house in Ripa where she lives with her sister, Argene. I am abreast of the news in Italy and am thankful Armida did not have recourse to take Silverio with her. No doubt he would be an Advance Guard in the Youth Movement now, as Armida is apparently employed by a high-ranking Fascist officer in Forte dei Marmi. She has only written us a few times since she left, so I know very little of what is really happening in her life. I believe, however, that she will soon miss Silverio and Violenza. They do not show their pain to the world, but I know it will take its toll. Perhaps she will come to her senses and return to America. Despite our past, if she could resolve her bitterness, I believe it is possible we could start over *again. Tell Alberto and Carilda I miss them also, and please send pictures of the children. As always, enclosed is money for you all. Love, Egisto."*

Bianca looked up sheepishly, lowering the letter onto her lap. "I didn't know uncle Egisto was *divorced*!"

Luigi held an arthritic finger up to his lips, charging her to keep the news confidential. "Are you sure you read everything to me, Bianca?"

"I think so. As I told you, I am not a good reader."

"Read the last paragraph to me once more."

When Bianca did as he asked, he quizzed her again. "Egisto said there was a divorce settlement, is that correct?"

"Si."

"And he said Armida bought a house here in Ripa where she lives with her sister?"

Bianca shook her head "yes."

"He said she is employed by a Fascist officer in Forte dei Marmi?"

"Si."

"He didn't say who it is?"

"No."

"Did he say Armida wanted to bring Silverio with her?"

"I believe so."

"Did it also sound to you that he thinks it is possible Armida may change her mind and move back to America?"

"That is what the letter says."

"Why did Francesco hide this from me?"

Luigi asked the last question more to himself than to her. As he pondered the mystery, Bianca carefully refolded her uncle's letter, placed it back in the envelope, and slid it across the table near Luigi's fingertips. Lost in thought herself, she sipped her soda, gazing absently at the throngs of people lining up outside the café to order drinks from the counter inside. She knew it was a sign it was getting late and that they should head back home, but she feared it would be rude to disrupt her grandfather while he was absorbed in thought. Patiently, she waited for him to come back to life. As she did, a dozen little boys dressed in dark shorts and jackets with bright wolf pins attached to their berets marched in formation toward them followed by a female chaperone. They weaved in and out among the tables and halted in front of the Café Rivolti, at the back of the line that snaked out into the street. Moments later, they began commanding those in front of them to move so they could be served before everyone else. At first, their demands were ignored, but when one of the boys loudly warned of what would happen if the Wolf Cubs' demands were not accommodated, everyone stepped aside, allowing the troop to advance to the front of the line.

During the disturbance, Bianca heard the name "Carditi" whispered in fearful tones and struggled to recall where she had heard it before. She was sure her father, Barlaam, had mentioned the name recently when arguing with a friend about politics. She glanced at her grandfather.

Meeting her gaze, he growled, "Fascists!"

"What's wrong, nonno?"

Luigi lowered his voice. "I can't speak openly in public, Bianca, but let's just say that I have seen too much in my seventy-five years of life to be fooled by an egotistical bully like . . . " Instead of saying the name, *Mussolini*, he craftily traced the initial "M" on his chest.

"When I was young," he continued, "Italy had real heroes like Garibaldi. Our kings were kings, not common thugs. I have seen my country through good times and bad; even when we were poor, we were strong in spirit. Yes, perhaps we are becoming rich now, but we are becoming weak also. We are giving all our power to one man everyone is afraid not to follow."

He glanced cautiously at couples sitting at tables near them before pointing discreetly to the lamppost. "Understand?"

Although Bianca was, indeed, beginning to understand, the fact remained that she was simply too young to care, so she humored her grandfather by nodding in affirmation, thinking to herself that she was much more concerned with the sad fate of her motherless cousins in America than she was with the implications of a troop of Wolf Cubs getting preferential treatment at the Café Rivolti.

"What's the point?" lamented Luigi, raising the flats of his hands level with his shoulders in a sign of surrender. "What will be, will be. I'm an old man now and good for little else but running errands for Carmela and tending my vineyard." He finished off the rest of his wine and wiped his mouth with a napkin. "We may as well go now, bambina. We're going to be late as it is."

As they rose to leave, the Wolf Cubs tumbled out of the café, drinks in hand, scouting out available tables.

"Armida!" shouted one of the boys, pointing at Luigi and Bianca. "I want to sit at this table here. The old man and girl are leaving. Can we get some more chairs?"

The woman escorting the troop approached Luigi. "Is this table available?" she asked.

Their eyes locked. Having only seen each other in person once before—years ago, the night Egisto married—they had to rely on the family photographs that had criss-crossed the Atlantic over the years to identify each other.

"Armida Sigali?" Luigi's voice was strong and clear.

Armida lifted her chin.

"I am Luigi Bertozzi."

"I know."

"You know?" he growled. "You stand here like you have no children, as though you were never married to my son?"

Mutely, Armida began sliding tables together and gathering empty chairs to place around them.

Luigi grabbed Armida by the elbow. "What do you have to say for yourself?"

"Leave me alone," she snapped, her lips curled back. "You have no right to touch me."

"I do have a right, as your father-in-law. How dare you divorce Egisto."

"You *were* my father-in-law. You are nothing to me now." Armida broke free from Luigi's grip. "Your son thinks of no one but himself, signore. He is a liar and deceiver. How little you know. It is Egisto who divorced me. It is all his fault."

"You are the liar, Armida, and it is you who are the selfish one. For years Egisto has sacrificed for us, for all of his family. Even now, after everything you have done to him, after abandoning your own children, he wants you back. He has more character in his little finger than you could ever hope to have in a hundred lifetimes."

At first, Armida responded with a high, nervous laugh that could have been perceived as almost maniacal if it wasn't for her otherwise reserved composure. But, ceasing to laugh as quickly as she had begun, her face deadened. Taking a step closer to Luigi, she said threateningly, "Don't ever speak to me again, or I'll see to it that you will no longer have a tongue to spew your venom with."

Luigi's eyes bulged from their sockets. "I'd like to see you try."

"I don't need to," she said evenly. "I have friends in high places."

Bianca had never seen her grandfather so angry. Her stomach churning with anxiety, she knew if she didn't do something quickly the situation would escalate out of control. Grasping his suspenders, she yanked on them firmly. "Nonno! Please!" she pleaded. "It's late. We must go."

Luigi inched away from Armida, maintaining eye contact with her as Bianca retrieved their bikes. When she returned with them, she noticed Armida had turned her attention to waiting on the Wolf Cubs, now milling noisily outside the café.

Luigi and Bianca mounted their bikes and spun out into the street. Before they turned the corner, onto via Provinciale, Luigi turned and yelled, "You are no mother, Armida Sigali! You have a heart of wood, like those bundles of sticks you are a slave to. Shame on you!"

❧

THAT WAS THE one of the few times in my life I was self-conscious, embarrassed actually, about my limp. When nonno and I jumped on our bikes—the day Armida Sigali stormed back into our lives—I was so rattled, I nearly fell off. It was all I could do, with my bad leg, to recover my balance and continue without crashing into a lamppost. I know Armida saw me; her standing there immutable, straight as a washboard with her eyes boring a hole in my back.

When I told mama about Egisto's divorce and our run-in with Armida, of course she cried. But, when I told her about feeling intimidated by Armida, she perked up and said, "You

*must never let anyone intimidate you. Your limp is a gift from
God and someday you will understand why. We must pray,
Bianca, harder than ever."*

You see, mama wasn't a woman to just go to Mass on Sunday. God was not a concept to her; He was real. She prayed
every day, many times a day, and she believed that no matter
what, God could turn people inside out, break their hearts and
change them.

I knew better than to doubt mama. But recalling Armida's
fierceness that day at the Café Rivolti, I wondered how someone so self-assured and commanding, so unafraid and outspo-
ken, could ever be broken.

❧

MEANWHILE, BACK AT the café, everyone within hearing distance who had just witnessed the scene rebuked Armida with
silent, withering stares. Armida, unflinching, stared them all
down in return until each person gave up and turned back
to what they had been doing. None of them had seen the
panic that had seized Armida when Luigi confronted her,
nor could they see the mental battle she was still fighting to
maintain an innocent façade.

Faking a smile, she picked up an envelope she noticed
sitting on the table Luigi had vacated. It was the envelope
Bianca had placed at her grandfather's fingertips earlier; the
envelope containing Egisto's letter to his family. Discreetly,
she tucked it into her dress bodice.

I'll read it when I get home, she thought, her heart racing.
*Egisto must have told his family about me. How much do they
know?*

chapter eighteen

✤

BEING CAPTIVE IN such a complicated world as it was then, I found myself a student of human nature. I often wondered what it was that induced us to make certain choices in life and came to the conclusion that it was Passion—an irrational, capricious spirit activated most profoundly by desire and/or pain.

Italy, in 1935, was infected with it.

You could see it everywhere, from Mussolini's mad obsession for power, to his insatiable appetite for women. He milked us to death, all so that he could restore Rome's former splendor, finance colonization in Africa, and make himself a god.

Meanwhile, our family—along with most other Italians—suffered, and our pain, our fear, instilled a passion in some of us to do things we never thought we would do.

Armida's passions, I decided, were motivated by both her desire to survive and live well, and the haunting pain of her past.

✤

SEVERAL MONTHS AFTER the Café Rivolti incident, Bianca's father, Barlaam Frediani met his fate in the form of a

Shell tanker, which claimed his life when it jumped a curb at the precise moment he was waiting to cross a street in Pietrasanta. Since his oldest daughter, Rina, was married, and his youngest, Lida, was still a young girl, it was left to Bice and Bianca, Carilda's middle daughters, to supplement their widowed mother's income with their sewing skills.

Luigi and Carmela, still living in their home near Carilda on Monte di Ripa, helped Carilda as much as they could. They provided her with fresh vegetables from their garden, wine from their vineyard, olives from their orchard, and rabbits and chickens from their own stock. No longer young, they required considerable aid themselves. Francesco and Alberto, struggling to keep their families afloat, invested the money coming from America into the marble business in the hope that someday it would provide an income for all.

The year 1935 also found Armida Sigali continuing in the role of a domestic for the Carditis. Ironically, though few people would have thought of her—a common housekeeper—as a passionate woman, she was. But in her repressed, subterranean world of passions, people could no longer be trusted, indulged, or obeyed—with the exception of Bruno Carditi, whose paycheck assured the survival of her and her sister Argene. Not surprisingly, it was Argene, and Argene only, who could say things to Armida no one else would dare say.

For example, the day before Christmas Armida flew into a rage because the butcher at the local *macheleria* demanded she pay in cash rather than put the purchase on the Carditis' account.

When they got home, Argene asked, "Why did you yell at signore Grandinetti? Don't you like him, Armida?"

"I didn't yell at him."

"Yes, you did. You were mad at him. You still are. Are you mad at me too?"

"Of course not."

"Because I don't like it when you're angry, Armida. It scares me. And it's almost Christmas. Baby Jesus wouldn't like it."

"I'm sorry, Argene. If I ever act like I'm angry at you, I don't mean it. It's only because . . . well, maybe I'm angry at myself."

"And I heard you crying in bed last night. You said you were happy here with me. Are you not happy anymore?"

"I'm very happy here with you, Argene. I just cry sometimes because of memories I'm trying to forget but can't."

"I have those kinds of memories too; a lot of them. Maybe some of them are the same ones you have . . . from when we were young?"

"Some of them, yes."

"Oh, and I forgot to tell you," she added excitedly, completely changing the subject. "Someone named Carilda Bertozzi came by this morning when you were at work. She said she and her daughter Bianca were going to bring some gifts over to us tomorrow for Christmas! She was so nice, Armida. You would like her. And she didn't look at me funny, like some people do. There was love in her eyes!"

When Christmas came, Carilda and Bianca did, indeed, bring gifts for the Sigali sisters. It would be the first of many attempts by the Bertozzi women to bridge the impasse between their families. For example, after the New Year, one frigid January day when word had gotten around that Armida was ill, Carilda sent Bianca to Armida's house with a wagon full of stew, bread, vegetables and a wool blanket.

Until Armida's health returned, either Bianca, Bice, or Carilda came by daily to check on her.

Never once did they mention Egisto. And never once did they mention her children.

❧

ZIO EGISTO WOULD always ask us to tell him how Armida was really doing; he said he couldn't rely on Armida to tell him the truth. Funny, but he would never tell us how he was really doing. Mama and I would have to read between the lines of his letters to find out. Oh, there weren't tear-stains on the paper, no blurred ink marks or anything, but his handwriting was tired, as though he wasn't sleeping well and his letters weren't folded as neatly as before. The creases were crooked, a sure sign of distraction, and they were stuffed into their envelopes rather than slipped into them—something most people wouldn't notice, but we did. We had to rely on nuances in those days since we couldn't call and talk to Egisto or see him face-to-face. The changes worried mama. I remember her chin trembling as she said, "Destiny is coming to Egisto and Armida's doorstep."

❧

EGISTO CONSIDERED ST. Paul's Cathedral, patterned after St. Peter's in Rome, to be one of the most magnificent structures adorning the entire Midwest landscape. Within its spectacular interior, his creation—the statue of St. Matthew, sinner turned saint—held an unnatural fascination for him, and he often visited his inanimate friend for no reason other than to stand at his rough stone feet in contemplation. Allegedly inspecting the statue for repair and maintenance while doing other work in the cathedral, he would wait until the sanctuary was empty to conduct these clandestine conversations. On one such occasion, while softly rubbing the hem of Matthew's robe with a cloth, Egisto felt a hand on his shoulder.

"Mr. Bertozzi, do you have a moment?"

"Certainly, Father Murphy." The priest motioned Egisto to a nearby pew. "St. Matthew is my favorite also," he said, grinning.

"I was only polishing his robe."

"His robe gets polished more than the other disciples, I think."

"He is one of my finest." Egisto admitted. Groping for an explanation, he added, "I carved him during a time in my life when perhaps I put more of myself into him than the others."

They both fell silent as they reflected on the four apostles standing sentinel along the cathedral's imposing inner colonnade.

"Matthew is outstanding," said the balding priest, finally. "He appears to be the keeper of many secrets. Perhaps you identify with him somehow?"

Bracing himself for an inquisition, Egisto asked, "In what way?"

"People rejected Matthew because they saw him only as a tax collector, but Christ saw the real man and called him forth into a different destiny."

Egisto reddened, but said nothing.

Father Murphy changed the subject. "How are Silverio and Violenza?"

"Fine."

"Good. They are beautiful children. Do you hear from Armida?"

"I'm sorry, Father," said Egisto, rising to leave, "but I have work to do."

Father Murphy tugged at Egisto's sleeve with an authority people rarely used with the sculptor and in his County Cork brogue ordered him to remain sitting. "I'm not going to bite. I simply want to talk for awhile. I sense you need someone to talk to."

"I have friends," countered Egisto.

"And you are able to tell them your deepest pain?"

Egisto lowered his eyes.

"I have watched you for a very long time, Egisto. When you thought no one was looking, I was praying for you. Pain cannot be swept under the rug. It is like trying to patch a rotted roof. When the rains come it will leak again. Only a new roof will solve the problem. When I see you with Matthew," he paused to point at the statue, "I imagine he knows your confession, that he is hearing the cries of your soul."

"No one hears my confession. I don't believe in God."

"You say that, but I cannot look at you with your Matthew and believe it."

"If there were a God, my wife would not have lost her mind and left us."

"Something that can be lost can be found again, Egisto. If there weren't a God, you wouldn't be sitting here with an artistic gift that others can only dream of."

"I worked hard for my talent." Egisto stiffened before letting his shoulders sag. "I can create beauty from a slab of marble. That is easy. But I could not stop the beauty of my wife from turning into stone."

"Armida's divorce is not recognized in Italy, you know," ventured the priest softly. "In the eyes of the Church, and your family in Italy, she is still your wife."

Egisto blinked.

"Are you seeing anyone, Egisto?"

"Why would I?"

"You must be very lonely."

Egisto hesitated before nodding.

"Do you fear the Church?"

"I do not belong to the Church," Egisto snapped. "Why would I fear it?"

"Be sure that you don't fear it! Christ is forgiving and sees your circumstances, Mr. Bertozzi. Although I pray that your marriage is restored, it is possible someday you could find yourself a widower. I say this only to remind you that under those circumstances, should you remarry, as long as the woman is not divorced herself, you may not be disqualified from returning to the Church . . . should you change your mind."

Squirming uncomfortably, as though he were chained to the pew and couldn't get up, Egisto said, "I am not interested in anyone because there is no one who interests me, nor do I plan to marry again. Besides, Silverio and Violenza do not even know about the divorce. They think their mother is gone only temporarily. They think she will come back someday. At least that is what they tell themselves and their friends. I let them believe it. It has been difficult enough for them without the added shame of divorce."

"As for the Church," he added, "why would I want to return? It is because of the Church that I married Armida and not someone else."

Father Murphy asked Egisto what he meant and listened

intently as Egisto recounted how he had refused to marry Marietta Tarabella in the Church, how he had felt pressured to marry before leaving for America, and how—after meeting Armida by chance in a drunken jag—he had impulsively asked her to marry him the day before his departure. Being an intensely private man, Egisto explained that in all the years since his marriage he had told no one his story. Not even his friends.

The priest shook his head. "You realize you have only yourself to blame for all this, Egisto. Failure is not an excuse to hate. It is an opportunity to defeat your weaknesses. It was your stubborn decision not to marry your first love in the Church that has led to this heartache. Do not blame Christ for your pride."

"I blame the authority that tries to force men to make decisions against their conscience."

"You forced Marietta into making a decision. Don't you find that hypocritical? I suppose you think she compromised her conscience by obeying her father's wishes, rather than following your will for her? I do not believe so. You refused to respect her conscience when she chose to respect her father." Nodding toward the statue of Matthew, he added, "Matthew was a stubborn man. He thought he was above the law, until he met the man who showed him what real love is. Real love, Egisto, is surrender."

Egisto crossed his arms. Gazing up into the gilded recesses of the cathedral's cupola, he asked, "What would you know about love? I have suffered for it more than you could ever know."

"Certainly, you have suffered, but have you surrendered? It is important that you address these feelings of yours, my son, and deal with them. Do not hold them captive in your mind any longer. The truth will set you free."

"The truth is, I did love Marietta," blurted Egisto. "Sometimes, even now, I wonder if I still do."

"Did you ever love your wife?"

"Yes, and I love her still. She and Marietta were complete opposites. Marietta was vulnerable, shy and predictable; Armida impulsive, unconquerable. Before my wife's breakdown, she was my strength when I was weak. She had the power to change my heart, my mood, with one look of her eyes, and at times, even though she is in Italy, I feel as though I'm still under her spell."

"You do not believe in God and yet you say you are under a *spell?* Come, Egisto!"

"I speak figuratively, Father. Perhaps I am not communicating my feelings well."

"You will never be able to articulate true love. It is why your sculptures are so brilliant. They reflect the very longings you deny yourself."

Egisto fumbled with his hands. "Maybe you are right."

"Marietta—is she married?"

"Yes. I understand she has two children and a good, decent husband."

"So, you love two women. The first you denied and the second denies you. You must clear up this confusion, Egisto."

Genuinely eager for a word of wisdom, Egisto asked Father Murphy how he could do so.

"You must forgive them both and you must ask God to forgive you and help you forgive yourself," the priest replied. "Only then will you have the peace of mind you long for."

"I have not had my confession heard since I was twelve years old," said Egisto, assuming that is what the priest meant. "I told you, I do not believe in God."

"Someday you will ask God to forgive you because His love will compel you to do so. You will not be able to resist Him. Until then, you must forgive Marietta and Armida. It is in here it must be done." Father Murphy pressed his hand lightly on Egisto's heart. "No one else in the world needs to hear you say the words out loud—except, perhaps, Marietta and Armida themselves. But, even if you never tell them, if you forgive them, you will be free from this spell you say you are under."

The hush of the cathedral was interrupted by the footsteps of parishioners entering the sanctuary for 6:00 Mass. Father Murphy rose and offered his hand to Egisto. "I will continue to pray for you and your children. And for Armida also. You may not believe in God, but He believes in you. God bless you, my son."

"I am sorry if I have offended you, Father."

"Not at all. We priests are not so naïve and narrow-minded as you might think! I will be here if you need to talk with someone, all right?"

Casting a parting look full of sympathy and knowing, Father Murphy made his way to the altar and genuflected before disappearing into the sacristy. Egisto, feeling lighter than he had in years, passed St. Matthew on his way out of the church. Touching the carved hem of the saint's stone garment, he thought, *I am ready for a change, but not so radical as you, Matthew. There are many things to consider yet. We shall see. We shall see.*

chapter nineteen

1939

❧

DANILO AND I talked at great length about whether or not we should invite Armida and Argene to our wedding. It wasn't an easy decision. Since that Christmas Day in 1935 when mama and I first ventured into their home with gifts, we had continued reaching out to them. Armida was usually working, so she wasn't always there when we stopped by to visit, but Argene was. I felt sorry for her, alone so much, and would often take her with me on various errands just to get her out of the house. She became very attached to me, and I to her.

Through Argene I learned much about Armida. I learned that beneath her hard exterior was a woman of deep sensitivities and insecurities. She was a perfectionist; a devoted sister and a shrewd negotiator whose drive to be self-sufficient was nearly equal to her determination to protect her pride. I don't know if it was fear or pride that kept her from ever talking to Argene about her life in America, or her children; I just know she never did. And if Argene remembered that her sister had been gone from Italy for over ten years, she didn't seem *concerned about it. Argene lived completely in the here and now and I think Armida envied her for it. I know she did.*

❧

"Attenzione! All ticketed northbound passengers to Genova! The 11:15 express from Rome is delayed approximately one hour. The estimated time of arrival is now 12:10."

Armida, perspiring and out of breath, listened to the announcement blaring over a loudspeaker behind her and thought, *Great. I raced to get here for nothing.* She brushed aside some strands of hair that had fallen over her left eye and looked about for a vacant seat inside the train station. Seeing only one was left, she claimed it. Despite the cool marble-tiled interior, the heat emanating from amidst the milling throng of passengers was too much for her. She pried open an adjacent window, settled back into her chair and took a few moments to collect her thoughts.

She was there to pick up fourteen-year-old Alessandro Carditi, returning from Campo Mussolini in Rome where he had joined his older brothers, both leaders at the Youth Camp, for two weeks of fun and indoctrination. Bruno and Chiara, far too busy—not to mention far too uninterested—to retrieve their youngest son and listen to childish recitations of his adventures in Rome, had ordered Armida to do the job. In a rare flash of introspection, she stopped long enough to ask herself why she was so eager to please the boy and realized she was transferring her previous affections for Silverio unto him, even though Alessandro was nothing like her son.

Silverio never threw fits like Alessandro, she thought. *He wasn't spoiled and self-absorbed, and he always treated me with respect, even when I was . . .*

She felt her throat splinter, as though it were made of tree bark. Terrified that she would begin to cry openly in public, she forced herself to think about more practical matters.

Thank God the Carditis don't know I have children, she thought, relieved that Bruno and Chiara weren't from Versilia. They were outsiders; too elite and too aloof to be privy to Ripa's rumor mill. *I probably should have told them at the beginning, but then I was afraid they'd think I was a . . . I was afraid they wouldn't hire me. Oh, well. If they find out someday, I'll just tell them I hated America and was homesick. I'll tell them my husband kept my children from me as punishment for my insubordination to him.* She smiled at the thought. *The ultimate sacrifice for my motherland. Bruno would love that.*

A group of S.S. officers getting directions from an Italian *carabieneri* patrolling the station grabbed her attention. The Germans were louder than everyone else; their barking, guttural voices ricocheted off the ceiling and walls. One of them felt her looking at him and turned to glare at her, his delft-blue eyes ordering her to lower hers, but she wouldn't.

Armida held his gaze. *Stare all you want, Tedesco. This is my country, my town. I won't let you intimidate me.*

A moment later, he turned when one of his fellow officers asked him for a cigarette. Armida stared at him a few more seconds, for good measure, and then turned her attention to one of the bags she had brought to the station with her. She picked it up and emptied its contents onto her lap and began to sort through numerous magazines, letters and bills, placing them in organized piles on the corner table next to her.

One magazine—P.N.F. *Gioventù Italiana del Littorio, III*

Campo Roma, XII Leva Fascista, a special issue of the Fascist Youth Movement commemorating the twelfth gathering of 52,000 Italian youth—she tagged by placing it on top of the pile. Alessandro would go crazy over it. The bills she bound up together with a piece of string and placed back in her bag. Letters she always saved until last. There were three.

The first was from Egisto, dated May 23. She smelled him—a blend of roasted pine nuts and Chianti—when she split the seal of the envelope with her thumbnail, and she felt him in the thin layer of marble dust that coated his letter, leaving white powdery smudges on her fingers. He must have written it in his studio at Drake. She resisted the temptation to savor his closeness and castigated herself for allowing him, after all these years, to put even a tiny dent in her armor.

> *Cara Armida,* it read, *I hope you are well. The children are fine. I have asked them to write to you. It is not that they don't want to write more often, they are just very busy these days. Violenza is still dating the neighbor boy, Dick Neumann. Silverio is now engaged to Ruth—the young woman I told you about in my last letter. Our Violenza has a problem with her thyroid and must have surgery soon. The doctor assures us there will be no problem. She will have most of it removed and must take medication the rest of her life. It is a difficult time for her, but she has many friends and I do all I can to support her.*

The rawness in her throat returned. Dim images of what her children must look like now flashed through her mind. Silverio was getting married and she wouldn't be there. She couldn't grasp the change; she didn't want to. Next, she would be hearing that she was a grandmother. Involuntarily, she slipped one hand down to her stomach. *Babies.* A tear splashed on to the letter, jolting her back to the present. Angry with herself, she wiped her cheek, and continued reading.

> *I have just heard that Mussolini signed a "Pact of Steel" with Adolph Hitler. It is a disgrace. Hitler cannot be trusted. The tyrant has lied to the entire world. Where was Italy when he invaded Austria? Now he has attacked Czechoslovakia and no one says a word! Next it will be Poland.*

Armida glanced warily about the lobby. The Germans were gone.

Why must Egisto always write about politics? Of course, I don't dare ask him not to. He would guess that his letters could put me in danger and he would know how bad things have gotten here.

Granted, she didn't like the ever-increasing presence of Germans in Ripa, but what did she care about the Fascists as long as she got her paycheck every month? With a sigh, she continued reading.

> *Why Mussolini continues to ape Hitler is beyond me. He is obviously seduced by the German. The Duce used to have a mind of his own, but no longer evidently. Italians, I understand, are now forbidden to marry Jews? I have warned you before, and will continue to warn you, that Europe is ripe for war. It cannot contain two such egos as theirs! I plead with you again, Armida. Please return to America. I do not presume that you would come back to Minnesota, although if you chose to do so, we would*

be happy to have you near us. I will help you in whatever way I can, should you decide to return. I expect nothing from you, so please do not be afraid. I cannot rest knowing that your life could be in danger in the coming months and years. I await your next letter. Julia and Duke send their love.

—Egisto

Unnerved by Egisto's warnings, she decided she would burn all of his correspondence when she returned home that evening. She placed his letter back in the envelope and opened the next one. It was from her children.

Mama,

How are you? We are fine. I am engaged, as papa told you and am almost finished with school. I am helping papa on a grand onyx statue in the St. Paul Courthouse—the Indian God of Peace—36 ft. tall! Very modern. Papa is also doing some work for the Mayo brothers at their clinic in Rochester. Papa is a great artist. I wish I were as good. Babe is doing well. Julia Barghini comes here often and teaches her how to cook. We don't know what we would do without her . . .

Armida didn't bother reading the rest. *They only write to me because Egisto makes them.* She folded their letter and placed it with the others. *Obviously, Julia is the mother in their lives now. Well, they have more than I ever had. When my mother died, my older sisters were married. I had to be the mother to Argene and the others. There was no one there for me. Violenza and Silverio don't know how lucky they are.*

She opened the last envelope. It was addressed to "*le sorelle Armida e Argine Sigali*" and was from Carilda Bertozzi. Armida read the embossed invitation, announcing Bianca's wedding in two weeks, on June 10, to a certain signore Danilo Corrotti. A handwritten postscript by Bianca expressed hope that both Armida and Argene would attend.

Armida cradled the invitation in her hands, pondering what she should do. She hardly knew Carilda and her daughters and although they had visited her and Argene several times, they were the only Bertozzis to do so. Argene had fallen in love with them. Rarely did anyone pay attention to her, so—because Bianca had gone out of her way to spend time with her—she responded like a seed to sunlight. No doubt, she would insist on going to the wedding, but how could Armida face Egisto's parents? The last time she had seen Luigi Bertozzi was in front of the Café Rivolti eight years earlier.

Brooding over her predicament, Armida started as the station attendant shouted over the loudspeaker, "Attenzione! Attenzione! The 2:15 train from Rome will be arriving in three minutes."

Gathering up her belongings, Armida made her way out to the crowded tracks to greet Alessandro and pretend she was dying to hear all about his Roman escapades.

"Shh, Argene!" Armida slapped her hand over her sister's mouth. "Be quiet or I swear we'll leave!"

Armida's devotion to her senseless sister had increased dramatically since their father's death. Marginally intelligent, Argene was more than capable of caring for herself for short periods of time. Her real neediness came in the form of adult supervision, which Armida provided every evening, even after doting over Alessandro Carditi all day. Occasionally, when Argene got overly excited, her immaturity caused Armida untold humiliation. Like now, these moments before Bianca's wedding.

"Argene, I said *be quiet!*" Vexed, Armida led her sister away from the fringes of a crowd gathering in front of San Luigi Gonzaga, the little church in Ripa where Bianca was soon to be married. They crossed the street and slipped around the corner of an abandoned storefront where Armida could conceal their identities.

"Why do you insist on talking so loudly and acting like an overgrown child, Argene? We cannot stay to see Bianca get married if you cannot be still. If I have to tell you one more time, we will just have to leave. That's all there is to it."

"I'll be good!" Argene pleaded. "I promise!"

"This is a sign we should not even be here. I knew we shouldn't have come." Nervously, Armida peered around the corner of the building at the church.

"Please, let's go back. Please?" Argene pressed her hands together back and forth, her body swaying in desperation. "*Please!*"

"Oh, stop it. Let me think a minute."

"I want to see Bianca in her pretty dress."

Armida spied the swelling throng of people outside the church and began chewing on her thumbnail. "I haven't seen Luigi and Carmela yet," she mused out loud. "Dear God, what if Marietta is here?"

"Who?"

"Never mind."

"I want to see Bianca!" Argene jumped up and down, her voice dangerously on the verge of shrieking.

Struck with a sudden idea, Armida grabbed both of her

sister's hands and steadied her. "Listen to me, Argene. Calm down. Do you remember Carilda?"

"Of course!"

Armida gently inched Argene around the side of the building and pointed toward the church. "See her? Right over there?"

Argene spotted Carilda standing among a group of women. "Yes. I see her."

"Walk over to her, Argene, and ask her if Marietta will be at the wedding today. She'll know who you're talking about. But, don't interrupt her. Wait until she is finished talking to those other women, and then ask her. After she tells you the answer, come back here and let me know what she said. If she asks where I am, just tell her . . . " Armida paused in mid-sentence, "well, just tell her I'm waiting here for you. She'll understand. Carilda is not like the others. Now go—before I change my mind and take you back home."

Armida gave her sister a slight push, watching as she crossed the street and darted like a hummingbird up to Carilda, tapping her on the shoulder while she was yet talking with her friends. Carilda hugged Argene and after a brief interchange she took Argene's arm and made her way toward Armida. Seeing them approach, Armida shrunk back, flattening herself against the building's hot stucco wall as though it could render her invisible.

Rounding the corner, Carilda called out, "Armida?"

Armida didn't move.

"Why are you over here?" asked Carilda.

"I don't want to cause any trouble for you, or Bianca."

"Trouble?"

Armida snatched Argene's hand and pulled her close. "Argene insists on seeing Bianca get married," she explained.

"That's the only reason we're here. We can sneak into the back of the church after the ceremony begins to avoid a scene."

"What do you mean, Armida? If this is about my mother and father, you need not worry," Carilda assured her. "Bianca told them she invited you and made them promise they would be civil to you. They are old and realize they need to forgive you before they die."

Armida turned to her sister. "Did you ask her?"

"Ask her what?"

Rolling her eyes, Armida asked Carilda point-blank, "Is Marietta here?"

"Of course; she is a dear friend to our family." Carilda motioned for Armida to come and peek around the corner at the church. She pointed at a petite, attractive woman who had just arrived and was talking to Luigi and Carmela. "There's Marietta, talking to mama and papa. Her husband, Martino Tamagnini, is standing next to her."

Armida cringed and stepped back into the shadow of the building. "You invited me today knowing Marietta would be here also?"

"You've never met her? After all of this time?" Carilda seemed to reel from the revelation. "In such a small village as Ripa, it is impossible!"

"Why would I want to meet her?" countered Armida. "I am too busy to bother with people who have ruined my life. Besides, Marietta has avoided me as I have avoided her."

"I'm sorry," said Carilda. "Really, I am."

A car pulled up alongside the church, horn honking, and Carilda, who had been keeping one eye on the wedding activities as she talked with the Sigali sisters, waved at Danilo as he stepped up to the curb.

"The groom is here," she said. "I need to go back." Before leaving them, she placed the palms of her hands on the back of Armida's skull, behind her ears, forcing her to look into her eyes. "It is not news, Armida, that Egisto married you because Marietta refused him. Everyone knows it. People talk; they always have and they always will. Marietta has learned to go on with her life and you must also. She is not the type of woman to bear a grudge forever. I am sure she must be just as curious to meet you as you are to meet her, though honestly, we have never spoken about it! I wrongly assumed you both had met each other by now."

Letting her hands drop to Armida's shoulders, she added, "It is inevitable that you face this moment, don't you think? And, it will mean so much to Bianca if you come to her wedding. The decision is yours, of course, but ever since Bianca saw you for the first time at the Café Rivolti, she has hoped and prayed our family would be reconciled with you."

Armida's face contorted in agony; indecision paralyzed her.

Then, seeing all of the wedding guests start to make their way up the steps of San Luigi Gonzaga, Carilda turned from the Sigali sisters and crossed the street toward the church.

Seeing her approach, Marietta and her husband smiled and waved. "Carilda! Buon Giorno! It's a beautiful day for a wedding!"

FROM HER VANTAGE point on the church steps, Marietta had made out the forms of two women in the shadow of the building, behind Carilda's approaching figure. One of them was bouncing back and forth from one leg to the other while the second woman stared stiffly in her direction. Marietta felt intensely scrutinized, as though she were under a microscope, and slid her arm beneath her husband's for support.

I wonder who that woman is, she thought uneasily. *And what Carilda was talking to her about?*

When Carilda joined them on the church steps, they embraced and entered the vestibule together. "Who was that you were talking to?" asked Marietta.

"Friends."

"One of them was staring at me like she knew me."

"That would be Armida Sigali." Carilda cast a warning look at Marietta's husband.

Marietta dismissed Martino. "I'll meet you inside in a moment," she said.

"I *know* who Armida Sigali is," Martino replied with a frown. Turning his back on Carilda and his wife, he dipped his fingers into a small copper basin of blessed water, made the sign of the cross, genuflected, and lumbered into a pew near the front of the sanctuary.

"What is Armida Sigali doing here?" demanded Marietta.

"It's Bianca's wedding day."

"You called her a *friend?*"

"She was my sister-in-law for many years, Marietta. Would you have me ignore the fact that she is the mother to my niece and nephew in America? Yes, I now call her a friend. It is no reflection on you."

Marietta's bottom lip quivered. "How long have you been . . . her *friend?*"

"Since she came back to Ripa eight years ago. I pity her, Marietta. It is unbelievable that since her return you haven't met each other. It is time, don't you think, to get over that part of your life?"

"Armida Sigali seduced Egisto and stole him from me.

She was his ruination. She made a mockery of him, abandoned her children, and now thinks she can live a normal life here as though nothing ever happened?"

"How long will you let this go on, Marietta? For twenty years this fiasco has been the talk of the town. It has only gotten worse since Armida returned. Your daughter is no longer a baby. Surely Vittoria knows what is being gossiped about town, your obsession with a man who is not her husband. It is shameful! If you continue to avoid Armida, your fear and hatred of her will only reinforce the notion that you are still in love with Egisto."

Carilda lowered her voice and added, "Of course, you cannot deceive yourself, or your family, or me. You *are* still in love with my brother. I know it. But for Vittoria's sake, and Martino's, at least let go of your jealousy."

Lida, Carilda's youngest daughter, interrupted their conversation, saying Bianca needed her in the bridal room. "I must go," said Carilda, excusing herself. "Armida and her sister may come in after the ceremony has begun. If they do, I imagine they will sit or stand near the back of the church. I beg you, Marietta, if you have not yet done so, forgive her. It is time."

RESPLENDENT IN THEIR adulation of one another, Bianca and Danilo floated down the aisle in a time warp, an insulated bubble of ecstasy. As they recited their wedding vows, Carilda wept. She would have given anything to have Barlaam sitting beside her just then—soothing her frayed nerves with his strong calm hands—on this bittersweet occasion in which she was losing yet another daughter.

Marietta, sitting next to her brooding husband in the second pew behind Carilda, dabbed her eyes. Bianca and

Danilo's perceptible hunger for each other only served to remind her of her own paradise lost. Jealousy gnawed at her very bones, burning along her ribs, up into her skull and back down her spine. She set her damp handkerchief on her lap, folded the wedding announcement into the shape of an accordion and fanned herself. Discreetly, she eyed the wedding guests within her peripheral vision. Her own parents sat next to Luigi and Carmela Bertozzi. They could never imagine the anguish she had endured from refusing Egisto's offer of marriage so long ago, she thought bitterly. They took false comfort in believing they had helped their daughter make the best choice for a husband, and assumed she was happy.

She avoided looking at Martino, whose knee was touching hers. She lifted her leg and crossed it over the other one, smoothing her skirt over her knee. Perhaps he was entertaining the same thoughts as she. A perfect father and devoted husband, she knew that he loved her as completely as a man could possibly love his wife. The realization only furthered the guilt she bore for nurturing a divided heart. She had tried to give him her best, it was the least he deserved, but they both knew he would never replace her first love. She analyzed Bianca's three sisters, her bridesmaids, standing next to her at the altar. *Such pretty, unaffected girls,* she sniffed. With a mother like Carilda, of course they would be both strong and self-confident, transparent and sweet.

Egisto should be here to see them. She picked up her hankie and dabbed her eyes again. *He should be sitting next to me today, not Martino.* No sooner did she think it, but an electrifying tingle vibrated through her body. *She's here. I can feel her.*

Battling the urge to turn around, she barely heard the

priest intone the final benediction on Bianca and Danilo. The congregation rose to their feet as the couple kissed and began making their way triumphantly down the aisle. Bianca stopped to kiss Carilda and her grandparents. Danilo kissed his parents. Marietta smiled thinly at the bride and blew her a kiss.

Suddenly, from the back of the church, a high-pitched voice pierced the sanctuary. "Bianca! Look, it's me . . . Argene! I am here! Armida let me come!"

Every head turned to catch a fleeting glimpse of Armida dragging her sister out the door, and then every head turned back to Bianca and Danilo to gauge their reaction. Bianca lifted her bouquet. "Grazie!" she called to the retreating pair. "Thank you for coming, Armida and Argene. Please stay!" Impervious to the disruption, she whispered something to Danilo, who nodded in agreement. They then continued greeting their guests, gradually making their way out of the sanctuary.

Marietta eyed the vestibule as they filed out behind the wedding party for a glimpse of Armida, but saw no trace of her. Swallowing his pride, Martino put his arm around his wife's shoulder protectively. He wondered if fate had finally come to collect its due and resolved to stand by his wife, nobly, whatever the cost to himself. Together, they took their place in the procession leading up to the Bertozzi vineyard where the reception was soon to begin.

Surrounded by excited children and celebratory friends and family anticipating an evening of food, wine and laughter, Marietta let Martino take her hand. As the revelers wound their way up Monte di Ripa, however, Martino suddenly tightened his grip, pulling her closer to him. She tracked his gaze. To their left, easily within earshot, Armida

was chastising a sulking Argene while the wedding cele-
brants snaked past her.

"I want to go to the reception," Argene was wailing. "Look,
Armida, they're all going up to Bianca's house. Why can't
we?"

"I took you to the church," Armida snapped. "You saw
Bianca in her wedding dress. Now it's time to go home."

Marietta couldn't keep herself from gawking. She slowed
to a standstill, studying Armida's profile, her voice, her
posture, her mannerisms. She found her to be, unfortunately, lovely. Armida's hair was thicker, and longer, than
hers. She was also taller and slimmer than Marietta ever
hoped to be. The calves of her legs were shapely; her ankles
chiseled thin. Her facial features were far more delicate
than the picture of her in Carilda's home made her to be.
Egisto had sent that photo after Armida's release from
St. Peter's. In it, she looked emotionally absent, with puffy
eyes, a drawn mouth and the beginnings of a double chin.
Now, Armida's proximity revealed a woman whose eyes were
large and clear, her jaw line defined, her mouth moving flu-
idly as she spoke.

It was just then, as Marietta was succumbing to her insecurities, that Armida turned and saw her staring. For what
seemed like an eternity, while everyone noisily skirted
around them, the two women locked eyes with one another.
When they finally turned away—Armida pulling Argene
away from the procession and Marietta and Martino melting back into the crowd—it was as if a tempest had roared
between them, ripping loose shingles of fear and loathing
and leaving in its wake a fatigued calm. It was an unspoken
truce, born of utter emotional exhaustion.

For the first time in her life, Marietta looked at Martino with something other than resignation. She squeezed his hand. *Thank you.*

As Armida and Argene climbed the steps to their home, hand-in-hand, Argene pulled away. Refusing to go into the house, she sat down on the top step and began twirling long sections of her hair around her index finger. "What just happened?" she asked.

"What do you mean?"

"Back there. In the street. You changed."

"I don't know what on earth you're talking about, Argene."

"You'll find out. Change is coming. Everything's about to change."

chapter twenty

IT HAD BEEN ten years since Luigi had transplanted his friend Ferruccio's cuttings alongside his own vines, and true to their promise, the two friends celebrated their eighty-fifth birthdays together in the Bertozzi vineyard on the sun-washed western slope of Monte di Ripa. The tanned, white-haired vintners set aside an entire day to taste an assortment of their various wines, holding court with whoever had the good fortune to stray onto the premises. The family's long oak harvest table was dragged out and set up in a clearing at the edge of the vineyard closest to the house, next to a stained and scarred marble table carved long ago by Francesco. Luigi and Ferruccio threw red checkered tablecloths on both tables, lined the long one with over thirty bottles of wine and placed several chairs strategically around the perimeter.

Carmela supplemented the wine with mountains of food: wheels of firm Tuscan marzolino and stracchino cheeses wrapped in grape leaves to protect them from the sun; bowls of soft panzanella covered with thick muslin to keep the flies away; giant filone-shaped loaves of golden-crusted Altopascio bread and great flat dimpled rounds of rosemary

foccacia; brightly painted trays of stuffed black olives, prosciutto, and garlic-rubbed crositini; wooden bowls filled with
scarlet-tinged pears and fresh red-fleshed figs; shiny jars of
lemony fig jam; several ring-shaped buccellato cakes; buckets of sweet chestnuts; and countless other stomach-coating
accoutrements.

Gone were the glory days of the early Fascist state. Considering the colossal failure of *autarchia*—Mussolini's
attempt to make Italy a self-sufficient, economically autono-
mous country—the expense of such an extravagant spread
was exorbitant. Scrimping and saving for weeks, the entire
Bertozzi family had sacrificed in order to make the day a
memorable one for Luigi.

Wanting to distance themselves from the house, Luigi
and Ferruccio squabbled over where to move their chairs.
Luigi insisted on a sunny spot that allowed an uninterrupted
view of the sea, while Ferruccio demanded shade beneath a
spreading olive tree that marked the separation of the Bertozzi vineyard from the olive orchard. They compromised,
settling on a location that had both a view and some shade,
but was still within easy walking distance of the all-impor-
tant buffet table.

By mid-morning it was already warm. God, both men
agreed, had smiled upon them, granting them June-like
weather in October. Surely it was a portent, a sign that the
year ahead would be, they hoped—as they toasted each
other—better than the last. They crossed their legs and surveyed the terraced vineyards below them bathed in sunlight,
gradually fanning out into the green plains of Versilia. The
plains, in their turn, straddled a crescent stretch of brilliant
white sand beaches that extended north to south as far as
the eye could see. And beyond that, the mythic Ligurian Sea

glistened turquoise, melting into the earth's horizon. They heard wild geese take off behind them from the pine forest crowning Monte di Ripa, and watched from their high vantage point as the flock coasted west and then banked south, hugging the seashore, their flight an aerial ballet performed to the accompaniment of thousands of resident cicadas.

After sitting that way for nearly half an hour, silently soaking up the rich autumn air and sweeping vistas, Carmela's voice crackled out to them from the house. "I'm going to Mass now, Luigi. If you two want anything, you'll have to come get it yourselves."

"Si, si." Yes, yes, Luigi yelled. Carmela's hearing wasn't what it used to be.

Ferruccio's eyes followed Carmela as she went back into the house, emerging a moment later with a black scarf draped over her snowy head. She tied it beneath her chin and began making her way down the steep cobblestone path to Carilda's home nestled at the bottom of the hill. "She's a good woman, your wife," he remarked as she disappeared down the lane.

"She is a saint," Luigi replied. "So is Carilda. They go to Mass together every day."

"All women are saints."

"Not all," said Luigi.

"This Vermentino isn't bad." Ferruccio held his glass up to the sun before tasting it again. "Not as good as mine, though."

When Carilda arrived back home an hour later, she found her husband and Ferruccio commiserating on the future of the nation. Mussolini, she heard them swear, was taking them all to hell in a hand basket. Hitler was bulldozing his way through France and bombing London. The barbarian! He didn't need Italy; he was just using them to cover his backside. They were but pawns in his arrogant, Teutonic hands.

On and on they ranted. Instead of leading coveted lives as they had been promised, Italians were being reduced to ruination. Everyone was becoming anti-Fascist—even the Fascists. Such an upside-down, confusing world! The British, who had for so long loved Italy, were now their enemies thanks to Hitler and the Duce. If America entered the war, joining forces with Britain and Russia, it would spell the end. They would turn the war around for the Allies, and then where would that leave Italy? Like ancient Homerian warriors, the two old men frowned at the prospect. No one could be trusted anymore, they complained. Egisto had seen it coming all along, Luigi boasted sadly, adding that his son had been born with a knack for discerning political winds.

Ferruccio was impressed. "Well, whatever the outcome, Gigi," he replied, using Luigi's nickname, "at least one of your children will be safe in America."

Carmela had heard enough. She would rather go back indoors and do nothing than stand about listening to such doom and gloom. Only God knew the future. Ranting and raving about it was a waste of time. *Besides,* she thought morosely, *Luigi is ill. This will only aggravate his condition.*

She interrupted them, pointing an arthritic finger in their direction. "You two will make yourself sick, drinking all morning without eating a thing! Look at all this food going to waste. Carilda is coming up this afternoon, Luigi, and if she finds you drunk, don't come crying to me." She assumed an air of disgust as she watched them chuckle in response to her, their eyebrows raised in mock chagrin.

Carmela had a semblance of grace for her husband that day only because she knew it would be his last birthday. A few months ago, the doctor had told them that the sporadic but increasingly severe pain Luigi had been experiencing in his upper abdomen was the result of an untreated hernia which had weakened his heart. Since then, Carmela had fussed over him like an anxious mother hen, frustrated by his insistence on keeping his illness confidential. She knew he often heard her crying at night when she thought he was asleep, because he would try to console her by patting her arm, or caressing her wiry untied hair, giving her assurances that she would be taken care of after his death. Even so, she couldn't bring herself to express her true feelings to him. After all this time, she feared it was too late. If only she could hold him close to her—her body conformed to his—and whisper in his ear how much she loved him. Regret tortured her.

Casting one last withering look toward Luigi as he got up to approach her where she stood sulking behind the buffet table, Carmela stiffened. Shrinking back from his advance toward her, she announced she was going to her room for a nap. Before she turned to leave, however, Luigi made sure she saw him tear off a large piece of bread, dunk it in a jar of olive oil, and put it into his mouth. It was his way of comforting her without saying a word. He winked at her as their eyes met, but she, simulating disdain—even as her heart melted within her—turned her back on him and disappeared into the house.

You can't run away from me forever, Carmela, thought Luigi. *You can't pretend any longer that I am not sick. Later this afternoon, when our guests are resting, perhaps I will come to you and confront you again. It is time you surrender to your real feelings.* He tore off another chunk of bread and, deep in thought, returned to Ferruccio.

It felt as though it was a hundred degrees in the sun, although it was really hovering around the ninety-degree mark. The two picked up their chairs and moved deeper into the shade to resume their conversation.

"How are your children?" asked Ferruccio.

"Bene. Good. Francesco is struggling, but he still has the business. His boys are . . . *whoosh* . . . this big now." Luigi stood up to demonstrate, placing his hand horizontally along the center of his forehead.

"No!"

Luigi sat back down. "Si."

"And Alberto?"

"Alberto is struggling in this economy like everyone else. His girls are big also. I believe they will marry soon."

"Where has the time gone?" Ferruccio shook his head in wonder. "And how are Egisto and his children?"

"Egisto is doing well. He has much work in America. Without his checks we would no longer have this home."

Ferruccio, nodding, understood completely.

"Silverio and Violenza are now married, both to Americans. I have seen the pictures." A faraway look settled in Luigi's eyes. "Can you believe I have never met my own grandchildren? It is not right."

"No," agreed Ferruccio, swishing his wine around and around in his glass. "It is not right. But, what can you do?"

"*Niente.* I can do nothing, because at first Egisto could not leave the children, motherless, to come here. Now that they are married, and he can leave them to come home to visit, the war makes it impossible to travel."

In the distance, paralleling the long stretch of beaches to the south toward Livorno, Luigi noticed a squadron of Sparrowhawk bombers performing war maneuvers. He pointed to them and exclaimed, as though he were talking to thin air, "If only I could fly to America, I would do it to see my son again."

Ferruccio detected desperation in his friend's voice. "You will see Egisto again, Gigi."

"I think not."

"Why is that?"

"I just do not believe it, that is all." Changing the subject, Luigi asked, "You know Bianca and Danilo have a new baby . . . a boy, Renzo?"

"No!"

"They have moved to Bientina, near Pontedera."

"Why is that?"

"Danilo has a job at the Piaggio factory building war planes. It is a losing battle of course, but at least he has a job."

"Poor Carilda! She must miss Bianca terribly. It is difficult to be a widow these days."

"It has been very hard for everyone. But, Danilo is a fine son-in-law to Carilda. Bianca is in good hands."

"And Carilda's other girls?"

"Her youngest, Lida is seventeen; pretty like her sisters. Rina has two children, and Bice is dating a pilot in the Air Force, from Pontedera. A handsome man and daring, I hear. Benedetto Viti is his name."

"A pilot!" exclaimed Ferruccio, impressed. "You are fortunate to have your grandchildren living so close."

"Unfortunately, life changes when we least expect it, Ferruccio. Take my Bianca, for example. She is an exceptional seamstress and very busy with her work but she needs help, so Carilda and the girls have made a decision. Carilda will rent her home and move in with mama and me. Bice and Lida will move to Bientina to live with Bianca and help her with the housework and the baby so she can continue her sewing business."

"I am sorry Carilda must rent her home." Ferruccio shook his head as he poured himself another glass of wine. "But the girls will be happy together in Bientina, no? And you will be happy with Carilda living with you in your house."

"God knows best."

Trying to cheer his friend, Ferruccio gushed, "You must be very proud, my friend. Not all men have such grand families. With my wife gone, and my son childless, all I have left are my grapes." He lifted his glass in the air. "At least, Gigi, we have no regrets, eh?"

Luigi winced. "I have many."

"No! What regrets could you possibly have?"

"I regret that I never learned to read, and I regret I wasn't more attentive to my wife." Luigi leaned back, rubbing first his abdomen and then his chest. "I regret that I was so hard on Egisto. I am to blame for his marriage to Armida."

"No!"

"It's true, Ferruccio. I did not trust that he could find a good Italian wife in America, so I insisted he find one here before he left." He stopped rubbing his chest, picked up his glass of wine, and stared at its dark contents like a primeval priest reading an oracle. "Then, when the marriage failed and Armida came back to Ripa, I regret the way I treated her."

Ferruccio tapped one finger on his temple. "Do not be so hard on yourself, Gigi. Any father would have been angry."

"There are no excuses for my behavior. It was ten years ago that I made a public spectacle of Armida . . . the very day I brought your cuttings back here to transplant. Since then, I have not stopped being ashamed of myself. No wonder she is afraid of me and will not come to see us. It is a miracle she came to Bianca's wedding! I do not like to think of dying without resolving our conflict."

Luigi stopped staring at his wine and took a long drink before concluding, "Yes, Ferruccio, I have many regrets."

Ferruccio could think of nothing to say. He waved his hand over the vineyard. "Shall we?"

Both men rose at his suggestion and began to inspect row after row of Luigi's vineyard. Ferruccio was especially interested in the vines from the cuttings he had given his friend. After carefully studying them in detail, he grumbled that they did not look as healthy as his own.

"Impossible!" Luigi scoffed. "My vineyard is on a broad hillside, you have only your back yard. Your grapes are thriving here."

They continued sparring, until they were interrupted by several neighbors dropping by to congratulate them both on eight-five years of good health. Card games and bocce ball followed, accompanied by an abundance of good-hearted bantering and braggadocio. At noon, Luigi announced there would be a wine-tasting contest. They all gathered around the table as Ferruccio poured four different *vino di Strettoias* into four separate, marked, communal glasses. The men stood in a circle and took turns tasting the contested varieties, passing each glass to the next person. After several rounds, Luigi and Ferruccio demanded a consensus. Which wine was the best? Overwhelmingly, of the four wines—one of them from the vines Luigi inherited from his father—they chose the wine that had come from Ferruccio.

Ferruccio was jubilant. Slapping Luigi on the back, he shouted, "What did I tell you?"

A HYPER-ACTIVE BUMBLE bee buzzed back and forth between Luigi and Ferruccio, circling their nodding white heads like an orbiting satellite. With mouths wide open, they dozed blissfully, their bodies occasionally shaking with involuntary spasms. Ferruccio, sweat streaming down his fat-rippled neck, had rolled up his sleeves and unbuttoned the upper part of his shirt, exposing a chestful of gray hair, which rose and fell atop his protruding belly with each breath. Luigi, lean and lanky, had likewise unbuttoned his vest, hanging his silk tie on the lowest branch of the olive tree, which now only partially shaded them. Their friends and neighbors had judiciously returned to their own homes to take naps, despite their attempts to retain them.

Thrusting his head back in a single mammoth head-to-toe shudder, Ferruccio inhaled. It was an operatic grunt—a colossal snore—that woke both he and Luigi. Shaking themselves awake, they stretched out their arms and legs and yawned.

Ferruccio checked his pocket watch. "Mamma mia, it's late! I must go."

"Go where? You are eating dinner with us tonight, of course."

"No, no. I do not want to intrude on your family celebration."

"You would prefer to eat dinner alone . . . on your birthday?"

Ferruccio's response was more of a question than an answer. "Si?"

"Ferruccio! Eat with us!"

"Well . . ."

"I insist."

"All right, if you insist. But first I must go home to feed my cat."

"Fine, fine. We will eat around seven o'clock." Luigi stood and escorted him to the rutted path intersecting the vineyard and the lane. "Thank you, Ferruccio for your friendship today." He hugged him, embracing him longer than usual, and then planted a kiss on each of his cheeks. "I mean it sincerely."

Ferruccio grinned and thanked Luigi for being such a generous host. As he shuffled down the lane toward via Strettoia, he turned and called, "Which is the finest Merlot in Versilia?"

Luigi lifted his wineglass and shouted, "Ferruccio's!"

"Ah-ha!" Ferruccio's laugh echoed off the stone walls. "I will bring another bottle when I return!"

Just as his friend rounded the bend near Carilda's house, Luigi spotted Carilda and Bianca making their way up toward him. They passed the jocular Ferruccio, exchanging greetings with him, and upon seeing Luigi standing at the top of the path, they yelled, "Papa! Nonno!"

Luigi held out both of his arms to them, meeting them half-way with a bear hug. "Bianca, what are you doing here?"

"Do you think I would miss your birthday, nonno?" she teased.

He hugged her again. "It has been too long! Six months since I last saw you. I do not like you living so far away, bambina."

"Bientina is not so far away; only forty miles. You could come visit me easily."

"Oh, Bianca, I am too old to travel that far," he protested. "As expensive as it is, and with the war going on, you might as well be in America." The truth of his statement stung her.

Changing the subject, Luigi asked, "Where are your sisters?"

"They stayed in Bientina with the baby. They are a great help to me. I will be helping mama move out of her house tomorrow. They send their love."

"Good girl." Luigi led them both to the spot where he and Ferruccio had been napping and pulled up an extra chair for Bianca.

"Here, sit," he instructed them. "Mama must still be sleeping or she would be out here with us now. Nothing escapes her, you know."

Carilda suggested they go inside the house and begin preparing supper.

"No," said Luigi firmly. "I need to talk to both of you."

The fact was, dread had been hounding Luigi ever since he had woken up from his nap, in no small part because as he slept—as the over-zealous bumblebee burrowed through his bristly hair and explored the thick wool fibers in his vest— he had dreamed he was dead. All of that talk with Ferruccio about war and tensions in Italy had not sat well with him.

In his dream, he hovered over Monte di Ripa watching helplessly as bombs destroyed his home and obliterated his precious vineyard. Through sulfurous clouds of smoke he saw Carmela, bloodied and hysterical, screaming for him to come back to her. He could still hear his wife's keening. His skin crawled at the recollection.

Finally addressing his daughter, Luigi explained, "Carilda, I am very ill. Often my heart struggles to beat, and I have much pain here." He touched his upper stomach. Carilda's eyes widened with understanding but also dread of what he was going to say next.

"Mama knows how sick I am," he continued. "But she will not allow me to talk to her about the things that are important to me . . . and to you. So, we must talk now."

Carilda's hand flew to her mouth.

"You must be strong," he warned her sharply, hoping the tone of his voice would prevent her from panicking.

Bianca and Carilda reluctantly listened as Luigi then explained his dream to them and laid out his plans and concerns for the future. "My dream was a premonition. I cannot dismiss it. I fear the war will get much worse before it is over and it may well bring devastation here to Ripa. I will not be here much longer, and it grieves me to know that you, Carilda—and mama—will be alone. Letters from Egisto have been censored for the last two years and some of his checks stolen. If America enters the war, he will no longer be able to send us letters or money. You know what that means?"

Bianca put her arm around her mother who continued to mop her face with her apron.

"Our only source of aid will be gone." Luigi said out loud what he knew they were thinking. "Francesco has had to pour much of the family income into the business, but with the war, it is for nothing. He is barely able to take care of his own family. The same is true with Alberto. You know what that means?" he asked again.

Carilda and Bianca steeled themselves. "Si," they answered in unison.

"It means you have no one to depend on but yourselves."

Calmly, he turned his attention to Bianca. "You and Danilo will have your hands full with the baby and your sisters."

He looked at Carilda. "It is a good thing you are moving

in with us. Mama will need you. She is too old to live by herself."

Carilda's eyes, large and brown like a lioness, brimmed with tears. "What are you saying, papa?"

"I am saying that I am worried about what will happen to mama after I'm gone. I could ask Francesco and Alberto if they think they would be able to care for her when I die. They may think that they can, but reality may be different. If our house remains when the war ends and mama is healthy, then she will be fine. But, if not, I am asking you, Carilda . . . do you think that mama would be a burden to you?"

"You know the answer, papa!"

"I know *you*, Carilda. You are the most dependable daughter a father could ever ask for. If all else fails, knowing that mama will be with you, gives me great peace."

To their left, the sun melted into the silvery curvature of the earth, casting shafts of amber and saffron light throughout the shadowing vineyard, while to their right a giant pearl of a moon crested atop Michelangelo's illuminated peak. A wide, twilight trail of undulating stars connected the two orbs, tossed like diamond confetti from east to west. A sacred hush fell over the three—father, daughter, and granddaughter—as they soaked up the spectacle. Perhaps if they didn't move, or speak, the moment might never end. Luigi inhaled the pungent smell of burning chestnut leaves wafting up toward them on tendrils of smoke from the purpling valley below them. He closed his eyes, remembering all of his children when they were young and still living at home; innocent, full of hope, dependent on him. He remembered his wife on their wedding day, and the memories strengthened his resolve to press ahead.

"The laws of inheritance in Italy are not kind to women,"

said Luigi, breaking the silence. "Francesco, Egisto and Alberto will inherit most of my estate when I die. My sons may not agree, but Carilda, I am leaving you the vineyard."

"It is not necessary, papa," she protested, stunned. "I still have my home."

"It is not enough. And it is not fair to you. You did not receive an education like your brothers and you have no husband to help you in this life. I know that it will fall to you to take care of mama after I am gone. Do you think I care about tradition when it comes to my only daughter? No doubt, your brothers will be angry with me, but I have made up my mind. It is your just reward, Carilda. Whatever you do, do not let them talk you out of your inheritance."

"Carilda! Bianca!" shouted Carmela from the doorway to the house. "Buona sera!" As she drew close to them, her eyes fixed on Luigi and her smile disappeared. Carilda and Bianca turned to see their father, ghostly pale, clutching his chest. Seconds later, he collapsed to the ground.

"Bianca!" Carilda screamed. "Find a doctor—hurry!"

While Bianca raced to find help, Carilda dropped to the ground frantically trying to unbutton Luigi's shirt. Unsuccessful, she finally tore it open. "Papa! Keep breathing!"

A gurgling sound, deep in Luigi's throat, surfaced on his lips. It produced a thin stream of bloody drool that ran from the corner of his mouth, down his jaw and then fell into Carilda's cupped hand. His eyes bored intensely into hers for what seemed an eternity, and then, in one convulsion, one heart beat, he was gone.

Pushing her daughter away, Carmela broke out in an eerie keen. She lay down on the ground next to her husband, curling up in a fetal position with her head nestled on top of his shoulder, her hands resting on his stilled chest, refusing to look at his face. An hour later, when she finally allowed herself to be led away from his stiffening body, she called out to him, for all to hear, "Forgive me, Luigi! I did not deserve you."

❧

NONNA REMINDED ME of Armida in that she was a difficult woman. Even my mother, Carilda, was afraid of her. Well, not afraid really, but we all walked on eggshells around nonna because she was so sensitive; so predictably unpredictable. When we thought she'd be angry with us for something, she wasn't, and when we thought she'd be happy about something, she was angry. At least, that's how she appeared. If I ever said anything derogatory about nonna—how I didn't like how she treated nonno, or how she would sometimes yell at my mother, or how she didn't talk to me very often—mama would scold me. "Your nonna had a hard life, Bianca," she would say. "Only God knows a person's heart. She may not be perfect— she may not show her love like nonno did—but she's a good woman."

Still, it was hard for me to not confront nonna about her sharp tongue, her bitterness and her hypocrisy. She would wail for hours about how much she missed nonno; how much she had loved him. I felt like saying, "Then you should have treated him that way when he was alive, nonna!"

The truth is, we all missed nonno terribly. I felt he had, like a bird, taken a part of me—a morsel of my me-ness—with him to heaven, just like I felt he had left a part of himself with me. Maybe that's what communion is. I've never told anyone this until now, but when I get homesick for nonno I tear off a piece of bread and chew it for a long, long time and then I wash it down with a glass of wine. I think that Jesus enjoyed eating with His disciples and said they could remember Him by breaking bread together. Well, I loved eating and drinking with nonno, and sitting and spending time with him, so every time I have communion at church I remember Jesus, but every time I have communion at home, I think of nonno.

I hope that's not a sin. I also hope it's not a sin to believe there are vineyards in heaven because that's where I picture nonno living now, making Jesus wonderful—bellisimo—wine. After all, his last thoughts were of giving his vineyard to mama and it's where his spirit left his body. Surely, that means something.

❧

PART IV

1943–1944

Caduto dalle Nuvole

"Fallen from the Clouds"

chapter twenty-one

July 25, 1943

❧

LESS THAN THREE *months after a somber funeral proces-*
sion accompanied nonno's body to his final resting place in the
Strettoia cemetery, Japan attacked Pearl Harbor and Amer-
ica entered the war. Four days later, on December 11, 1941,
from the balcony of the Palazzo Venezia in Rome, Mussolini
declared war on the United States. That month, the Duce also
forbade newspapers to mention Christmas.

"It only reminds one of the birth of a Jew," he said.

Can you imagine? Clearly, he had underestimated our egal-
itarianism and our devotion to the Church. Not only that,
but he had miscalculated our soldiers' abhorrence of fighting
against Italian-Americans. I'm not a historian by any means,
but we all knew that with America now allied with the British
and Russians, and with the British Royal Air Force surprising
Mussolini by using their long-range Wellingtons to bomb the
port of Naples, it could signal the beginning of the end.

But, it got worse before it got better.

The shortage of men in the private work sector forced Mus-
solini to abandon his Battle for Births initiative and recruit

women into the workforce. The cost of living doubled, the use of private automobiles was prohibited, and taxis were banned after 10:00 in the evening. Listening to American jazz was forbidden, as well as reading books by English or American authors. In blacked-out cities across the country, flashlight batteries could not be replenished after running out because there were no materials available to make more. Pedestrians resorted to wearing luminous buttons on their clothing to prevent running into others in the dark. Citizens were asked to observe four meatless days a week.

Soon, it came out that Mussolini was spending $10,000 per month on his mistress, his "Rasputin in Skirts." He went from being a beloved leader to one of the most hated men in the history of Italy.

Then, the inconceivable happened. Civil war descended upon us.

❦

ALONE IN THE sprawling Carditi villa, Armida groped about in the fading light of dusk, searching for mementos and pictures of Alessandro for a scrapbook she was asked to compile in honor of his upcoming eighteenth birthday. With Paolo and Arturo now stationed in the south, Alessandro remained the only son at home. He was embracing manhood—on this sultry, jasmine scented Sunday night— by going out and carousing with his Fascist friends. Bruno, summoned to Rome on urgent business, had been gone for over a week, while signora Carditi, increasingly absent from her home and her husband, was supposedly in Pisa visiting family. Her long absences forced Armida to work at the villa for days on end, during which—when necessary—Bruno allowed her to go home for brief amounts of time to check on Argene.

Stifled by the heat, Armida went over to the shuttered windows facing the sea and opened them, hoping to coax some ocean breezes into the stuffy house. They were still without electricity, so she lit an oil lamp and wandered from one room to another talking quietly to herself.

Why is Bruno so adamant that someone be here in the villa at all times?

He had told her he feared someone might break into the house. Also, he said, though no longer a child, Alessandro expected her to be available if he needed her.

That was a sorry excuse, she mused. *Alessandro is hardly ever home.*

Armida knew Versilians loathed the Carditis, and she suspected that Bruno's vanity prevented him from realizing his residence was despised as a symbol of Mussolini's excesses.

Well, it's not my concern. I'm not really a Fascist. I'm just a housekeeper, a danger to no one.

Deciding the second-floor study would be the best place to unearth items for Alessandro's scrapbook, she climbed the steps and opened the windows there as well before setting the lamp on Bruno's desk. The daily newspaper, *La Nazione,* lay folded where she had left it earlier that day. Ever since the Allied bombing of Rome a week ago she had avoided reading the news or listening to the radio. The hysterical rumors swirling about Forte dei Marmi were disturbing enough without reading endless details about it, most of which were, hopefully, fabricated. Nevertheless, a sudden urge compelled her to open it.

In giant letters the headline screamed, *"King Will Decide Mussolini's Fate."*

Armida collapsed into Bruno's chair and continued reading. Sixteen hundred Romans were confirmed dead from the recent Allied bombing. Pope Pius XII had fled the Vatican.

Unthinkable! Why, less than a month ago Italy had seemed impregnable! Now, the Grand Council, the newspaper noted, convening in an emergency session, was set to vote on removing Mussolini from power, and Mussolini, in a last ditch effort to preserve his dictatorship, was expected to seek support from King Victor Emmanuel. Government officials were scrambling to make peace deals with the Allies, while Hitler vowed he would occupy Italy before allowing Allied troops victory there.

Armida gasped. The implications for her were staggering.

She refolded the newspaper and sat for what seemed an eternity, staring at the flame in the oil lamp as she frantically measured her options. If Mussolini was deposed, all the Fascist positions in his government—including Bruno's—would be defunct. If Hitler occupied Italy, as he was threatening to do, war would certainly be fought on their soil. The Führer would never expose Germany's backside to the Allies; he would make Italy a shield to protect the Rhineland. Realizing the danger she was in, she wished she was back in America. She began to formulate a plan of action, deciding then and there to leave a note of resignation for the Carditis after which she would return home to pack her belongings and . . . and what? Her connection with the Carditis would follow her everywhere she went. She would be a liability to her entire family. She had no friends she could turn to. Her mind still racing, she opened the top drawer of Bruno's desk and pulled out a slip of paper and a pen. Trying to steady her hand to keep it from shaking, she scrawled:

Signore e signora Carditi:

It is with great sorrow that I must inform you of my inability to continue in your service . . .

The pen stopped working. She shook it several times, tried it again, and then set it aside. As she rummaged through the desk drawer for another pen, her eyes fell on a letter bearing handwriting that looked oddly familiar. She peered intently at it in the dim light and saw that it was addressed to her from Egisto.

From the darkened doorway came a deep voice: "The light from that lamp becomes you, Armida. You look like an angel. Really."

Startled, she jumped to her feet. Reaching out to recover her letter of resignation, she knocked the oil lamp off of the desk, sending it crashing onto the carpet where it immediately burst into flames. Instinctively, she fell to her hands and knees, grabbed the edge of the carpet and pulled it over the spreading flames, smothering the fire until it was extinguished. She could discern, squatting in the pitch darkness, through the sound of her own blood pounding in her ears, footsteps coming closer. She felt a rough brush of fabric on her forearm, and knew he was right next to her. A moment later, the icy silence was broken by the scratching of a match being lit, followed by a tiny flash of light illuminating the leering face of Bruno Carditi. He bent down and stared into Armida's eyes while he held the match to his cigarette. When the light went out, he tossed the match carelessly on the still smoldering carpet. The round orange glow of the cigarette's burning tip flashed brighter when he inhaled.

"Faithful Armida," he rasped.

When she didn't respond, he lit another match, held it up near her face and said, "There are some candles in the bottom right-hand drawer of my desk. Get one out for me."

Armida crawled back to the desk, feeling her way with her hands until she found the drawer. Opening it, she felt around for the candles and retrieved one, offering it up to her master. He took the candle, lit the wick with the tip of his cigarette and handed it back to her.

"Here," he smiled, plopping down in his chair. "Do something with it."

Armida floundered about looking for a candlestick. When she found one, on a nearby shelf, she pressed the burning candle into it and placed it in on his desk.

"What do we have here?" inquired Bruno. He picked up the note she had begun to write and inspected it. "Don't tell me you're resigning?"

"Yes."

"A bad idea, don't you think?"

"No."

Bruno let the note slip from his fingers. "What did you say?"

"No," repeated Armida, firmly.

"No?" he shouted. "Italy is going to hell and you choose a day like today to bite the hand that has fed you all these years?"

"I'm . . . sorry."

He picked up the pen Armida had been using and flung it at her. She deflected it with her hand, sending it skipping across the floor.

"Sorry?" he hissed. "You pathetic liar." Yanking the top desk drawer open, he pulled out the letter from Egisto she had been reading earlier. "What is this?"

Knowing she was trapped, Armida lowered her eyes and said nothing.

"No doubt you wonder how this letter of yours is in my possession. Alessandro found it in your room just before I left for Rome. How foolish of you to leave evidence like this around the house, Armida. It appears we have been employing a stranger in our home."

He waited for a reply and when there was none, he demanded shrilly, "What do you have to say for yourself?"

Armida kept her lips tightly sealed, terrified her voice would crack, or worse, that she would start crying if she tried to answer him.

"You have two children in America," he snarled, aroused by the scent of fear rolling off her damp skin. "You would have me believe you have no attachments to them?"

"I don't."

"Oh, but they are attached to you, aren't they?" He unfolded the letter from Egisto and read it with difficulty in the faint candlelight.

"Armida, the children have not forgotten you. It has been hard, but if you are willing to come back and live near us, they are willing to forget the past and start over again. They need their mother. I know that deep inside, you love them. If it were possible, we would come to see you, but Mussolini has ruined Italy. It is not safe for us to come to you, and although you would have us believe you are safe, I know you are not. Nothing good will come of working for the Fascists. Please, you must try to find work elsewhere. Again, I beg your forgiveness and ask that you write soon, accepting my apologies . . ."

Armida interrupted him. "That was written a long time ago."

"Of course." Bruno inserted the letter back into the envelope and tucked it inside his shirt.

"I never wanted to go back to America. I hated it there."

"I wish I could believe you." He rose from his chair and walked toward the open window. "You realize this puts us in an awkward situation."

Just then, the lights in the house sputtered back to life. An RAI program, which had been tuned in before the power went out, crackled over Bruno's radio. Armida moved to turn it off.

"Leave it!" Bruno ordered, looking at his watch. "I want to hear the news."

The radio played in the background as Armida waited silently for Bruno to continue. He studied the moonlit garden beneath the window and then raised his sight toward the town's crowded piazza. A sudden, sporadic round of fireworks showered fiery, brilliant sparks over the town's roofs, illuminating scores of revelers spilling out onto the streets.

Suddenly, through intermittent static, they heard a radio announcer shout, "It is official! Today, after a vote in the Grand Council, Benito Mussolini, in the presence of His Majesty the King, resigned as Prime Minister of Italy. As he was put under arrest and taken to an undisclosed location, the King appointed Field Marshall Pietro Badoglio as Premier . . . " Breathlessly, he listed multiple theories of what would happen next.

"Turn it off," growled Bruno, still gazing out the window. He nodded toward the street mob that now appeared to be gravitating in the direction of the Carditi villa. "Let them celebrate the fall of the Duce. They think he made life miserable for them. The Führer will make their lives insufferable."

He turned and looked at Armida standing next to the radio cabinet with the moonlight full in her face and the faint glow of the hallway light, come back to life, backlighting her trembling body. The candle on his desk flickered fitfully in the warm breeze wafting in from the sea.

"So, here we are," he said. "We have some decisions to make, you and I."

"I have already made my decision."

"Why, you can't leave us now!" He waved his finger back and forth like a metronome. "No, no, no, no, no."

Armida bit her tongue and waited.

"Actually, I have a very special job for you," he continued, taking a step toward her. "It will be far more exciting than cooking or cleaning. You like to travel, don't you?"

"No."

"You will learn to like it." Another step closer. "You are familiar with the Piaggio plant in Pontedera?"

"Everyone knows the Piaggio plant."

"Well . . ." Bruno swung his arm out, flicking his spent cigarette out the window. Reaching into his shirt pocket he pulled out a white package of German Regie 4 cigarettes. He tapped the box against the back of his hand and pulled out another cigarette, cupping both of his hands near his mouth as he lit it. "This is top secret, Armida."

At precisely the moment he said her name, he lowered his right hand to caress the black handle of a Beretta in a holster strapped across his chest.

"I don't want to go to Pontedera."

His hand froze on the gun. "This isn't a request."

A bead of sweat rolled down the side of Armida's face and tumbled down her neck, disappearing between her breasts.

"Let me explain," he continued. "You have put me in a very awkward position. Here I am, a top officer, with a house-keeper who has lied to me for thirteen years about having children. American children, no less. Who would believe that a mother could not miss her children so far away? My superiors, or worse yet, the Nazis—if they knew about your deception—would suspect me of harboring an American sympathizer. Indeed, Armida, how do we know that you are *not* a spy?"

"You know I am not."

"Do I?" The smoke from Bruno's cigarette veiled his face for a moment. When it cleared, he said, "Alessandro and I, so far, are the only ones who know the truth about you. Of course, once we were made aware of your lies, we had to have you thoroughly investigated. Quite an interesting history you have Armida, I must say. Your family, the Sigalis, seem harmless enough: poor, uneducated, always struggling. But you are the exception to the rule, aren't you?"

Armida lifted her chin defiantly.

"Your sister, Argene," he continued, "has been very help-ful to us."

Taking a step toward him, Armida clenched her fists. "Leave my sister out of this!"

"Now, now; there's no need to get so worked up. It's obvi-ous your sister is . . . " Bruno pointed to his forehead. "Not all there?" He laughed as he rolled his cigarette between his lips. "Still, we were able to glean some valuable information from her. She seems to be very infatuated with your hus-band's family; particularly your sister-in-law, Carilda, and her daughters. They would be your nieces, is that correct?"

"You already know that."

"Bianca and her husband seemed to especially capture Argene's imagination."

"That is only because she went to their wedding. As you said, my sister is not normal."

"Then it is only coincidence that Danilo Corrotti, who has risen with stellar speed through the ranks of aeronautic engineering at the Piaggio plant, is not only a very important designer, but very popular with the citizens of Bientina as well? They say he is so well-liked among the citizens of Pontedera that he functions as the unofficial mayor of the city. Quite impressive, wouldn't you say?"

Armida realized her answer could mean life or death for Bianca and Danilo. "I have never spoken with Danilo Corrotti," she said evenly. "As I told you, I have only seen him at his wedding."

Bruno exploded. "And you have no children in America, right? I came this close to killing you," he shrieked, raising his hand and holding his thumb and index finger together closely to demonstrate. "The satisfaction of slitting your throat was the only thing that kept me going in Rome when the cowards in the Council said they would vote against Mussolini; when Nazi agents threatened us if we refused German plans to occupy Italy; when American envoys warned us of the consequences of not surrendering to the Allies."

"Do you realize we now have two guns pointed at our heads?" he screamed. "The Germans *and* the Allies!" Taking a deep breath, Bruno struggled to regain his composure, speaking partly to Armida and partly to himself. "Rome is in utter chaos. The new government thinks they can surrender to the Allies without any penalty. Ha! Can you imagine? The humiliation of it all was more than I could bear. When I left

Rome this morning, my comrades were defecting right and left. I watched one of my own officers throw himself in front of a train. I have no idea where Paolo and Arturo are and Alessandro will surely be devastated when he hears the news."

He lowered his voice. "But through it all, I thought of you."

Armida avoided Bruno's corrosive eyes by looking over his shoulder, through the window, at the soft moonlight reflecting off the sea.

"So, today is your lucky day, Armida! You see, I had an epiphany just before arriving in Forte dei Marmi this evening. I thought to myself: *Bruno! If you play your cards right, Armida might be more valuable to you alive than dead.* Isn't that good news?"

When Armida didn't reply, he began circling around her, sniffing like a panther closing in on its prey. "Let me explain. Soon, we are all going to have to make a very important decision. We will be forced to side with either the Germans or the Allies. I have made my decision; of course, I had little choice. As a Fascist officer, do you know what the Allies would do to me if they win the war?" The glint in his eyes as he pressed nearer to Armida made her recoil. "So, I made a deal with the Nazis. I will help them strengthen our northern borders and ferret out insurgents while Nazi forces move in to occupy and prepare for an Allied invasion. It will happen any day."

"Hitler boasts that we will win, but you know the Germans always have a backup plan, just in case." Holding his index finger to his lips in a secretive gesture, Bruno added, "I know what that plan is, but naturally, I can't tell you. Top secret. Shall I just say that we will be in the thick of it?"

His orbit brought him close enough to Armida to touch her. He reached out and tapped her collarbone. "This is where you come in, my *preziosa*. Part of my assignment is to oversee Pontedera, particularly the airplane factories; iden-tify Allied sympathizers, execute deserters, recruit new troops, etc., etc. If the Allies should somehow gain control of the Piaggio plant, we would lose one of our greatest resources in the war. Understand?"

Bruno's face was now next to hers. She felt his hot breath on her; saw the hairline cracks in his pale lips. He removed the gun from its holster and shoved it hard against her tem-ple. "Understand?"

"Sì."

"I can't hear you."

"*Sì!*"

Drawing the nose of the Beretta through her hair, he relaxed, dropping the gun to his side. "Within the next few months, you will go to Pontedera and deliver information from me to some Nazi agents working within the Piaggio plant."

"Why me? It makes no sense."

"It makes perfect sense. No one will suspect that my housekeeper is my courier. The only thing you need to understand," he added, "is that from this point on you will never know when someone is watching you, following you, listening to you. I will be made aware of all of your comings and goings." He slid the gun back into its holster. "How else will I know if you can be trusted if I don't test you?"

Bruno turned his back as if he was dismissing her, but when she made a move toward the door, he spun around and grabbed her. Twisting her arms behind her, he asked, "Don't you want to know why I am sparing your life?"

"You're hurting me!" Armida tried to pull free of him, but when he put all of his strength to bear on her, she sunk to her knees.

"Remember that I said you could be more valuable to me alive?" he asked. "You haven't asked me why. Are you not listening to me?"

She hung her head so he couldn't see her face and nodded.

Bruno yanked her arm backwards so hard that she had to arch her back and look up at him. "Germans aren't the only ones with back-up plans," he yelled over her cries of pain.

Letting go of her with one hand, he reached into his pocket and retrieved Egisto's letter. She struggled to keep her mouth closed as he tried to shove it into her mouth. "This letter could condemn me," he said.

Lifting it back up, as though he were having second thoughts, he added, "But, it could save me also. The father of your children is now a U.S. citizen. Your children are Americans. If the Germans discover this I would be guilty by my association with you. They would accuse both of us of being spies. If, however, the Allies win the war, this letter will prove that I have been harboring and protecting an American sympathizer and thus the case could be made that I was supporting the Allies all along. I can protect you from the Germans and you can protect me from the Americans."

He tucked the letter back into his pocket and then twisted Armida's arms tighter. "You will be given many opportunities to redeem yourself."

"Please," Armida begged. "You're hurting me. I am nothing. I am nobody. I will disappear. You'll never hear from me again. I swear it!"

Bruno shook her like a rag doll. "You will go nowhere, save where I say you will go!"

"Fine! Just let me go home now," she pleaded. "I must let Argene know what is happening."

Hesitantly, Bruno let go. "From now on," he warned, "your home is here with me. Permanently."

Armida, by now nearly prostrate, jumped to her feet.

"Alessandro will accompany you to your home when he returns," said Bruno. "Someone else in your family will have to take care of your sister. Be sure of this, Armida: Your family will pay for your stupidity if you dare to tell anyone about our discussion tonight. Do I make myself clear?"

"Si."

Bruno ran the palms of his hands through his hair, slicking it into place. "Very well."

Armida held her breath, afraid to move. The sound of merry-making began to die down in the streets. Erratic gunfire and the whine of sirens attested to the fact that, with or without Mussolini, the military machine was still keeping law and order in the region.

Striding over to the desk, Bruno took one last hit off his cigarette and then squashed the butt into an elaborate marble ashtray.

"Are you afraid of me?" He asked it almost as an afterthought, his voice emotionless. "I don't mean afraid for your life," he added. "I mean afraid of me as a man." He strolled back toward her, his reptilian eyes eating her in anticipation.

Armida blinked, unable to reply.

"I'll take your silence as a 'yes,'" he said. "Well, let me give you some final advice, *mia ragazza*. This place will be crawling with Germans soon; angry, hungry soldiers. Don't ever forget that I am Italian, not German. I don't think like them; I don't love like them. You may be afraid of me now, but the time will come when you will prefer my company to theirs."

Armida edged backward, toward the door, but Bruno intercepted her. He placed his hands around each side of her ribcage and shoved her against the wall. Pinning himself against her, he reached under her blouse and groped her, slathering her face and neck with violent, mucid kisses.

She knew if she put up a fight he would kill her. *God, help me!* she prayed. *Oh God, please help me.*

Literally seconds later, the voice of Chiara Carditi called upstairs from the foyer. "Bruno! I'm home. Are you up in the study?"

Bruno pulled himself off Armida. "Yes, I am in the study!" he called out. "I'll be down in a moment. Armida is helping me with something."

"Hurry, Bruno. I have heard the news of Mussolini and I am frightened out of my wits. What will happen to us?"

"We will discuss it when I am finished, Chiara. I said I will be down in a minute."

While he was yelling at his wife, Armida remembered the many times Bruno had flirted with her, told her she was beautiful, pinched her while she was cooking a meal, leered at her while she scrubbed floors or did laundry. She had been flattered then. She'd even entertained the thought of returning his advances. It would have been so easy. But now, wiping Bruno's saliva from her neck and cheeks, feeling his perversion deposited on her skin like viscous slime from the underbelly of a snail, she recoiled.

Her revulsion aroused him. Touching his lips to Armida's ear so Chiara couldn't hear him, Bruno whispered, "Other

than Alessandro, no one is to know our little secret. Chiara knows nothing. As far as she is concerned you are still
our housekeeper, but you and I know differently. You are my
slave; your pay will be my mercy. And remember, if you so
much as breathe a word of this to another soul —if you dare
try to escape from here—I will not only kill you with my
bare hands, I will make your family pay as well."

Kissing her hard, one last time, he shoved her toward the
door. "Now get out of here."

chapter twenty-two

June 5, 1944

NEARLY A YEAR after Bruno assaulted Armida, warning that he would test her, she was ordered by him to take part in an undercover operation in Bientina. The town, a short distance from Piaggio's impressive aeronautic complex in Pontedera, was a bustling hive whose residents were either employed by Piaggio or related to someone who was. Once a prosperous and proud community, the destitute citizens of Bientina and Pontedera now found themselves under increasingly intense surveillance by Nazi occupiers infuriated by Italy's surrender to the Allies almost a year earlier. Italians, according to the Germans, were fair-weather friends who could no longer be trusted.

Double-checking an address scrawled on the edge of a mangled bus schedule, Armida tucked it back inside her skirt pocket and crossed the street amidst a throng of jittery Bientina pedestrians. Alighting on the other side, she glanced over her shoulder. Alessandro, masquerading as a partisan, slouched against a lamppost opposite her, a glowing Gauloise dangling from his lips. He wore a fisherman's cap pulled down low to shade his hawkish eyes, and a greasy striped shirt with a red bandana twisted around his neck—the universal badge of a communist.

She continued walking, stumbling through the chaos enveloping her. People whispered, chattered, shouted, shoving their way past her as though they were responding to an air raid siren, except there was none. She fine-tuned her hearing, listening intently to what was being said, and soon realized, with a sickening jolt, that what was being hawked was the latest news: Rome had fallen to the Allies. Dazed and confused, she stopped to check her bearings, but was jostled about so roughly she was forced to continue walking, adrift in the crowd like an inflatable ball at sea. Hoping to keep panic at bay, Armida tried to evaluate her current predicament.

Fortunately for her, Bruno was rarely home anymore; he was too absorbed with resurrecting the crumbling Fascist Party under pain of death from his Nazi overseers. Still, she slept with a chair wedged against her bedroom door every night as a precaution, even though, so far, nothing had happened. She chalked her good fortune up to the fact that Bruno's many mistresses were still keeping him occupied.

Signora Carditi on the other hand, now finding herself on the wrong side of Fascist popularism, could no longer busy herself with the shallow social trivialities of the past and almost never left the villa. Taken to drinking, and too depressed and consumed with herself to be aware of anyone else, she was, Armida admitted grudgingly, nearly the mirror-image of Armida before she left America. Alessandro, when he wasn't out rounding up and killing Fascist deserters with his father, was Armida's perennial chaperone during the rare times she *was* allowed off the grounds of the Carditi estate. Her once innocuous ward despised her for deceiving them about her American children and double life. As far as he was concerned, she might as well have had the word "traitor" branded on her forehead.

The crowd began thinning. Sensing Alessandro continuing to track her from across the street, she snapped back to the present, to the streets of Bientina, and a cold, calculated determination filled, strengthened, her bones. She could feel it harden inside of her, gripping her skull like a vise and then racing down her spine to her heels. More focused now than before, she stopped at the next intersection, looking up at a long, two-story, salmon-colored stucco apartment building directly across from where she stood.

"That must be it." She checked the address once again. She was almost there.

While they waited to cross the street, a toothless, ulcerated old man jabbered away at a skittish woman standing next to Armida.

"Just you wait," he crowed, spit flying from his lips and landing on the woman's shoulder. "The Americans will be here before you know it and those damned Nazis will go back to Hell where they came from!"

"What are you?" the woman shot back, elbowing him away from her. "A prophet? Just because Rome is liberated doesn't mean the Allies will be up here anytime soon to liberate us! Hitler will make them walk over our dead bodies before he lets them into the Rhineland."

"That's for sure," grumbled another pedestrian, a skeletal, middle-aged man with cheeks like shriveled apples. "My brother disappeared three days ago. Where do you think he is?"

"Either in the mountains with the partisans or . . . " the toothless old man retorted. He produced an exaggerated gurgling sound from his throat as he slid his hand in a slicing motion across his neck.

The traffic finally thinned, allowing them to cross the street. When they reached the curb, Armida skirted around them, listening to the skeleton man spell out in detail what he was going to do to the Fascists if he discovered they had killed his brother. Yet another passer-by piped up, offering to give them the names of people who could connect them with some partisans operating out of Bientina.

If these people talk rebellion so openly in the streets, the situation is much worse than I thought! She shuddered, imagining Alessandro was hearing the same kind of talk. *They are not even afraid who hears them! What if these people can all see through me? What if they know why I'm here? They would string me up on the nearest lamp pole if they knew.* Taking a deep breath, she regained her composure. What was she thinking? She had nothing to worry about. She'd been ordered to dress as a peasant before leaving that morning on the train, so she would blend in with the citizens of Bientina. No one would ever suspect what she was up to.

By now she was standing directly in front of the stucco apartments. Checking the address one last time, she gathered her courage, walked up to Apartment #3 and knocked several times. No one answered, but a young girl who was digging in the vegetable beds lining the sidewalk, asked who she was looking for.

"Bianca and Danilo Corrotti," Armida answered.

The girl, dressed in an oversized tattered cotton dress, pointed behind the apartment. "Go around that way," she said. "They might be in the backyard."

Armida walked around the building to a gated, fenced-in area where two golden-haired toddlers, clad only in sun-bleached underwear, played with crude toy airplanes whittled out of wood. A large barrel of rainwater was stationed nearby, apparently meant for their enjoyment and relief from the heat. A round, grandmotherly woman with steel-grey hair wound in a tight knot at the base of her neck, sat in a low canvas chair. She was snapping peas into a large wooden bowl on her lap.

"Buon giorno," ventured Armida.

"Buon giorno," returned the old woman, setting the bowl on the ground and rising to approach the gate where Armida stood.

"I'm looking for Bianca."

"She's not here. They are all at the church preparing for the wedding."

"What wedding?"

"Why, Bice's, of course. Bianca's sister. You didn't know? Bianca has been working for weeks on Bice's wedding dress."

The woman rolled her filmy eyes, yellowed from too much sun. "Oh, you should see it!" she exclaimed. "It is magnificent. As you well know, Bianca is a true artist with her needle. Why, even the wives of German officers . . ."

"Isolina!" A lizard-skinned man with one shoulder hitched higher than the other leaned over the fence dividing the two properties and growled, "Stop exaggerating! You don't even know who you are talking to!"

"I'm *not* exaggerating!" Chagrined, the woman looked at Armida and apologized. "My husband, Alfredo—forgive his rudeness. We are Bianca's neighbors. We watch the babies for them sometimes. Who are you?"

"An old friend from Ripa," Armida replied. "I was just stopping by to say hello."

"She's an old friend from Ripa," the woman shouted to her

husband, repeating what Armida had just said. "Just stopping by to say hello!"

The old man grunted, grabbed a *zappe*, a forked type of hoe, and attacked a patch of untilled ground as though it were his mortal enemy.

Isolina ignored him, opened the gate and invited Armida in. "Renzo! Lucia!" she cooed to the little boy and girl. "We have a guest. Come greet her."

The two approached Armida, staring intently at her before holding up their chubby arms for a hug. "Ciao!" they sang in unison.

Their undefiled smiles disarmed Armida. How long had it been since she had touched and smelled such innocence? She couldn't help but remember Silverio and Violenza at that age. As Bianca's two children clung to her, a stab of remorse pierced her heart. She came back to her senses only when Isolina asked her if she would like something to drink. Renzo and Lucia scurried back to their play.

"No, grazie," she told the woman. "Danilo is not here either, you say?" Nervously, Armida pretended to pick some lint off the sleeve of her dress while scanning the surroundings for Alessandro. There he was; directly in her line of vision, standing beyond the fence across the street, leaning against a bus stop sign, still dragging on his Gauloise.

"No," sighed Isolina. "Danilo went with Bianca. Bice and her fiancé, Benedetto, were going to meet them at the church. What a terrible time for a wedding! But, what can you expect from the young ones when they are in love?" In a hushed tone she added, "And Benedetto, what will happen to him if the Allies reach Pontedera?" She shook her head in amazement. "To think they will soon be brothers-in-law! Benedetto, a Fascist, and Danilo, a Parti..."

"Isolina!" shouted Alfredo. "How many times must I warn you about your loose tongue!"

"Why, everyone knows Danilo Corrotti is a hero," Isolina retorted. She waved her hand dismissively. "This is not news. If it weren't for Danilo—and Bianca—half the people in this town would be without food and clothing."

Addressing Armida again, Isolina said, "I don't know what they're doing to survive in Ripa where you live, but here, in Bientina, Danilo has gathered families into groups to forage the countryside for food. He has organized cooperatives to combine resources and share surpluses from their gardens. And Bianca? Well, she has worked her fingers to the bone, day and night, to make clothing for the children and orphans. So many orphans from this war!"

With an air of melodrama, the old woman wrung her hands in despair. "I tell you, we don't know what we would do without them. They are saints! You are a friend of the family, so you know all of this, of course. But, did you know that the people of Bientina begged Danilo to be their leader?"

Armida lied. "Of course."

"See, Alfredo? Loose tongue, ha! Don't mind him," she said, pointing to her husband. Holding one hand up to shield her mouth from him, she added confidentially, "This has not been a good year for him."

Alfredo's hearing was just fine. "Not a good year? That is an understatement," he spat. Addressing Armida, he said, "Signora, have you by chance any family in Rome?"

"No, I don't."

"Well I do. Or, shall I say, I did. I was the oldest of four sons. Now, I am the only one left. Two of my brothers are dead and one has disappeared. My brother, Giuseppe tried to help his Jewish neighbors. The priests had already filled

the monasteries with Jews, so my brother hid his neighbors in his cellar. When the Gestapo swept through Rome
in October they rounded up over 1,000 Jews—men, women
and children—and sent them to Auschwitz. Do you think
they will ever be seen alive again?"

Armida glanced over the fence at Alessandro. He flicked
his cigarette on the pavement, ground it with his heel and
stretched. The jerkiness of his motions indicated he was getting impatient.

The old man continued. "My cousin is a Fascist. A filthy
Judas is what he is! When he found out that my brother was
hiding Jews, he turned him in for a reward. His own flesh-
and-blood! The last I heard, my brother was in a labor camp
in Germany. Only God knows his fate."

Alfredo paused to swipe his forehead with the back of his
hand. "I will never forgive the bastards who killed my family.
Never."

Isolina dabbed her eyes with the edge of her apron. "Al-
freeedo," she cooed, touching his arm gently. "Who is the one
with the loose tongue now? The signora does not need to
hear your stories. Look at her." She held her hand out toward
Armida. "Look at her face. She has enough sadness in her
own life. Remember what Danilo and Bianca always say:
'Never take your eyes off of tomorrow.'"

Alfredo's shoulders hunched over even lower. "Forgive me,
signora," he said. "I don't know why I am telling you all this."

"He is usually a man of few words," said Isolina, "but this
war has changed us all."

"Isolina is right," admitted Alfredo. "Here, in Bientina, we
can no longer afford to live under any pretense of safety. It is
wonderful that the Allies have taken Rome, but they want
to push Hitler completely out of Italy and they will have to

fight their way through Florence, Pontedera and Pisa to do it. Now that Mussolini has escaped to Lake Garda, do you think the Germans will let the Allies get close to him? No. They will make a stand near us; near Florence. They must."

"Now, if the Allies can break through the Apuanes," he continued, pointing to the mountains behind them, "they will have a clear shot to Mussolini and then it will be over." Alfredo emphasized his last word with a flick of his wrist. Bowing his head to Armida, he apologized again. "Forgive me. But I am a realist. The Germans will destroy everything in their path when they retreat, just like they did in Rome. They will wreak their vengeance on us in retaliation for surrendering to the Allies."

Isolina began to protest, but Alfredo held up his hand as though she need not say a word. "I am finished, Isolina," he promised. "You know that everything I said is true. Danilo knows it also. We are prepared. It is good that you hope, Isolina, but hope in the impossible is foolishness. What is possible will come only at a great cost to all of us. Perhaps tomorrow will be our day of reckoning, but it is the days that will come after many tomorrows that we must keep our eyes fixed on."

Three sharp whistles from Alessandro were Armida's signal that her time was up. Discreetly looking his way, she saw that he had crossed the street and was now standing so near to them that he could have heard their conversation if the breeze were blowing in the right direction.

Quickly, Armida reached out her hand to Isolina. "I'm sorry. I must go."

At Isolina's command, Renzo and Lucia, splashing each other with water from the rain barrel, stopped and toddled over to Armida. She opened her arms, stooping down to hug them, and in doing so she was able to momentarily disappear from Alessandro's direct line of sight. She looked up at Isolina, mouthing her words so that only the old woman could hear. "Tell Danilo to leave immediately. He is not safe here."

Another whistle, louder this time, pierced the air.

"Good-bye." Tearing herself away, Armida bolted out of the yard, through the gate, and disappeared around the corner of the house.

It took several moments for Isolina and Alfredo to recover from the shock of what Armida had just said.

"*Who* was she?" asked Alfredo, mystified. "What did she say her name was?"

"She didn't say."

Alfredo threw his hoe down and yelled, "Watch the children. I'll find her." But, by the time he unlatched the gate and hobbled out to the street, Armida was nowhere to be seen. He looked in both directions, crossed the street and frantically scanned the jostling crowds for her, but like a ghost she had vanished into thin air.

�֍

WHEN ALFREDO AND Isolina described to me the "angel" who had come to warn them, I knew it had to be Armida. Clearly, she was being broken. I felt great fear and joy for her because once the battle came to Tuscany, she would have to choose between the Carditis and the Allies. If she chose the Fascists, it would make her a traitor to the majority of Italians and we all knew what happened to traitors in the war. Perhaps her warning us was a sign, I thought. A sign that Armida was ready to leave the Carditis.

✿

UPON LEAVING THE old couple, Armida—anticipating they would try to follow her—hailed a bus marked for Pontedera that happened to be stopped at the corner of their street. Alessandro, seeing her board the bus, had to chase it through two busy intersections before he was able to get on it himself. Livid, he shoved his way to the rear of the bus where Armida was fanning herself with a newspaper someone had left on the seat next to her.

Ripping it out of her hands, he threw it across the aisle. "What do you think you're doing?"

"They would have followed me if I would have just kept walking. I had to make a quick decision. The bus was my easiest escape."

"*They?*"

"The man and woman I was talking to. You saw them."

Alessandro sized up the people sitting nearby. No one was paying attention to them. "The Corrottis, you mean?"

"Sure," she quipped sarcastically. "Just how old do you think Bianca and Danilo are?"

"Don't get smart with me, Armida." He grabbed her arm, squeezing it until she flinched. "Who were you talking to?"

"Bianca and Danilo's neighbors."

"My father didn't send us here to talk to their neighbors. Your instructions were to talk with Danilo and draw him away from the house to me."

"I told you, he wasn't there. Neither was Bianca."

"Where are they?"

"I don't know."

Alessandro threw his arm around the back of the seat, put

Armida in a head lock and pulled her toward him, her neck crooked down at an unnatural angle. She cried out in pain, causing several heads to turn. Alessandro smiled at the passengers, making as though he was playfully teasing Armida.

"At least you picked a bus that was going in the right direction," he hissed, letting loose of her with a shove. "We should be in Pontedera soon."

He pulled his last Gauloise out of his pocket—swearing he would have to get another pack before the morning was over—and continued his interrogation. "Why wasn't Corrotti there? We picked today because we knew he wasn't scheduled to be at the plant."

"The old man was suspicious. Neither of them would tell me where Danilo was."

"You're lying."

"All they would say is that Bianca and Danilo were helping someone get ready for a wedding, but they wouldn't tell me who, or when, or where."

"We know that Danilo is a partisan," Alessandro explained, casually lighting his cigarette. He threw the match out the bus window. "An important one. He has been spying for the Americans. Apprehending him alone at his home was the plan; arresting him while he is on the job at Piaggio, or in any public place, could spark a riot."

"I don't know why," said Armida. "You arrest important people in public all the time."

"In Forte dei Marmi, maybe. Not in Pontedera. Not in Bientina. It must be done discreetly. Corrotti is a hero here. Arresting him in the open would bring the entire city out in his defense."

He unsheathed a Swiss army knife from under his belt and ran his finger along the razor sharp blade. "You should have given me a signal, Armida. We could have taken the children and the old man and woman hostage and waited for Danilo's return."

"You should have given me better instructions. I didn't know what to do."

"You are worthless," he grunted, raising the tip of the knife to beneath his chin and then tilting it out in a flicking motion toward her. "Why my father wanted you to be in on this operation is beyond me. 'I'm testing her,' he said. 'We need a woman for this; someone no one will expect. Someone no one will remember.' My father actually thinks keeping you alive means you could eventually serve some redeeming purpose for him. That's a laugh."

The bus rounded a sharp corner causing everyone to lean in the opposite direction to stay balanced, and then heaved to a stop. In the distance, Armida could make out the gleaming Piaggio complex, an enormous beehive of activity. A military airport to their right was swarming with Italian Kangaroo, Stork, Sparrowhawk, and Kingfisher bombers. She knew the huge cargo planes were laden with pillaged goods for German forces occupying northern Italy. They were commandeered by Luftwaffe pilots who did double duty as aviation spies, reporting any suspicious activities detected from the air enroute to their destination. The scale of operations was incredible. She noticed Alessandro's chest swelling visibly with pride at the sight.

"Nothing can stop us," he gloated, half to himself, half to Armida. "Soon, the Allies will be drawn into our trap and victory will be ours again. The Duce will once again rule in Rome."

"What trap?"

"You'll see," he snapped. "We're almost there. This time

you *will* get it right, Armida. No slip-ups." With his free hand, Alessandro removed a small envelope from his shirt pocket and handed it to Armida. "When we arrive, you are to walk up to the reception desk and ask for the Personnel Director. His name is Carlo Rossotti. He is one of us, but you will forget his name and his face when you walk back out the door. Understand?"

Armida turned away from him. Staring out the window she nodded slightly.

Alessandro reached over her shoulder and grabbed her chin, jerking her back around to look at him. With his other hand, not caring who saw him, he pressed the flat edge of his knife blade into her cheek. "I asked you a question. Do you understand?"

Armida simply returned his threat with a look that said, *Don't think for a minute that I wouldn't turn that knife on you if I had the chance.*

"We will be conducting a sweep of the entire plant at 3:00 this afternoon," he whispered into her ear, pulling her close to him. "The letter you deliver will give the Director ample time to warn our spies throughout the plant so they can act as though they know nothing."

Armida tried to tilt her cheek away from him, but he pressed the blade in even further. "We knew that Danilo Corrotti was not scheduled to be at his office today, but there are other partisan leaders there recruiting co-workers. If we don't nab them before they get better organized, the Germans will see to it and then it will be *our* necks that will be on the chopping block. The more partisan blood we can placate the Nazis with, the better."

"So it's civil war now?"

"Idiot!" he snarled. "It has been civil war ever since

Mussolini was voted out of office. Only now, as the Allies advance toward us in the north, it is much worse."

"And," she asked testily, "if one were to choose to remain neutral?"

"Neutral? There is no such thing. Every Italian will have to choose whose side they will be on. Of course, your choice has already been made for you."

Alessandro laughed before continuing. "When we arrive at the plant, we will walk in together. If there are any questions, use your sister's name, Argene Sigali. I am your son, Alessandro Sigali. Under no condition can anyone other than Rossotti see the letter you have. If someone asks why you want to see the Personnel Director, you are to say that it is personal business. Rossotti expects us. He will speak directly with you at the counter and take your envelope. Everything will be done openly so no one can suspect him of meeting clandestinely with you today. In the event that after the sweep suspicion is raised, it can only be traced to your sister—a stupid peasant woman. Brilliant, no?"

Hard knots appeared beneath Armida's ears, on the edge of her jaw line. She hated Alessandro with a passion she would never have dreamed possible a few months earlier. "I told your father to leave my sister out of this."

"Not a chance. All is fair in love and war."

The bus coughed its way up to the main entrance of Piaggio and shuddered to a stop, waiting for passengers to disembark. Alessandro kept Armida in the back, corralled into her seat, until the bus was nearly empty.

"Remember, we walk in together and I will be acting like I am your son," he warned. "I will be watching your every move and will be close enough to hear every word you speak. Rossotti knows the raid is sometime this week, but doesn't know the exact time until he receives the letter from you. Don't worry, the message is coded and he is aware of our back-up plan in case things go wrong. All you have to do is give him the letter."

He slid his knife back into its sheath and lifted her up, escorting her down the aisle of the bus and out onto the steps in front of Piaggio. Together, they pushed their way through the company's sleek revolving glass doors and entered the vast, semi-circular lobby, its white marble floors and walls blindingly bright from sunlight pouring through windows ringing the small domed cupola above. The reception desk, a mammoth Nero Portoro work of art, was situated on the flat end of the lobby, but because several people were milling around it, Alessandro slipped Armida aside to wait until it was clear.

While leafing through some literature on Bientina's aerial history on a visitor's display rack, he rebuked her again. "Don't think I have forgotten about Danilo. When we are finished here, we will call my father. We cannot return home without taking Danilo dead or alive." He broke out into a wide grin, his teeth perfectly straight and white and against his nut-brown skin. "The reward for him will be huge."

Then, seeing that the reception desk was suddenly open, he gave Armida a shove. "Go."

Armida's heart hammered within her chest, her legs wobbled as though they were made of mascarpone instead of flesh and sinew and bone. It seemed like an eternity before she finally reached the black granite desk, so highly polished it reflected her image almost perfectly, even catching the pearlescence of the abalone comb in her hair. Two guards, Breda machine guns cradled in their arms, stood at each end of the desk, like book ends, critiquing her. Could they detect the panic radiating from every fiber of her being? She thought of the tens, maybe hundreds, of people who would lose their lives that day because of the one letter she was about to deliver. Just as quickly, she dismissed the thought, reasoning that the sweep would happen sooner or later, regardless of her. It gave her the resolve she needed to proceed.

"May I help you, signora?" asked the receptionist, flawlessly groomed, her voice condescending, no doubt, by the fact that Armida appeared so *ordinary*.

For a fleeting moment, Armida wished she could tell the red-lipped, raven-haired beauty who her employer was. The name Bruno Carditi would put the fear of God into the smug little tart! But instead she replied curtly: "The Personnel Director, please."

"That would be signore Rossotti. Just a moment while I ring him." She placed her thin secretarial fingers on the telephone receiver. "And who may I tell him is here, and what is the nature of your visit?"

"Argene Sigali. It's a personal matter."

The receptionist smirked. "Personal?" she asked.

"That's what I said." The acidic edge in Armida's response achieved its intended effect. The call was put through.

While Armida waited, the moments seeming an eternity, she agonized over what would happen afterwards; when Alessandro continued to hunt down Danilo, when she returned to the villa and had to face Bruno, when . . . when the Americans broke through the Arno Line in Florence. The Fascists wouldn't admit it, but everyone knew they would. Her gut twisted, making her stomach growl as she thought dismally, *If only the Americans were here now. I could tell them who I am and they would protect me.*

A stolid, balding man of no particular age—he could have been thirty or sixty he was so nondescript—emerged from an office behind the receptionist and addressed her. "Signora?"

Armida handed him the letter, her hand shaking so strongly the director had to take it and hold it to up to his lips in a gesture of false intimacy in order to deflect Armida's nervousness from the inquisitive eyes of the receptionist. Even as he kissed her fingers, she could see the wheels of his mind spinning, trying to come up with an explanation for his relationship to her should he be asked. He didn't bother looking at the envelope, but muttered an almost unintelligible thank-you as he let go of her hand.

"Is there anything else I can help you with, cara mia?" he asked, using a term of endearment.

"No, grazie." She felt Alessandro's eyes boring into the back of her head. Turning, she began to make her way to the door of the lobby. Out of the corner of her eye, she saw Alessandro take a step toward her.

Then, without any warning, she collapsed. It happened in slow motion, she realized later, recalling the incident. First, came the blood rushing to her head, the pressure behind her eyes so intense it split her vision, then the letting go, her legs giving out first, crumbling into each other, and finally her head—cracking onto the hard, unforgiving stone floor. She remembered Alessandro hovering over her as consciousness slipped away from her. The last thing she heard was him pretending to be alarmed.

"Mama!" he shouted. "Someone bring my mama some water!"

chapter twenty-three

A MONTH LATER, while Armida was being raked over the coals for the millionth time by Bruno for failing to locate Danilo, Danilo Corrotti was shivering uncontrollably beneath a threadbare blanket wrapped tightly across his bony shoulders. He wasn't shivering because it was cold; indeed, it was a balmy July evening. He was shaking because his brain was racked with fever and his sick, malnourished body was on the verge of giving up his soul.

"Things could be worse," he whispered aloud through chattering teeth. "It could be winter instead of summer."

The position he found himself in was so utterly beyond hope that trying to convince himself otherwise was ridiculous. He stifled a laugh and toyed with the idea of standing up to peer over the edge of the four-foot stone wall next to him. From the top of the church, he would be able to see out onto the sleeping city below. Sometimes, when he thought it was safe, he would do just that. But days had passed since he had last done so, and he knew his knees would not support him now. Instead, Danilo gazed up at the calm, crescent moon with Mars dangling off its lower hook, and slipped in and out of consciousness.

The bell tower of the fifteenth century Church of the Assunta in Bientina was Danilo's prison, though he preferred to think of it as his throne of salvation. It was in this same medieval church that Bice had married Benedetto just a month earlier, under the immense pressure of civil war. Had there been enough moisture in his body to manufacture tears, he would have wept at the recollection.

Perhaps all of this is a dream, he thought, letting his mind drift along in a stream of unfettered, disconnected memories. Wincing with pain, he shifted his body so that he could lie flat on his back, exposing his soul to the night sky for all the stars to see. Soon, only semi-aware that he was hallucinating, Danilo was conversing with unseen guests, reliving the events leading up to his solitary confinement.

In his mind's eye, he remembered the day he and Bianca were at the church preparing for Bice's wedding. He saw his frantic neighbor, Alfredo, bursting into the church swearing that an angel had come to warn them about his safety and insisting that Danilo run for his life.

"We must trust Alfredo," Bianca had insisted. "Why would he be so frightened for nothing?"

"This is not the first time I have been warned to go into hiding because my life is in danger," he had replied.

"This time is not like the others. Now that Rome has fallen, the Allies will be here soon. The Germans are desperate. Please, Danilo, for the sake of our children!"

"How can I leave Bientina, Bianca? Too many people here depend on me. And what about your sister's wedding? We will talk about it after the ceremony this afternoon."

"Bice will understand," pleaded Bianca.

"If I think it is necessary, I will go to the mountains."

"You know very well the Germans are combing the mountains as we speak, slaughtering entire villages where they think partisans are hiding."

Danilo remembered how he had raised his voice in exasperation. "Well, then there is no where to go, is there? Better I stay here and face the enemy on our terms than run and face them on theirs."

As if by divine appointment, the affable priest of Assunta, Padre Tullio, popped his head into the small ante-chamber to announce the bridegroom's arrival. "Bianca, your sister is asking for your help fitting her dress." He then raised one eyebrow toward Danilo. "And Benedetto looks as though he could use a drink. I'm not so sure he'll survive the next few hours without one."

Both Bianca and Danilo pounced on Padre Tullio at once, pulling the startled priest into the room with them, closing the door to keep prying eyes and ears at bay. Danilo recalled their conversation in fitful spurts, like an old recording that annoyingly speeds up and then slows down again.

"Father," confessed Danilo, "it is possible that my life is in danger. I am with the Resistance."

Padre Tullio was not surprised, having long suspected Danilo of anti-Fascist activities.

"I have been working with undercover agents through my office at the Piaggio plant," continued Danilo. "They know me as il Gatto, The Cat. Of course, I know many partisans around Bientina and Pontedera as well."

Gravely, the priest nodded.

Bianca asked him if he knew of a monastery or convent in the countryside that would take Danilo in and hide him. Without hesitation, Padre Tullio offered refuge in his church.

Just as quickly, Danilo declined. "No, Father, I will not put you, this church, or Bientina in jeopardy."

"It is you we must think of, Danilo," said the priest, his eyebrows knit in consternation. "Not me."

Danilo had asked Bianca at that moment to leave the room, telling her that no one must know what they were to decide. Not even her.

She hesitated.

"Bianca, we agreed on this long ago. If the squadristi were ever to interrogate you, it is imperative that you know nothing. Would you put me, the children, Piaggio—the entire town in danger? Don't worry. When it is safe I will return."

Danilo had placed his wife's hand on his heart to seal his promise. "I swear it, darling. You have my word."

Just remembering the warm closeness of Bianca's final embrace, the smell of her hair in his nostrils, the feel of its softness on his fingertips, was like a shot of morphine injected directly into his bloodstream. Danilo's shivering subsided. A smile played at the corners of his cracked, bleeding lips. Here he was in Bientina, right under everyone's noses, and no one but Padre Tullio knew it! The semi-enclosed, partially concealed rooftop of the church offered several escape routes if he ever received the pre-arranged signal from the priest that danger was imminent. Of course, they both knew the odds were against the luxury of any warning at all, since searches were often done in the middle of the night and few people survived to talk about it.

Besides, thought Danilo with chagrin, *if troops stormed the church now, I couldn't stand on my own two feet, let alone scale the wall to escape.*

Turning his head slightly to the right, he saw Padre Tullio sitting on the pitted granite floor next to him and breathed a sigh of relief, even though he knew it was an apparition.

"Well, Danilo," he heard the priest say, his voice soothing, melodic. "The Allies are preparing to face the Germans over the Arno Line in Florence. It won't be long now."

"They are that close?!" Danilo's voice cracked with excitement.

"Si."

"That is wonderful news, Padre. But it is the Gothic Line near Ripa I am really worried about."

"I, also, am worried about the Gothic Line, my friend."

※

I KNOW THIS *about war: it's a series of actions and reactions; a game of offense and defense. When the Allies seized Rome, German troops retreated up the peninsula to Florence behind the Arno Line—named for the river flowing through the city. We all knew it was just a matter of time before the Allies broke through it though.*

In anticipation of the loss of Florence, the German's Field Marshall, Albert Kesselring, drew another line of defense extending through the Apennine Mountains from the naval port of La Spezia—just north of Forte dei Marmi—to Rimini on the Adriatic Coast. In Versilia, it ran directly through Strettoia on Monte di Ripa; less than a quarter of a mile from mama's—and my—home.

It was called the Gothic Line, and because it was literally the Fascist's last stand, they made it impregnable. If the Allies broke through the Gothic Line, nothing would stop them from flooding into Milan—and from Milan they would have an open door into the Rhineland; into Hitler's lair.

As much as we feared being trapped in the crosshairs of an

epic battle, we thanked God that all the uncertainty—all the
evil—was finally coming to a head. We prayed for victory, and
we prayed we would survive.

❧

"MY FAMILY," ASKED Danilo, still hallucinating. "How are
they doing?" Somewhere in his subconscious, Danilo realized this imaginary conversation he was having with Padre
Tullio had really transpired several days earlier, but he didn't
care. He indulged in reliving it.

"Bianca and your children are fine," replied the phantom
priest. "Bice and Benedetto are happy, but very frightened.
Benedetto is a valuable pilot for the Fascists. They cannot
afford to lose him. They watch him like a hawk."

"What about the Germans?" Danilo's voice broke. "Have
they . . . ?"

"No, no, no." the priest, reading his mind, assured him.
"The only time the German's harassed Bianca was the day of
Bice's wedding. They threatened her, but she convinced them
she had no idea what had happened to you. Of course, it
helped that the following day the Allies invaded Normandy,
no?"

In tandem with the fall of Rome, the news of the Allied
invasion of Normandy had signaled the turning point of the
war in Europe. Danilo envisioned the pincer movements of
the Allies pushing toward Germany from the west through
France, from the south through Italy, and from Russia in the
east. The implosion of the Third Reich was inevitable. How
he wished it was over!

"In any case," Padre Tullio concluded, "the Germans
believe you are hiding with the Partisans in the mountains."

The priest weighed his thoughts carefully before adding, "The reports coming from the south are not good."

"Tell me. What is it?"

"The Nazis know it will be impossible to hold the Allies back at Florence on the Arno Line, so all of their focus is shifting. They have infested Versilia with troops and weapons because it lies right along the Gothic Line. There are reports that flatbed cars in the tunnels above La Spezia are rigged with long-range cannons. The Nazis will use them to blow the country south of the Gothic Line to high heaven. Ripa, Massa, Forte dei Marmi—they are all within the cannons' range."

Danilo cringed.

"Everyone is starving, Danilo. It is worse now than it was a month ago. Who would have thought it was possible?"

Seeing the effect the negative news had on Danilo, the priest apologized. "We will talk about something else."

"No, I want to know everything," said Danilo, adding half-jokingly, "I thought you looked rather thin, Father. Is there nothing left to glean in the hills?"

"The Germans have stripped the countryside bare. Some people have their own gardens, but it is not enough. There are no cats left in Bientina. They have all been eaten. Some dogs remain, but they too will soon disappear. I have turned a blind eye to the children who hunt rats and mice around the church." He shrugged. "I have seen worse. I saw an old woman yesterday crushing locusts and eating them. Meat is meat—as long as it is not human, eh?"

Unable to refrain from asking the ultimate question, Danilo blurted, "My wife? She is . . . ?"

"Bianca is Bianca," smiled the priest. "She is a sign from heaven. Her garden is no bigger than average, but somehow it seems to produce twice as much as everyone else's. She is the most generous woman in Bientina, and the more she gives, the more abundant her harvest is. When the Germans do their sweeps through town, they see her limp and dismiss her as unimportant. They are incapable of seeing past any weakness. Bianca's handicap is a blessing in disguise. Do not worry, Danilo. God is taking care of your family."

Whether the conversation Danilo was having with Padre Tullio was real, or not—whether it was happening now, or yesterday, or last week, or never at all—it no longer mattered to him. The Father's exhortation, regardless, had a medicinal effect on Danilo. He relaxed, rolling over on his side in an effort to get more comfortable.

"Any other news I should know about?" he asked.

"The Germans are beginning to dismantle the Piaggio plant. They want to leave nothing for the Allies. They will plant bombs everywhere so that they will inflict as many casualties as possible when the Allies break through. Everyone knows the bombing will begin soon. Bientina will not be spared. We are too close to Pontedera to escape it."

Padre Tullio caressed the smooth, ancient stones cemented into the wall next to him and added, "It must have been an angel, indeed, who warned Alfredo about you that day."

Danilo nodded. He remembered the shock of hearing about the Piaggio sweep shortly after Alfredo had come to the church to warn him. It was that announcement that had finally convinced Danilo that he must flee for his life.

Gingerly, Danilo ventured, "Do you think Bianca knows that I am here?"

"No." Padre Tullio shook his head. "She couldn't possibly know where you are. But she would like to think that you are close." He drummed his fingers along the edge of Danilo's tin water cup set out near him to catch any rainwater. "At any rate, our ruse was thoroughly brilliant, no?"

Amused, Danilo flopped over onto his other side. "It was your idea."

A shooting star streaked across the diamond-studded sky. After spending a few moments surrendering to the siren call of deep space, Danilo and his imaginary companion recalled the last-minute plan they had hatched only a month earlier.

By all appearances, during Bice's wedding ceremony, Danilo had appeared highly confident. No one that day would have guessed he knew his life was in danger. Bianca was equally cool and unruffled. Then, seemingly out of nowhere, a thunderstorm broke over the Church of the Assunta, forcing the unprepared wedding guests to cover themselves with jackets, shawls or scarves in their mad dash from the church to a large home several blocks away where the reception dinner was being held. It was assumed Danilo Corrotti was among the huddled, cloaked forms side-stepping the rivulets in the flooded street.

Upon entering the villa, Bianca and her sister Lida immediately busied themselves in the kitchen with the little food they had to serve. Less than twenty minutes later, SS officers arrived, faces all stony and red with anticipation and their guns drawn, demanding Danilo's surrender. Bice, new blushing bride that she was, shook beneath Benedetto's protective arms, while Bianca, acting as though her husband was within earshot, cried, "Danilo! You are in danger!"

"Shut up!" shouted the burliest officer, slapping Bianca full in the face. The impact sent her reeling backwards, her arms knocking glasses and silverware off the table as she tried to catch herself. Padre Tullio raced to her side, asking if she was hurt; no one else dared to breathe. Methodically, the soldiers searched every room, indiscriminately pistol-whipping the terrified on-lookers whenever they felt the urge. Finally realizing they had been duped, the soldiers herded the guests out of the villa and into the street.

They would have set fire to the building had a Fascist officer not shouted, "Why waste time here? Corrotti can't be far. Come on, let's go!"

So, as quickly as they had appeared, the Germans departed, roaring out of town in their black, BMW sidecars, their swastika-stamped rim helmets gleaming pewter in the sunlight, leaving the wedding guests shaken, but alive.

Violent cramps suddenly racked Danilo's frail body and the pain made it no longer possible for him to imagine that he was talking with a friend. "What's the point?" he groaned. "Padre Tullio is probably dead, and I will soon follow." He was tired of fantasizing, rationalizing, hoping.

The truth was, the priest had, indeed, mysteriously disappeared and his absence had left Danilo utterly alone, despondent and paranoid. Gone, along with his daily crust of bread and cup of water, was his only contact with humanity.

I'm probably dying, Danilo reasoned soberly, *like Padre Tullio, and who knows how many others.*

Danilo gagged at the stinging taste of bile in his throat and fought the urge to dry-heave, the muscles in his stomach contracting in nauseous waves of hunger-induced convulsions. His strength was so diminished that when the sky suddenly exploded in a searing maelstrom of fiery smoke and debris, pitching the very foundation of Assunta with a sickening jolt, he could not even command his own body to take cover.

The Allies were finally bombing Piaggio and the surrounding area. Hysterical screams erupted throughout

Bientina as residents awoke to the nightmare descending upon them. Danilo prayed for his wife and children. Another blast, closer this time, rocked the church, lurching Danilo's helpless body out into the center of the exposed, flat roof. The pulsating, surrealistically painted sky was a scene out of Dante's *Inferno*; scorching, crimson flames hungrily sucked the oxygen-rich atoms out of the once-tranquil night air. Danilo drew a blistered hand across his eyes.

"I'm still alive!" he shouted into the raging inferno. "And, I will live to see tomorrow! Bianca—do you hear me? Tell the children. I am coming home! Deliverance is here!"

chapter twenty-four

WHILE DANILO CORROTTI shouted victory atop Bientina's Church of the Assunta, twenty miles due southeast—near the incomparable, art-drenched city of Florence—Allied forces fought and routed German troops standing their ground along the Arno Line, soundly defeating them and finally forcing them behind the heavily fortified Gothic Line.

Among the victors in that battle were two Italian-American soldiers: Privates First Class Sal Passarelli and Vinny Del Vecchio. The former, a confrontational Chicagoan with a huge chip on his shoulder, was a know-it-all playboy without the resources to match his ambitions, while the latter, the sheltered son of a San Francisco clothing merchant, was a typical Mr. Nice Guy, but a card short of a full deck. They had just completed two and one-half years of active service in General Clark's Fifth Army, 34th Infantry Division. From North Africa to Cassino to Rome, and now to Florence, Sal and Vinny were slowly, but surely, beginning to lose heart. Their souring attitudes manifested in bickering and brawling usually instigated by Sal. A nearly fatal outburst had recently occurred inside a centuries-old cantina in Tavarnelle, a newly liberated village just south of Florence, in which Sal and Vinny stupidly picked a fight with soldiers from the elite

10th Mountain Division, the Japanese-American 442nd Reg-
imental Combat Team, and some African-American Buffalo
soldiers of the 92nd Infantry.

Of course, the battle-weary Italian-Americans lost, and
lost badly.

By the time the MPs arrived, scraping the soldiers' mangled remains off the liquor-and-blood soaked floor, the two
GIs had learned three important truths:

- The frontiersmen of the 10th Mountain were not
  the amateurs Sal and Vinny had presumed they
  were.
- The Japanese-American "Go for Broke" soldiers—
  deceptively staid and detached—relished invitations to demonstrate their focused ferocity.
- Sal and Vinny underestimated the simmering,
  explosive vengeance of their black countrymen
  who gladly seized the opportunity to level the
  playing field outside the confines of a still racially
  segregated nation back home.

All told, said soldiers from each division beat the living
daylights out of Sal and Vinny and would probably have
killed them had the tavern owner not called the police when
he noticed Sal brandishing a switchblade.

Now, three days after the fall of Florence, having been
bandaged by flirtatious but unsympathetic nurses at the
Army's field hospital, the bruised and humiliated duo found
themselves wallowing in self-pity in the correctional treatment facility hastily constructed near the scene of their last
battle. Their superiors, well aware of the toll that years of
fighting was having on the morale of their men, had decided
that a few days confined together in jail would make the two

sick of each other, get their tempers under control, and give them some much needed R & R.

"If only your mama could see you now," growled Sal, sneering at Vinny. Vinny touched his swollen, black-and-blue face. Not known for his quick-wittedness, he could never rally a creative comeback to Sal's smart remarks. "Lay off, Sal. If it weren't for your big mouth, I'd be lookin' just fine."

Sal impersonated Vinny, repeating what he said with a snicker. He was bored out of his mind.

"One of you boys got some mail," drawled an on-duty guard, showing up at their cell to thrust a chewed-up looking envelope through the bars. He watched with perverse satisfaction as Sal and Vinny leaped simultaneously to retrieve it, banging heads as they did.

"It's for me!" Vinny got to it first, madly tearing into the letter.

Sal skulked off into a corner to pout, sliding down on to the floor in a lethargic heap. The guard watched them for a moment before sauntering away humming the chorus of *G. I. Blues.*

"Who's it from?" asked Sal.

"My folks."

"Did someone die or something?"

"No. Most of it's in Italian. I don't understand it."

"Man, I swear!" Sal jumped up and grabbed the letter out of Vinny's hands. "You California Italians can't even speak the mother tongue."

"Like you were born here."

"Hell, I wasn't!" bristled Sal. "I was born in Sicily. Moved to the States before I could crawl. You must be second generation. That would explain it."

"Explain what?"

Sal gestured impatiently, sliding back down to the floor with the letter in his hands. "Forget it, stupid."

While Sal read the letter, Vinny rushed to explain that his mother had written a short note in English to ask a favor of him. A friend of a friend, whose wife was apparently trapped in Italy somewhere, had sent a letter asking if her son—Vinny—could find her. The husband had written instructions and a personal letter in Italian to be delivered to her if she was found.

"So," asked Vinny breathlessly, "what does it say?"

"The guy's real frustrated. His name is Egisto, uh . . . Bertozzi. Says his friend—some broad named Julia Barghini—recommended writing to your mom because you were stationed here in Italy and he can't get any mail through any other way."

"Wow, aren't you lucky?" Sal added, his lacerated upper lip furled into a sarcastic grin.

"Just read it, will ya?"

"Relax! Let's see. The lady's name is Armida Sigali. She's with some Fascist family named Carditi in Forte dei Marmi." He looked quizzically at Vinny. "Where the hell is Forte dei Marmi?"

"How would I know? You're the big expert."

Intrigued, Sal kept reading. "Uh, here it is. It's in Tuscany, north of Pisa, on the coast. Well, we're damn close now, aren't we?"

"There's a little something called the Gothic Line in the way."

"You got that."

"What does the guy's letter say to his wife?"

Sal lifted his finger as a sign he was in the midst of reading it. "Just a bunch of love-stuff." He kept reading hungrily. "Wow! This Egisto guy's willing to pay big bucks to get her back. Says that if you find her and get her amnesty, he'll give you a reward."

"How much?"

"It doesn't say. It just says, 'I will reward you handsomely'—which usually means, you name the price and he'll fork it out."

Vinny shuffled his feet. "I got more morals than that. You can't put a pricetag on someone's head. Besides, I'd be doing it for my mom . . . I mean, her friend."

"Friend, schmend!" mimed Sal, rolling his eyes. "It says here he's got other family, same name of Bertozzi, living around here somewhere and a niece, Bianca Corrotti, in Bientina. Her husband's some big shot at Piaggio in Pontedera. He says if we can't find his wife, maybe we can find them."

Disgusted, Sal handed the letter back to Vinny.

Thoughtfully, Vinny refolded it. "What's with you anyway, Passarelli?"

"Well, for starters, this guy thinks we're gonna just roll into the exact village where his family lives? What—we're supposed to stroll up to some stranger on the street and ask where his wife is? Or, did it occur to you that maybe the Fascist she's living with is some big honcho goon? C'mon, Vinny. You've seen what it's like from Rome to here. These people are living like animals and it's only getting worse the farther north we get. Chances are this guy's wife is either dead or close to it. Same goes for his family."

"I don't care, Sal. I'm gonna try to find them."

"Oh, yeah, you're on a mission now, right?" Sal spit a blood-clot into the corner of the cell and then shot his hand up to massage the spot on his jaw where he was now missing a tooth.

"Whatever you say, Hero-man." Vinny tucked the letter into his pocket, turned his back on his friend and lay down to sleep, tuning Sal out but thinking that what Sal said was probably true. The chance of finding this woman—Armida—would be like finding a needle in a haystack. He had seen enough death and wretchedness in their march from Naples to Florence to know *not* to expect anything different on the next march to the Gothic Line. Starving orphans and widows lined the roads everywhere begging for food. Grown men, once strong and now shadows of themselves, wept openly. Visions of massacred, mutilated, bodies—innocent women and children gunned down en masse for no other reason than living in a village that might, or might not, harbor a partisan—robbed him of sleep many nights. But now, after two grim years of slugging it through one battle after another, he finally saw a glimmer of hope. Suddenly, unexpectedly, he had a personal incentive to survive.

The fact was, at only twenty-one years of age, Vinny Del Vecchio missed his mother with an ache that nothing could touch. He longed for the day when he would be back home, eating her home-cooked meals, sleeping in his own big warm bed, pushing paper at some mindless, risk-free desk job. It mattered little to him if he was greeted upon his return as a victor by his community, as long as his mother was proud of him. Smiling contentedly for the first time in months, he crossed his arms, placing his battered hands beneath his sweat-stained armpits, and drifted off to sleep.

In the morning, Vinny told Sal he'd dreamed of Armida Sigali.

"And?" asked Sal.

"Forget it."

"Whenever you say 'forget it,' it's either bad news or something stupid. Which is it?"

"You're superstitious. I don't know if I should tell you."

"Where do you get that I'm superstitious?"

"You think the worst of everything."

Sal growled. "Just tell me, will ya Vin?"

"Okay. I dreamed we found her at the bottom of a lake . . . digging in a vineyard."

"Digging in a vineyard at the bottom of a lake. Yeah, that makes sense. So we're looking for a mermaid now."

"It doesn't matter what you think." Vinny turned his back on Sal. "I know it means something. You'll see."

chapter twenty-five

"PA, WHAT'S GOING on? You don't look well."

"It's nothing, Babe. I'm fine."

Violenza exchanged looks with her brother, Siv, and continued fixing dinner. They had all gathered at the little house on Margaret Street to celebrate Columbus Day, which just so happened to be Violenza's fourth wedding anniversary as well. Though Egisto reveled in having his children and grandchildren in his home again, he nevertheless bore the air of one carrying the weight of the world on his shoulders.

Babe persisted. "It's mama, isn't it?"

Egisto ignored her. "When will dinner be ready?"

"Papa!"

Siv's wife, Ruth, took off her apron and announced she was going to go outside with Babe's husband, Dick, to keep an eye on the kids. As the back door slammed behind her, Siv picked up a dish towel and began to dry some dishes.

"I told you, I'm fine, Violenza," repeated Egisto. "Just a bit tired, that's all."

"Maybe you should cut back on your hours at Drake, pa," suggested Siv.

"My work is what keeps me going."

Siv seemed to accept the explanation at face value, but Babe paused from peeling a potato and pointed her paring knife at her father. "There! If everything is fine, papa, then why do you need something to keep you 'going' as you say?"

Egisto scowled. Hiding anything from his perceptive daughter was impossible. He didn't dare tell her that she had her mother's tenacity. It would infuriate her. Babe might remember the ugly years of her mother's life—the cold shoulders, insane accusations, spiteful fits—but Egisto knew the real Armida Sigali: the woman who braved public ridicule and an ocean of separation from her family to embark on an adventure with a man she thought loved her. Or at least would learn to love her. Even her insistence on a divorce and return to Italy were, he believed, simply manifestations of a wounded, granite-shelled character driven to put actions to words, whether right or wrong. It was that same stoic stubbornness, that "dare-me" dogged determination, Egisto hoped was keeping Armida alive on the other side of the globe.

"All right, Violenza, you win," he sighed. "I have been worried about your mother. Do you have any idea what is happening in Italy?"

"Yes, pa, I read the papers, too."

"Then you know I have much to be concerned about."

"I can understand you being concerned for your mother and your brothers and Aunt Carilda, but mama made her choice a long time ago. She left us and never came back. When are you going to accept that?"

"For all I know, my family could be dead. At best, they are at least homeless, starving and destitute. Since you've never met them, I cannot expect you to feel the same desperation I feel for them. But your own mother, Violenza! Her life could also be hanging in the balance. Don't you care?"

Babe gripped the handle of the paring knife and tore into another potato. "I never said I didn't care. I just can't allow myself to be emotionally involved in this and neither can you. What can you or I do, anyway? It's out of our control. If mama dies in Italy, it will make little difference in the way we live our lives here now."

"Violenza!"

"It's true. What did she ever do for you? It makes me sick to think of you losing sleep over her. Look at you! It's been almost fifteen years, pa. Fifteen years! And she still has you wrapped around her little finger."

Siv tried to intervene. "C'mon, Babe. Forget it."

"No, we need to talk about it," said Egisto, shaking his head. "Is that what you think also, Siv?"

Babe prodded her brother to answer truthfully.

"Pretty much, pa," he answered. "Babe's right. It's out of our control. Why make yourself sick and lose sleep over mama? There's nothing you can do about it."

"I wasn't going to say anything," said Egisto, clearing his throat, "but you may as well know what's happened. Julia Barghini has an Italian friend in California whose son is serving in Italy. She suggested that if I wrote a letter and sent it to her, perhaps her friend's son could deliver it to your mother. There is no other way of communication until the war is over. I was hoping that if this young man could not find Armida, he could at least find someone in my family."

Babe held the pot of peeled and pared potatoes under running water until it was full and then set it on the stove, turning the burner on to high. Wiping her hands on her apron, she sat down next to her father. "I hope they find her, pa," she said.

"I do too."

Siv placed his hand on his father's shoulder; a gesture of support, one man to another.

Egisto reached up and covered Siv's hand with his. "Both of you need to know that I worry about your mother because I am the one responsible for her situation."

Babe began to protest, but he dismissed her. "No. Listen to me. You do not know how your mother and I met. You do not know what I was like before you were born. There are many things you do not know. Perhaps someday the right time will come for me to explain it all, but not now. For now, you must trust me and understand that I do not suffer unrealistic expectations as you think. If your mother survives the war, I do not expect her to marry me again. But war changes everyone, and if she survives, I believe she will be changed. We can visit her and she can visit us. You can have a relationship with her again."

Marking the skepticism on Babe's face, he added, "One thing is certain, Violenza. Your mother does not deserve to die an ignoble death. I cannot bear the thought of her dying in horror or shame. The fact that she could be suffering is bad enough, but a lonely, cruel death is unthinkable. When I look at you, my baby, I see her. How can I possibly forget your mother? No, I will not rest until the war is over and your mother and my family are found. Think, Violenza. Put yourself in my shoes."

Chastened, Babe hung her head.

"Dinner will be ready soon, pa," she finally blurted, getting up from the table. "It's a holiday, and my anniversary. We won't spoil it with any more talk about mama or the war. All we can do is hope. That's all we can do."

Egisto smiled weakly. "And we can seek the truth. Even if the news of your mother, or my family, is bad, it is better than knowing nothing. It is the waiting that is killing me."

chapter twenty-six

❧

THE GERMANS HAD moved north and Danilo was home again, but the fear that Danilo and I wouldn't be able to feed our children consumed us. There were days when all we had to give them was a handful of moldy chestnuts from last year's harvest and, if we were lucky, a scraggly onion or under-ripe tomato from the garden. Marauders got the rest.

We heard—through our partisan connections—that those living directly along the Gothic Line were bearing the brunt of the war now. We were told Monte di Ripa was being bombed and that residents had fled to the hills and were starving to death. Later, my sisters Rina and Lida told me that they—and my mother and nonna—had hidden in the mountains with shepherds and partisans. They ate grass to survive.

I'm glad I didn't know it at the time; it would have killed me to think of them suffering like that. Danilo and I prayed, hoping and believing they would survive. We prayed for Armida and Argene too. Armida, especially, because we knew she was in the most dangerous position of all.

❧

BY LATE AUGUST, with the Germans hunkered down behind the fifty-mile-deep defenses of the Gothic Line, anxious Italians watched the Allies' Fifth Army rumbling out of Pisa, pausing briefly to split up into two groups before continuing their advance north toward the ominous mountain bastions looming before them.

A small unit from the 1st Armored Division, to which Sal and Vinny were assigned, was ordered to accompany the Buffalo Soldiers of the 92nd along the western flank of the Apennines. The plan was for the bulk of the Fifth Army to attack the Germans near the center of the peninsula at the Futa and Il Giogo Passes, while the British Eighth Army advanced to the east, toward the Adriatic Coast. The primary objective of this pincer strategy, designed to divide and conquer German resistance along the Gothic Line, would only be achieved if the western assault by the 92nd was successful.

Sal and Vinny were ambivalent about their role in accompanying the 92nd on its way up through Viareggio and Forte dei Marmi to Massa. Their earlier encounter with some of the black soldiers on the barroom floor in Tavernelle had earned the Buffalo Division their respect and Sal, who had until then never before met his match, was particularly ingratiating. As the army lumbered through the flat, straight abandoned streets of Viareggio, Sal leaned over the edge of the Sherman infantry tank he was perched atop and shouted down to the sweating soldiers marching behind him.

"Hey! Bo! Gotta smoke?"

"Not for no white boy, I don't!"

"I ain't white!"

Bo's ivory teeth blazed beneath the shadow cast on his

face by his helmet. "You ain't white?! What color you think you is?"

The men roared. He shouted to his companions, "What color do he look like?"

"He look white to me," replied a behemoth warrior striding alongside Bo, shifting his rifle from one bulging forearm to another. He removed his helmet, shading his eyes for a better view. "Ya-suh, he white all right."

"I ain't white!" Sal snorted indignantly. "I'm Italian!"

"Say what?" Bo laughed so hard he had to hold his ribs. "If you be Italian, boy, you be white."

The behemoth bellowed, "You prove you ain't white and I'll give you a smoke!"

Sal sprang to his knees, reached into the commander's hatch and held up the freckled, tattooed, bare arm of gunner Private Patrick O'Malley. "That's white, my friends."

O'Malley wrested free of Sal's grip, giving him the finger before resuming controls of the vehicle's long-barreled 75mm artillery. Sal scooted back to the edge of the tank, dangling his feet over the caterpillar tracks and rolled up his own sleeve, exposing his russet skin to Bo, who was still laughing at O'Malley.

Flexing his biceps, Sal crowed, "But this here's a hunk o' *brown* beauty! Tell me you don't love it."

"You one proud mother, man," said the colossus, retrieving a cigarette from his pocket. "You still be white, but you a sight darker than that white-boy gunner. Here," he shouted, tossing the cigarette up to Sal's waiting hands, "Brown-boy!"

Sal gave them a victory sign and hungrily lit up, his loose helmet straps slapping against his sand-paper cheeks in sync with the swaying tank.

Vinny, who had been sitting quietly near Sal during the exchange, suddenly spoke up. "Give me a drag."

"No way. I earned it."

"You're full of it."

"Get your own."

"Gimme!" Vinny grabbed the cigarette, taking at least three long drags before Sal whacked him on the helmet and grabbed it back.

"What's eatin' you anyway, Del Vecchio?" asked Sal.

"You."

"*Me?*"

"Yeah, you."

"What'd I do now?"

Vinny pointed to the great sweep of mountains angling parallel to them. "Don't you know what's waiting for us up there?"

"German sons-of-bitches?"

"All you ever do is joke around. It's gettin' old."

"Well, I'll be . . . " Sal was stunned. "You're scared."

Vinny avoided looking at Sal. "Yeah, and you should be too. I have a feeling about it."

Sal was superstitious. He squirmed. "A bad feeling, Vinny?"

"Real bad."

Sal took another hit off his cigarette and then handed it absently to Vinny. His hands were shaking.

"I wanna find that woman," whispered Vinny, caressing the pocket that contained the letter he had been carrying around for weeks.

"The hell with her," spat Sal. "Forget the damn letter, Vinny! What happened in Pontedera, huh? Nothing. People acted like they'd never heard of Danilo Corrotti. It was a waste of time, not to mention dangerous. Now you think we're going to find someone here in this rat hole? The whole thing's probably a hoax anyway. Your mother got suckered into some scam and you're buying right into it."

"It's no scam, Sal, and you know it."

Sal swore under his breath. "How'd I ever end up with you?"

"Maybe it's fate."

"Quit talking like that. You're spookin' me."

"Don't you ever think about it? About fate?"

"No." Sal stole the cigarette back from Vinny, inhaled the remains and flicked the butt over his shoulder.

They were now entering the narrower outskirts of Forte de Marmi, hemmed in-between the intoxicating sea with its seemingly endless white beaches to their left and the hushed pine-green Apuanes to their right. Just beyond Forte dei Marmi, to the northeast, they caught sight of their destination: the little village of Massa resting near the base of Monte di Ripa. And north of Massa was the strategic, German-occupied seaport of La Spezia. Their mission was to break through the Gothic Line at Massa and then take the seaport. On paper, it appeared simple enough, but in their eyes, as they drew near Massa, it looked like suicide.

Sal gulped and turned around to look at the hundreds of black faces scoping out the landscape as they marched behind the tank toward certain death. *We're sitting ducks*, he thought morosely. He had lost a lot of buddies in this war, but never once had he considered losing Vinny. Del Vecchio was like a brother he had never had. If something happened to him . . . Sal stopped. What was he thinking? God, this war was getting to him.

One of the commanders in the Ford GPW jeep ahead of

them stood up and pulled out his binoculars, scanning the mountain ridges. Moments later, he sat back down and conferred with another officer as they made notations on a huge field map spread out between them.

Vinny squinted in the direction the officers had been studying. "I see flashes of light up there."

"Where?" demanded Sal, staring hard in the same direction. "I don't see anything."

"I know I saw it. They're sitting up there waiting to take us out."

"I can't believe we haven't hit any road bombs yet," Sal noted, trying to change the subject. "You know the bastards planted them everywhere."

"Let the explosives squad up ahead do their work, Sal. That's what they're here for."

As the division rolled through Forte dei Marmi, inching their way toward Massa, they began to see the familiar, methodical devastation encountered all along the march from Rome. The Germans had sent the approaching troops a clear message by leveling everything beneath their Gothic fortresses so that the Allied soldiers would have nowhere to hide. Not one building along the route had been left intact. Smoke still billowed up from several neighborhoods. Human putrification permeated the air. Vinny tucked his nose and mouth down into the inside of his shirt and gagged. They passed the stiff, bloated corpse of a middle-aged woman dangling from the end of a rope attached to the second-story balcony of a partially razed building, her hands tied behind her back.

Choking down his breakfast, Sal could almost understand Vinny's obsession with finding the mystery woman in the letter.

The soldiers continued marching somberly, silently, like

remote-controlled robots, conserving their energy for what lay ahead. They passed a sign telling them they were entering Monte di Ripa. The hypnotic pounding of hundreds of pairs of boots on pavement, along with the metallic whining of the tanks' engines and an occasional backfire, deadened the deceivingly pleasant, warm air. A nerve along Sal's trigger finger twitched involuntarily. Suddenly, the ruins of a recently destroyed church came into view. The name of the church was still visible over the blackened doors: San Luigi Gonzaga. Providing adequate cover with its spreading trees and protective walls of rubble, the commanders, having received radio verification from their advance scouts that the place was clear, announced they would bivouac there, rendezvousing with other troops from the 92nd approaching from Pietrasanta.

Scuttling down from the tank, Sal and Vinny were immediately ordered into reconnaissance teams to secure the perimeter. Both of them, along with Bo and two other Buffalo soldiers, headed away from the center of operations at the church toward their assigned sector, creeping cautiously from house to house, shimmying their way around innumerable obstacles while looking for booby traps and any signs of snipers.

Motioning to Sal, Bo suddenly said, "Hey, white boy! Look-ee here! We got us some scared possum."

Sal looked in the direction Bo was pointing and saw two forms, covered in soot, huddled together in the hollowed-out cave of a blackened chimney. Sunlight pouring through a giant hole in the roof above them made the whites of their petrified, unblinking eyes glow like tiny moons in an eclipse. Sal had to bend low, displacing loose stones and mortar in his effort to reach them. Bo followed close behind, while Vinny stood guard near what had been the building's entrance. The other soldiers continued on to the next house. As Sal and Bo neared them, the pair recoiled in horror.

"It's okay," said Sal, solicitously, offering them a chocolate bar he had stowed away in his pocket.

"Po' things," clucked Bo as he watched the waifs devour the candy. "They be thirsty you think?"

Sal unscrewed the lid of his canteen, handing it to the smaller form, who gulped down nearly the entire contents, before giving it to the other, much larger form, who finished it off, wiping a sleeve-covered hand across its face. Sal's jaw dropped as he realized the larger form was actually a young woman, perhaps eighteen years old. Even with her hair matted flat against her head and charcoal smears criss-crossing her face, she was gorgeous. Curious, Vinny backed away from his station, lowered his gun and shimmied closer to where he could observe what Sal and Bo were doing. When he saw the girl, he let out a soft whistle.

Rita Hayworth don't have nothin' on her, thought Sal, using the palm of his hand to brush some debris off of her shoulder. Her moist cinnamon eyes, rimmed with thick black lashes, eyed him with caution.

"Come si chiama?" Sal asked her, gently.

Bo said, "What'd you just say?"

"I asked her what her name is."

"Why?"

"Cause when this war's over I'm coming back to marry her."

Bo shot a glance at Vinny, who shrugged in amazement. In the two and a half years he had known Sal, Vinny had never heard him equate women with marriage. Surely, he was kidding.

The smaller form, now distinguishable as a boy, nudged the girl. When she didn't respond, he lifted his chin. "Her name is Gianna!" he said in Italian.

Bo and Vinny watched with fascination as Sal spoke in their native tongue, asking them a flood of questions. They were brother and sister. The boy's name was Mario. Their mother had hidden them in the chimney when the Germans retreated less than twenty-four hours ago, instructing them not to come out until she returned. It was the last time they had seen her. Wide-eyed with fascination, they asked Sal about the black buffalo insignia patch on Bo's shoulder. Sal smiled at their curiosity.

"He's an American, like me," replied Sal. "He's a Buffalo Soldier." He pulled Bo's helmet back so the two could see Bo's dense, wiry curls. "He looks like a buffalo, don't he?"

The siblings smiled shyly.

Could a woman possibly be more beautiful? thought Sal, hypnotized by Gianna's smile.

Bo broke the spell. "We done been here long enough," he said, jittery as he repositioned his helmet on his head. "Best be going."

"Wait a minute," said Vinny. "Sal, ask her about the Sigali woman. Hurry."

Sal asked Gianna if she knew of any Sigalis in the area. When her brother nodded in affirmation, pointing across the room, out through the crumbling, gaping hole in the wall, toward a disheveled looking specter staring mutely at them from across the street, Vinny let out a quiet whoop.

"Argene Sigali is right there," explained the boy. "She is crazy."

Shocked, Sal looked at Vinny. "Is that the name of the lady you're looking for?"

"No, but it's close enough." Triumphant, Vinny raised his fist in the air in a sign of victory and then lowered it and gave Sal a thumb's up. "C'mon, we've got to talk to her."

"Nuh-uh," grunted Bo, shaking his head furiously. "Don't do it. She a devil."

Vinny slid along the wall to the crumbled opening, looked both ways, and motioned for the woman to come near. As though in a trance, she approached him, unblinking.

"She a *devil!*" hissed Bo again, taking cover behind Sal.

When Argene got close enough to get a good look at Vinny, she screamed, "Danilo!" and rushed through the opening to embrace him.

What sanity Argene might have had before the Allied invasion of Italy had long since been lost. Not bothering to brush her prematurely white hair for weeks, it hung down almost to her waist in oily, twisted, lice-riddled knots. Her clothing was ripped to shreds, her gums recessed, exposing rotten, yellowed teeth. She reeked of filth.

Vinny looked desperately at Sal with an expression that screamed, *What are you waiting for? Help!*

"Do you know Armida Sigali?" stuttered Sal in Italian.

Argene howled, "Where is she? Where is my sister?"

"Armida Sigali is your sister?"

"Where is my sister?" she repeated, ignoring Sal's question. "I want her back!"

After Sal interpreted her response, Vinny said, "Tell her we don't know where her sister is, Sal. Tell her we're trying to find her, too."

Argene seized Vinny's arms, trying to draw him out into the street, begging him to follow her.

"What's she saying, Sal?" asked Vinny.

"She keeps calling you Danilo. Hey, maybe it's that

Corrotti guy! She wants you to take her with you. Geez, Vinny, you got a wild one on your hands."

Even now, Sal couldn't help teasing Vinny. The image of his poker-faced friend with Argene wrapped around him like a pretzel was just too irresistible to pass up.

"Signora Sigali!" shouted Mario, crawling out from his hiding place next to his sister. "Stop it! These are American soldiers. Tell them where your sister is. Maybe they can help you."

Instantly, a different personality emerged from Argene. Backing away from Vinny, she said calmly and with precise articulation, "Armida escaped with the Carditis. She made sure I knew before she left, because she loves me."

"Where did she go?" asked Mario, in an authoritative tone far beyond his years.

"She went to one of the mountain lakes; the one near Garda, where the Duce lives now."

Sal again interpreted her answer, this time adding his own conclusion. "In other words, Vinny, Armida Sigali's number is up. I guess the mission to find your mystery lady is over."

Argene, sensing Sal's sarcasm, gushed, "Armida is coming back for me. She promised!" Then, blithely, she turned, climbed through the hole in the wall and began to pick her way back through the rubble, crooning and clucking like a chicken as she crossed the deserted street: "I'm going to the church to wait for Armida," she sang. "Danilo and Bianca are getting married today. I want to see Bianca's dress."

Vinny looked quizzically at Sal. *What in the world is she saying?*

Sal made a circular, rotating motion at his temple. "She's nuts."

Gianna had scrabbled out of the chimney crevice and was standing close to Sal. Mario positioned himself at his sister's side, satisfied that he had done what the Americans had expected of him.

"Ask them what they think, Sal," said Vinny, nodding toward Gianna and Mario.

As Gianna spoke, Sal, losing himself in her presence, slowly repeated in English what she was saying in Italian. "She said she thinks it's true that Argene's sister escaped to the north. They feel sorry for Argene. They say she didn't use to be this bad until . . ." He turned around and stopped in mid-sentence.

Vinny was gone.

In a flash, Sal was on his belly, peering over the hole in the wall where he could see Vinny following Argene down the street as though he were in a trance. Using his elbow to propel him along the floor, Bo followed right behind Sal, stationing himself on the other side of the opening, his back to the wall. They watched as Argene glanced over her shoulder at Vinny and sprinted over to a street lamp where a dead body lay, sprawled spread-eagle on the curbside. The man had been severely beaten, his face so disfigured it was impossible to tell how old he was. A bright red bandana was tied about his bloody, twisted neck. Next to his corpse rested a large wooden box and what appeared to be small, individually wrapped pieces of brightly colored candy scattered around and on top of it. Argene let out a squeal, picked up one of the candies and impulsively shoved it in her mouth, and then leaned over to open the box.

As she did, Vinny roared, "No!" and rushed toward her. Thinking he was going to tackle her, Argene bolted like a rabbit, hiding behind a collapsed wall just out of his reach.

Trembling, she peered around the rubble and watched as Vinny, tripping over the dead body, lost his balance and stumbled onto the box.

Sal, closing in on the scene, yelled at the top of his lungs, "V-i-n-n-n-y!"

A deafening explosion shook the street, shooting wood fragments, glass shards, nails, rocks, metal, bones and flesh at deadly speed in every direction. Bo, Gianna, and Mario ducked for cover as the grisly debris rained down around them. When the dust settled, all that was left of Vinny Del Vecchio was his helmet, which after flying thirty feet up in the air, crashed onto the street, clattering eerily along the cobblestones until it came to rest just outside the demolished wall of the house that, only moments before, he had been standing in.

Sal's mangled body lay motionless in the street, yards from where Vinny had last been seen.

Taking a deep breath, Bo shot out from behind his refuge with his gun drawn and drug Sal back into the house by his feet. Gianna leaned over him while Bo ripped the sleeve from his shirt and frantically fashioned a tourniquet to stanch the blood that was gushing from Sal's split abdomen.

It was too late.

Tenderly, Gianna felt Sal's neck for a pulse. Finding none, she pressed a hand over Sal's face, closing his eyelids and looked at Bo, her eyes hollow and cold, before ushering Mario back to their hiding place to wait out the next battle that was yet to come.

Before leaving them, Bo got down on one knee and lifted a chain out from beneath his shirt. A cross dangled from the end of it. Not caring that they wouldn't understand him, he said, "It's mighty bad for y'all right now, I know, but you pray to Jesus. Ya hear? You pray for me that snipers don't take me out while I carry Sal here back to our base, and I'll pray for you that someday you can forget all this bow-shet."

He watched Gianna and Mario make little signs of the cross on their foreheads and hearts and shook his head. "Don't know 'bout none of that," he said, tucking the cross back down into his shirt. "I just know ain't none of us getting outta here alive without Jesus."

Tipping his helmet in a farewell to the two, Bo hoisted Sal's corpse onto his back. He made his way to the opening and looked both ways before stepping out of the building. A moment later the sound of gunfire filled the air. Gianna and Mario shrunk back into their hole, listening intently. When the shooting stopped they heard a low deep laugh coming from outside, close by. Then they heard a deep, resonant voice singing a strange song in English completely foreign to them. The words sounded like, *"Oh, Lordy, ain't gonna tarry here; cause he's digging down in the ground, ain't going to tarry here."* Even though they didn't understand it, they knew it was Bo letting them know he was alive and well.

Mario turned to Gianna, smiled, and did a very American thing. He lifted his fist in a sign of victory and gave his sister a thumbs up.

PART V

1944–1945

La speranza è l'ultima a morire

"Hope is last to die"

chapter twenty-seven

❧

Iᴛ ɪs ᴀ regrettable vagary of war that the greatest loss of life often occurs in the most beautiful places. One could almost call it diabolical. Normandy, Dresden, Alsace-Lorraine . . . the lakes of northern Italy.

Lago d'Iseo, for example, is a jewel of a lake nestled amidst the yawning, glacial valleys of the Southern Alps. It encircles Monte Isola, the largest lake island in southern Europe, like a glittering wreath. It's a primeval refuge of sleeping hamlets connected by winding, narrow, cobblestoned roads. For over 800 years Monte Isola's crowning glory has been the Sanctuary of the Madonna della Ceriola, perched high atop the island's mountainous peak. A proud sentinel of Monte Isola's olive orchards, walnut groves and vineyards, the 360-degree view from the church has been labeled "stupendous."

The kidney-shaped lake itself is also ringed with scores of idyllic villages, not the least of which is the town of Iseo, known as the "Gateway to the East." Like a pendant at the end of a circlet of pearls, Iseo dangles directly south of the lower cusp of Monte Isola. Its handsome promenades and pleasant plazas lie a mere fifteen miles east, as the bird flies, from a much larger and more famous mountain lake: Garda.

The beautiful town of Gargnano on Lake Garda was Benito Mussolini's sanctuary after the collapse of his government in Rome. There, the Führer prepared elaborate accommodations to help resurrect Mussolini's reign, sparing no expense to restore his most valuable ally to his former vigor. Hitler even ordered Claretta, Mussolini's mistress, to join them there to comfort and inspire her disheartened lover, even though the Duce's wife, Rachele, was also living there with him. With Mussollini's headquarters set up in the nearby town of Salò, they called his new government The Salò Republic.

Lakes d'Iseo and Garda were home to two different factions of Fascists. Garda housed Nazi and Fascist elites, while Iseo was assigned to Italy's Naval Admiral, Prince Junio Valerio Borghese and his 10th Light Flotilla, aka Decima MAS. They were famous for their state-of-the-art submarine fleet and specialty-trained commando units nicknamed the "Sea Devils." Perhaps prophetically, the fleet's emblem was a skull holding a long-stemmed red rose firmly between its yellowed teeth.

Borghese was also known as "The Black Prince" but he shrewdly played both sides of the political fence, maintaining a half-hearted allegiance to Mussolini, while at the same time distancing himself from Salò in the event the Allies won the war. He and Mussolini clashed and as a result Hitler became so suspicious of Borghese he garrisoned a contingent of SS troops around Borghese's stunning villa on the island of San Paolo, near Monte Isola, to monitor the prince's every move.

Now, stretched between the Garda and Iseo lakes—some say like a woman basking in the sun—is a seductive landscape called Franciacorta. It's a breathtaking expanse of dreamy, terraced vineyards undulating through hills dotted with castles, ruins, manors and otherworldly monasteries and abbeys. Many believe Franciacorta carries within her earthly womb prehistoric seeds of the vine. Without a doubt, it is one of the oldest wine-producing regions of the western world. Legend has it that both Pliny the Elder and Virgil extolled the virtues of Fanciacorta's wine. Indeed, after the Fall of Rome in the fifth century, her monasteries kept viticulture alive in Italy. In doing so, they survived the Dark Ages even as invading barbarians pillaged Franciacorta. Plundering the countryside, they would reportedly drink the famed, looted wine from the skulls of their enemies.

Together, Lago d'Iseo, Lago Garda, and Franciacorta form the heart and soul of Lombardy, the idyllic province where Armida Sigali—in the late summer of 1944—was soon to find herself imprisoned.

How do I know all this? Me, a simple dressmaker from Tuscany? Danilo and I went there for a short holiday, before he died. We wanted to see where Armida had spent the final days of the war.

✤

BARELY ESCAPING WITH their lives, the Carditis, along with Armida, had first fled behind the Gothic Line in Tuscany when news of the Allied victory in Florence reached them in Forte dei Marmi. After receiving Bruno's transfer orders, they were hastily assigned to a military convoy destined for Lago d'Iseo.

Entering the outskirts of Milan on their way to the lake, they were shocked to see that Allied B-26 bombers had already begun fierce nighttime raids in the city. From the cramped back seat of one of the supply lorries rumbling through the chaotic aftermath of a recent air attack, Armida witnessed the abysmal plight of her countrymen. Thousands of fleeing refugees clogged Milan's roads. Orphans and widows, their bellies grotesquely distended from months of starvation, rushed the convoy as they passed, begging for food. Skeletal, ragged young boys, seething with contempt for both the Germans and the Fascists, defiantly threw rocks at them. Armida nearly leaped out of her skin when a jeering Fascist soldier straddling the roof of the truck just ahead of them shot one of the boys point-blank through the head as though he were nothing more than a jack rabbit. Callously, Alessandro had mumbled, "That will teach them to throw rocks at us."

Seeing first-hand the mounting violence of Italy's civil war, it finally dawned on Armida what it meant for her. *Italians blame the Fascists as much as the Nazis for all of this,* she thought. How foolish she had been to think that simply being Italian would protect her somehow from her countrymen's fury. Her close association with the Carditis would mark her as a traitor every bit as much as if she were German. If little boys were unafraid of throwing stones openly at them, what would organized bands of partisans be capable of? The realization prevented her from entertaining any thoughts of freedom once they arrived at their destination in Lago d'Iseo. If anything, she had a sinking feeling that Bruno's noose would tighten even more around her. Recalling her most recent ploy at feigning insanity before they had fled from Forte dei Marmi, Armida winced. By hysterically threatening to kill herself if she was forced to leave, she had banked on the Carditis leaving her behind, but the ruse had simply earned her a black eye.

"If you dare try that again, I'll break your arm," Bruno had seethed, shoving her down the steps toward Alessandro's waiting truck. "The Nazis don't tolerate insanity. They don't tolerate anything. They'll shoot you without thinking twice about it, and then I will have no alibi if the Allies win the war. You are the only person I know with American ties. You will vouch for me, in that event, no?"

For effect, Bruno had grabbed her arm, wrenching it behind her back so hard she thought it was going to break. "If the Americans capture us you *will* tell them I was looking for a way out of Mussolini's service. Know this, Armida. I still need you too much to kill you, but I swear, if you try to escape—if you try to kill yourself—I'll make your sister wish she'd never been born."

Knowing he meant every word, she had stifled her hysterics and meekly surrendered, letting him stuff her into the waiting truck. Sitting next to Armida, Chiara Carditi—like Lot's wife—had turned around to look upon their cherished villa only once, and then set her face like flint toward the mountains.

Armida's reminiscing was short-lived. As the convoy left the outskirts of Milan, winding higher up through the southern reaches of Franciacorta, the verdant landscape began to work a kind of magic in her. By the time the long procession reached the town of Iseo, she seemed to have forgotten her worst fears. It was early September; in the terraced fields sloping down to the lake, laborers were preparing for the grape and olive harvests. In the town of Iseo, scores of vendors plied their goods in a bustling open market in the sun-soaked city square.

They pulled up to a train depot doubling as a temporary military command center, and Armida stepped down from the truck and stretched her legs. While everyone else huddled together commiserating over what would happen next, she slipped away to the lakeshore, a stone's throw away. Lago d'Iseo was so still and clear that the reflection of the bisque-bellied cumulus clouds tumbling across the cobalt-blue heavens looked more real—mirrored in the water—than the actual sky itself.

Captivated, Armida felt her soul tear lose from its moorings and evaporate into the clouds. It lasted only a moment, a brief journey of self-awareness, but it had a profound effect on her. *Maybe this is what death is like*, she mused, bending down to scoop up a handful of water. She splashed it over her face, letting the cool liquid wash away the ugliness that had been so much a part of her past.

Tranquility. Newness. Peace.

Even the fear that had been plaguing her since being found out by Bruno seemed to dissipate with the water dripping off her chin and the tip of her nose. She felt ten pounds lighter. Although she was terrified of water, she was so completely mesmerized by it she had to battle the urge to cast her body headlong into the lake's dazzling incandescence.

Meanwhile, Bruno, impervious to everything but expediency in resolving his integration into the Salò military machinery, paced back and forth, waiting for his final orders.

"I want to be quartered on that island over there," Armida heard him demanding. She turned to see a pallid SS officer ordering Bruno to the front of the queue. The spell was broken. Hesitantly, she stepped back from the edge of the lake.

"We have just the place for you," the thin-lipped officer told Bruno, more than a hint of sarcasm in his voice. "First, however, we must issue you new Party membership cards."

Armida dried her face with her sleeve and rejoined the group.

Bruno pulled his billfold out of his pocket and opened

it, rifling through some cash and an assortment of business cards. "I have my card right here."

"I said *new* Party membership cards. The *old* Party has been purged. Your new membership card will reflect your current standing in the Repubblica Sociale Italiana." The German turned his head and coughed loudly, not bothering to cover his mouth. "Now," he continued, his voice nasally, "this document says you are accompanied today by your wife, a son, and . . ." He paused, squinting through his thick glasses, mispronouncing the name *Armida Sigali.* Peering over the top of his glasses at Bruno, he asked, "Who is she?"

"She is my servant." Bruno said this with a gilded air of supremacy.

"In that case, your wife, your son, and your *servant* will also be issued new membership cards shortly. Is that understood?"

Bruno began to argue, but the officer interrupted him. "Are the women with you *'stirpe ariana'* or *'stirpe giudeica?'*"

"Sorry?" asked Bruno. The German's Italian was pathetic. He could barely understand him.

"Aryan or Jewish? Is your wife, or your servant, Jewish?"

"Of course not!"

Systematically stamping a pile of documents, the officer droned on: "You will report tomorrow morning to Decima MAS headquarters where you will be given your assignment. Your request for residence on Monte Isola requires that you will be working with the Department of the Navy in their submarine division. We have no problem with that, *do* we?" His emphasis on the word "do" indicated there was to be no arguing.

"Whatever you say."

At Bruno's mocking response the German leaped up and walked around the table toward him. Though thinner than Bruno, he was much taller. Decidedly more menacing.

"Your son," he nodded toward Alessandro, "is being assigned to the Brigate Nere. The Black Brigades should be a perfect fit for him. His credentials seem to support the fact that he enjoys doing undercover work; especially the disarming of partisans. Such an assignment requires a certain, shall we say, callousness—a certain mercilessness—when it comes to dealing with rebels."

In a more conciliatory tone of voice, Bruno agreed. "The Black Brigades *will* be a perfect fit for my son, I am sure."

The officer thrust an envelope into Bruno's hands, instructing him to have his family and belongings at Iseo's main dock at 18:00 hours, and dismissed him with a click of his heels.

It was, therefore, at 18:00 sharp, just as columns of dusky vapors began rising over the lake, that the Carditi party was ferried to the village of Siviano, on the northern tip of Monte Isola. They were then escorted to a small, but elegant villa overlooking the village docks. Not only was it fully furnished, but the kitchen was stocked as well, prompting a relieved signora Carditi to exclaim, "Oh, Bruno! It has everything to make this house a perfect home!"

"I'm glad you like it signora," said their escort, who also spoke very poor Italian. His iron-black SS uniform set him distinctly apart from the other grey-clad Nazi officers. "We requisitioned it only a few hours ago."

Chiara Carditi, surprisingly naïve, yelped, "Requisitioned? Why, what do you mean?"

The officer and Bruno exchanged a fleeting look of amusement with one other. "The Germans have a very efficient way of providing for our needs, Chiara," said Bruno with a patronizing wave of his hand. "It is rude to question their methods."

Eager to settle in, Bruno tried to dismiss the German, but was ignored, the officer lingering near the entryway as he made notations on a clipboard emblazoned on the back with a black-and-white German eagle carrying a swastika in its talons.

"One more thing, signore," the officer said, pointing his pen at Bruno. "You will be sharing this residence with another family. Germans; a husband and wife by the name of Werner and Elsa Kolbe."

"That wasn't what I was . . . " Bruno blustered. He knew the German High Command was pairing up German officers with the arriving Italian officers to spy on and intimidate them.

"It is rude to question our methods, is it not?" snapped the officer, mimicking Bruno's earlier comment to Chiara. "Do not worry, Commandant Kolbe speaks Italian."

"But, how many bedrooms are there?" whined Chiara. "Where will we all sleep?"

"If it is not to your liking, signora Carditi," smiled the officer, "we have a cell in the town jail that might serve you nicely. Otherwise, I would suggest you allow Herr Kolbe and his wife to select the bedroom they desire when they arrive tomorrow. You may have the one they do not choose."

Chiara asked the officer if it might not be fairer to draw straws. Bruno, glowering like some fire-god on the verge of self-immolation told her to "shut up."

The officer next turned to Alessandro, who sat sulking at the kitchen table. "And as for you, signore, you will have to sleep on the floor, no?"

The expression on Alessandro's face barely masked his rage. He acknowledged the dig with a slight nod of his head. He pointed petulantly to Armida. "What about her?

Where will *she* sleep?"

Momentarily perplexed, the German scanned the documents on his clipboard. "Who is she? A sister? An aunt?"

"She is our servant."

"Ah-h, very good. I see you have come prepared like good Italian noblemen." The way he said it, Bruno couldn't tell if the German was being facetious or not.

"You and the Kolbes will get along fine," continued their escort. "If they do not bring their own servant, perhaps yours will suffice for both families." He pointed toward a closet. "In that event, that closet can be converted into a small room for her."

A jolt of fear cracked down Armida's spine. Her experience at St. Peter's Mental Hospital had left her severely claustrophobic. The closet he referred to was tiny; barely large enough for a child.

Sizing Armida up, the German muttered brusquely, "Yes, it should work . . . for a servant. Well, any more questions?"

Of course, no one dared ask anything more.

The officer placed his clipboard along with some assorted papers and documents back in his briefcase and saluted Bruno. "Heil Hitler!"

Bruno returned the salute. Alessandro stood at attention, a façade of respect plastered on his face.

"The Kolbes will arrive tomorrow," the German reminded them. "You will give them a proper welcome. Gute Nacht"

chapter twenty-eight

THE KOLBES ARRIVED on Monte Isola the following day, leading a procession of scowling natives pressed into lugging their suitcases, boxes, wooden crates, steamer trunks, and other sundry belongings up the steps from Siviano's docks to the newly confiscated villa. Werner Kolbe's exact age was difficult to gauge, although he appeared to be in his early forties. Sophisticated and aristocratic, his tall, muscular build, tanned face and thick dark-blond hair, packaged beneath a crisp S.S. uniform, imbued him with a fierce aura of superiority.

Bruno and Alessandro, upon returning to the villa after reporting on their first day of duty, discovered Werner Kolbe had assumed command of the villa. He had claimed the best bedroom, the finest linens, and the choicest wines for himself. To their astonishment, Kolbe had even conscripted some local men to construct a private office onto the house, an addition to be built off of their bedroom. He had, apparently, been unable to locate a suitable facility in Siviano for his office as the German overseer of Monte Isola. The villa would have to do. Not only that, but outraged that there was no direct access by automobile from the docks to the villa, he ordered the house below him condemned and torn down, and then commissioned a primitive road to be built directly from the docks to the villa, post haste. Amidst the chaos and din of moving and remodeling, the two families' first meeting was awkward at best.

Werner's idea of civility when introduced to any stranger was to acknowledge their presence with respectful detachment. But, Italians? In his estimation, they were traitors and cowards. So, with thinly veiled derision, Werner woodenly shook Bruno's and Alessandro's hands upon meeting them. Speaking their language, passably, with a thick, heavy accent, he formally introduced them to his wife.

Elsa Kolbe was stunning. Surely, lusted Alessandro inwardly, Herr Kolbe had robbed the cradle. The smoldering, Teutonic beauty couldn't be more than twenty-five years old. Provocative, sophisticated, yet childishly vulnerable, her presence in the room was disarming. Everything about her screamed for attention, from her platinum, bleached-blond hair curled softly around her perfectly sculpted face, to her voluptuous figure poorly concealed beneath a white linen shirt tucked in at her tiny, belted waist. She was a tantalizing sphinx, and Bruno and Alessandro—their hearts pounding within their chests, their faces red with the searing power of her sensuality—were rendered speechless by her. The splendor of Elsa absorbed whatever hostility her rude husband may have conveyed in introducing himself to the Carditis.

For her part, Chiara, incapable of concealing her jealousy, and incensed that they had to share the same living quarters, simply glared at her new rival and said nothing.

Werner explained to the Carditis that they had not brought a servant with them and that the German High Command had assured them Armida would be at their disposal. Left unsaid was the fact that Werner Kolbe far outranked Bruno, and as such, the Kolbes would lay claim to first rights over Armida's time and services. Chiara Carditi didn't give up without a fight. Their first Sunday in the villa was a battle zone.

"Armida," Chiara shouted from her bedroom. "Come in here and help me finish unpacking these boxes."

Elsa intercepted Armida on her way to Chiara's room. "Come with me, Armida. I have some unpacking that needs to be done immediately."

As Armida followed Elsa, Chiara burst out of her room. She grabbed Armida by the hand, looked at Elsa and hissed. "*Porca vacca!* I called her first!"

Elsa grabbed Armida's other hand and pulled, cursing at Chiara. "*Verdammt!* Leave her go you *weibchen,* or I'll call Werner."

The same scene played itself out nearly every day, with Armida never having a moment alone. She suffocated in the villa's close quarters. Nagging regrets and new fears began to haunt her in the late night hours when—lying upon a thin mattress on the floor of the closet-turned-bedroom—she was so exhausted she couldn't sleep.

What's happening in Monte di Ripa? Where's Argene? What if she's dead? How long will this war last? Will the Allies win?

If I had known it would end like this—trapped with Bruno here at Iseo—I never would have accepted the job. But then, I never should have left America. I was so proud! So blind. If I was in America, I would be safe right now. I'd be with my children. My children . . .

Who am I fooling? My children hate me. They'll never forgive me for leaving them. I can't even forgive myself . . .

Often, when she did finally fall asleep, she would dream she was trapped inside the crib at St. Peter's Hospital. Deliriously, she would thrash about in a cold sweat, pummeling the closet walls with her hands and feet.

But then fate intervened in the form of an unexpected visit. It came floating into Siviano, capricious, like the smell of pine trees in a desert, on a glorious day in early October. Armida had taken advantage of the fine weather to spend the entire morning doing laundry. She reveled in the methodic rhythm of scrubbing clothes in the large metal bucket set up on the patio, and hanging them up to dry in the warm fresh breeze blowing up from the lake. Shortly before noon she returned to the kitchen to do some ironing. Elsa emerged from the front of the villa where she had been basking semi-nude in the autumn sun. Using a crude form of sign language, she demanded that Armida do something for her.

When Armida failed to comprehend exactly what it was she was asking, Elsa threw her hands in the air and called for her husband. "Werner! Helfen sie mir!"

Werner pretended not to hear. The door to his office remained closed.

But Chiara, hearing Elsa's voice, pounced forth from her bedroom, having waited for just such an opportunity. She thrust a perfectly pressed gown into Armida's hands.

"Iron my dress," she ordered.

"Si, signora." Carefully placing Chiara's gown on the ironing board, Armida began to press it.

Gloating, Chiara tossed her head and positioned herself triumphantly next to Armida.

"Werner!" screamed Elsa at the top of her lungs. "Helfen sie mir!"

"What is it now, Elsa?" shouted her husband, storming out of his office. "I am trying to work!"

"Oh, Werner!" Elsa pointed to Armida, her flawless complexion temporarily marred by two deep lines between her eyebrows. "This idiot understands nothing I try to tell her."

When Werner looked as though he were going to dismiss his wife's tantrum and return to his office without taking any action on her behalf, Elsa pointed to the sniggering Chiara. "And that, that . . . *woman!*"

Werner's eyes narrowed. It dawned on him that the real issue at hand was Chiara's attempt to undermine their authority in the villa. Subsequently, it took only one look from his lethal blue eyes for Chiara to back down. She grunted, tore her evening gown from the ironing board and retreated to her bedroom, slamming the door behind her. Werner then proceeded to tell Armida in no uncertain terms that from now on she was always to tend to the needs of his wife—and himself—first, regardless of what the Carditis required of her. When Armida indicated she understood, he dismissed Elsa, suggesting she take a nap or lay down and rest. She gladly obliged, blinking away her tears and blowing him a suggestive kiss as she disappeared into their bedroom.

Alone with Armida, Werner turned toward her with an altogether different expression. Bending down so close she could see her face in his eyes, he spelled out in exasperatingly slow, broken Italian, what errand it was that his wife had been asking her to do. Elsa wanted Armida to go to Dr. Grassi's office in town to pick up some medications for her.

Trembling, Armida backed away. "Si, Herr Kolbe."

Werner followed her out of the kitchen and paused on the lower terrace to light a cigarette while Armida stumbled down the path to the lake shore, glancing nervously over her shoulder before disappearing into a throng of villagers.

UNACCUSTOMED AS THEY were to foreign occupiers, the inhabitants of Lago d'Iseo were doubly oppressed under the totalitarian boot of Hitler's regime. Those citizens who remembered well the days before Mussolini's New Socialist Republic—now headquartered not far from them—longed for his demise, even though their close proximity to Lake Garda meant their liberation would come at a very high, and a very dangerous, price. Little wonder also, that in such a volatile environment, the residents of Siviano viewed a Fascist-affiliated newcomer like Armida with deep suspicion. In fact, most of them treated her with open contempt.

When Werner Kolbe ordered Armida to town in pursuit of his wife's medications, he had assumed she knew where Dr. Leonardo Grassi's office was. She didn't. All she knew about the doctor was what she had gleaned second-hand from Chiara who had already paid him several visits herself. Leonardo Grassi had married a younger woman late in life and had fathered a daughter, Lara, when he was in his fifties. Now a widower at the ripe old age of eighty, he doted on his daughter, who lived with and also worked for him. Evidently, like most of the citizenry of Siviano, Lara Grassi adored her father.

As Armida made her way through the village, she stopped in several shops to ask directions to Dr. Grassi's office. The clerks, knowing that Armida was employed by the despised German commandant, turned their backs on her as though she didn't exist. Undeterred, she continued scouting the maze of streets snaking the bay, approaching several pedestrians with the same request. Like the clerks, they responded with icy recognition, brushing past her in disgust. Feeling exposed and vulnerable, she pulled the sleeves of her wool sweater down over her hands and crossed her arms. She continued walking with her eyes downcast until she crashed into an equally distracted woman who had stopped suddenly in her path. Armida regained her balance almost immediately, but the other woman tripped over her three-legged Yorkshire terrier tethered at the end of its leash.

After soothing her pet's shattered nerves, the woman stood up and introduced herself: "Buon giorno! My name is Lara Grassi, and this is Milo."

Armida reached down to pet Milo. "I hope I didn't hurt either of you."

"We'll live. And you are . . . ?"

Armida blushed. "Everyone in Siviano seems to know who I am."

"Perhaps everyone in Siviano *thinks* they know who you are, but I prefer to hear from your own lips who you are."

Her sincerity was so compelling, Armida gushed, "My name is Armida Sigali and I am the new commandant's domestic. I came here with the Carditi family of Forte dei Marmi."

"Here," said Lara, taking Armida by the elbow. "Let's walk along the bay while we talk. You look a bit disoriented. Is there something I can help you with?"

Armida swiped the edge of her sweater across her eyes and stared at signora Grassi. Something about her reminded her of Bianca. The eyes, blue as a robin's egg, the mischievous smile, a voice like lemon gelato . . .

"Did you say your name is Lara *Grassi?*" Armida asked.

"Si."

"You remind me of someone I know back home."

"Really? Is that good or bad?"

"Very good."

Lara's smile broadened.

"I am looking for Dr. Leonardo Grassi," Armida said. "Is he your father?"

Lara laughed. "He is."

"Herr Kolbe has sent me on an errand for his wife. Evidently your father has some medications for her."

"No doubt. They turned a corner and stopped in front of a two-story limestone building facing the lake. Above the arched door, etched in weathered marble was the title, *dott. Leonardo Grassi - Siviano.*

"Here we are," Lara said absently, untying Milo so he could stretch out on the sun-warmed stones in front of the office. She led Armida inside the building, swinging her satchel up on one of two large, cluttered desks.

"Papa!" she called out loudly. "Someone is here to see you."

From the back of the building, down a narrow hallway, a bent man with a white handlebar moustache and a pair of round, Pince-nez eyeglasses resting crookedly on his nose, shuffled toward them. His hair was white as well, rather long and curly, ringing his head like a halo, with a large bald spot on top which shone like a Florentine dome at sunrise. He passed several elderly, confused-looking patients squeezed together on a bench along the corridor. They sat listening dully to a German nurse barking unintelligible instructions to them in Italian, clearly not understanding a word she was saying.

As the doctor neared Armida, he craned his neck so as to better see her. Blinking several times, he held out his hand.

"Buon giorno, signora."

"Buon giorno, dottore."

"How may I help you?"

"My name is Armida Sigali, and I've come for Herr . . . "

"The courier from the pharmacist in Salò should be here with Frau Kolbe's medication any moment," he interrupted, frown lines splayed across his forehead. "If my pharmacist here on Monte Isola hadn't been shot for trying to poison . . . ah, well, never mind."

He lifted his hand toward a nearby chair. "Please, signora."

Armida sat down in the faded damask chair to the left of his desk. Nervously, she pulled the hem of her skirt down over her knees.

The doctor held a finger up to her as if to say, *just a moment*, and walked back to the open doorway.

"Nurse Mueller!" he called.

"Ja, doctor?"

"I have a private appointment now. You will excuse me?" It was not a request. "And Nurse Mueller," he added, before she could rebut him, "Please find someone to interpret for you. I am afraid your Italian is atrocious."

A volley of German expletives faded away as the doctor turned his back on the indignant nurse and closed his office door with a resounding thud. Wearily, he plopped down at his desk, muttering, "Doctor Schroeder I can tolerate; he is a decent man. But that impudent woman is a sorry excuse for a nurse."

"Dr. Schroeder came here with the Germans," explained Lara, while her father poured himself a glass of water and put two small white pills on his tongue. "Most Nazis consider Lago d'Iseo the backwater of Lago di Garda, but Dr. Schroeder was raised on a farm in southern Germany. He hates the pomp and ceremony of the Third Reich and fits in quite well here on the island. He travels around to all the villages on the lake and although he cares mostly for his own people stationed here, he and papa have become good friends. They have learned much from each other."

Lara signaled her father that it was his turn to speak, and then set herself to tackling the mountainous piles of paperwork overrunning her desk.

Dr. Grassi offered Armida some water. When she declined, he placed his elbows on his desk, clasped both of his hands together and rested his chin on his fists. Cutting to the chase he said, "When I asked you, signora Sigali, if I could help you, I was not speaking about your errand for Elsa Kolbe."

Without looking up from her work, Lara chastened him. "Start from the beginning, papa. She knows nothing."

"No, of course not," he apologized. "Forgive me."

Just then, an armed guard patrolling the neighborhood stopped outside the office window to peer in at them. Dr. Grassi saluted him with a slight, irritated nod, and mouthed, "We're fine . . . just fine. Grazie."

Lara acted as though she knew the soldier, rolling her eyes at him and brushing him away with a movement of her hands. Instead of moving on, he gazed in at Armida until he was distracted by Milo, wildly barking for his attention. He smiled, bent over to pet the dog, and with a tip of his cap went on his way.

"As I was saying," Dr. Grassi continued, "I asked if I could help you, signora, because I believe we may soon need each other's help. You see, we are both in unique situations here on Monte Isola. Like you, I am needed by both the Germans and the Fascists, but not trusted by either of them."

"How would *you* know what kind of position I am in?" she asked, suspicious.

The doctor looked surprised. "Everyone knows about everyone on the island, signora, and I—more than anyone else—know everything about everybody. Although," he added, rubbing his upper abdomen as though he had heart-burn, "I find it interesting that for some reason the Germans, though they trust no one, trust me to keep their secrets. Perhaps they think I'm too old to be a partisan; too feeble-minded to be a danger to them. And then . . . "

"Papa, for heaven's sake!" scolded Lara, scooping up some papers and tossing them into a small pot-bellied stove behind her desk. "Tell Armida what you know and how you know it!"

"Yes, very well then," Dr. Grassi cleared his throat. "Signora Sigali, surely you do not credit Chiara Carditi's apparent mental stability to her own strength of character? She came to me within forty-eight hours of her arrival on Monte Isola to ask me for tranquilizers to help her cope with her depression. But, before I could explain to her the process I must go through to prescribe medications to my non-German patients, and how long pharmaceuticals take to get here from headquarters in Salò, I was subjected to a sordid litany of reasons why she thought she needed to be medicated." He shook his head. "She is suicidal, you know."

Pensively, as though thinking of herself, Armida chewed on her lower lip.

"Your name was mentioned several times," the doctor added. "Signora Carditi is quite attached to you."

"Is that what she said?"

"In so many words."

"What else did she say?"

"She told me that her husband is quite attached to you as well."

Armida shifted positions, crossing her ankles and then wrapping her feet around one of the legs of the chair. "Did she tell you why?"

"They believe if the Allies win the war they can convince them they were American sympathizers because they kept you in their employment. They would expect you to corroborate their stories. You are their 'ace-in-the-whole.'"

"I don't understand why any of this concerns you, Dr. Grassi. I am well aware of the value the Carditi family places on me."

Leonardo leaned back in his chair, stroking the lower edge of his moustache. "Perhaps you are too familiar with Bruno Carditi to realize what a dangerous man he is. His son is even worse. And Commandant Kolbe? We won't even mention him. Sometimes those closest to us are the least understood."

"I didn't come here for you to analyze me," countered Armida.

"Do you imagine that Bruno and Alessandro's most recent, gullible conquests sleep well at night?" continued the doctor, unfazed by her growing discomfort. "Barely six weeks since their arrival, and I have already had visits from four different girls swearing they have been impregnated by either the father or the son."

Lara glanced up from her work, her mouth open as though she were going to say something, then thought better of it.

"Men talk, signora Sigali, and the women of Siviano are no different from women the world over." The doctor's eyes, magnified by his powerful spectacles, bored through her. "I know more about you, through them, than you could possibly imagine."

The blood drained from Armida's face. She hunched over, clutched her knees and began to rock back and forth in her chair.

"There, there!" the doctor exclaimed, taken aback by her reaction. He jumped up, rushing to her side, and placed his hand on her head, tenderly, stroking it with a kindness born of personal empathy.

"There, there," he repeated, until she finally shuddered to a halt. Lara, too, had come to Armida's side, and was gently rubbing her shoulders.

Gradually, Armida's tremors subsided until her breathing was no longer coming in shallow spurts and she was once again sitting up straight. "What did they tell you about me?"

"Nothing you don't already know," consoled the doctor, "I know you've threatened to kill yourself. I know you have a mentally ill sister who depends on you. I know Chiara suspects her husband has tried to bed you."

"Hurry, papa," said Lara, motioning toward the door, "before someone comes with the medication!"

"Armida," blurted the doctor, "I also know you have an American husband and children. Because of that, you are also a great liability to Bruno Carditi. What you must understand is that Bruno doesn't have the power in Lago d'Iseo that he had in Forte dei Marmi. Here, Werner Kolbe is in charge. Not only would the Germans—if they knew of your ties to America—have no use for you, they would have you executed immediately."

"I am sure you know that Alessandro despises you," he continued, his voice rushing with urgency. "But, even though he has other victims to hound, he brags that spying on his former nanny was the most satisfying assignment he ever had. You may have thought Alessandro's previous omnipresence in your life was a curse, but should the Germans get wind of your connection to America, you would gladly chain yourself to him for the protection it would afford you."

Armida's face clouded over. She slipped her hands beneath her armpits.

"Where is Alessandro now, signora?" asked Dr. Grassi.

Armida shrugged. "I don't know. He is on some assignment."

"You could say that. Alessandro Carditi is up to no good. The Brigate Nere is made up of hundreds just like him . . . criminals who enjoy torturing and killing innocent people."

"What my father is trying to say," Lara interjected, "is that Alessandro is no longer watching over you as he once was. The Carditis are gambling with your life."

Armida shrugged again. This was not news to her.

"It is not a good sign," continued Lara soberly. "It means you are no longer as valuable to them as you once were. Bruno Carditi is an opportunist. He realizes that he is subordinate to Werner Kolbe, so he will do anything to save his own neck, including letting go of his obsession with you, if it means that your American connections could *cost* him his life rather than save it. Believe me, signore Carditi does not have the courage to stand up to the Nazis at this stage of the game. The coward would betray his own mother, perhaps even his own wife and son, to assure his survival."

"Do you know where that leaves you, signora?" asked Dr. Grassi.

"It leaves you vulnerable; completely unprotected," said Lara, not waiting for Armida to answer.

Dr. Grassi nodded in affirmation. "Of all the poor souls on this island, your life is by far the most at risk."

"Why do you care about *me?*" mumbled Armida. "I don't understand."

Dr. Grassi raised himself to his full height. "I am the doctor of this island," he declared, "and I take personal responsibility for the health and welfare of every person on Monte Isola."

"That's it?"

"What do you mean, 'that's it?'"

In her entire adult life, Armida could not recall anyone offering her something for nothing. The concept was inconceivable. After all, everyone had their conditions. The only people who had truly shown her respect in Italy, who had come close to penetrating the walls she had built around herself, were Carilda and her daughters. She really could not comprehend what it was Dr. Grassi was suggesting.

"Signora Sigali," said Leonardo, searching for the right words. "By virtue of simply being on this island, you are now my patient, whether you view yourself as such or not. It is as simple as that."

"I have learned to trust no one, Dr. Grassi. There is always something people want from me in return. You said earlier that we may need each other's help. What is the catch?"

Puzzled, the doctor and his daughter looked at each other for a moment before Lara ventured, "It is wise that you trust no one, Armida, but truly, we expect nothing from you but what help you feely give us."

"Which is . . . ?"

Dr. Grassi poured himself another glass of water, while Lara explained. "Winter will be upon us soon. Many believe it will be an unusually cold one. Already, we have experienced a shortage of food on the island because of the war. It will only get worse." She paused and glanced at her father again, who nodded for her to continue.

"There are spies everywhere, as I am sure you are aware. Many of our own people in Siviano are partisans. We know who most of them are. Unfortunately, we also know what the Germans have done to villages that shelter the Resistance." Lara gulped, her voice sounding suddenly hoarse. "Werner

Kolbe's reputation for revenge has preceded him here."

Lara shook her head in affirmation.

"You see, child," the doctor interjected, "I believe that those in Siviano who survive the winter will face even greater hardships in the spring. I have no doubt that once the snow begins to thaw in the mountains, the Allies will sweep through Milan and make their way here to the lakes. Salò is their goal. This is the last hope for Mussolini and the Germans, so you know they will not give up without a fight to the death."

"It will be a bloodbath," whispered Lara.

"Yes," agreed the doctor. "A bloodbath it will be."

He put his hands behind his back, walked to the window and set his gaze out onto the lake. For all practical purposes, it could have been any autumn day of any other year in Monte Isola's recent history. Sailboats skipped across white-capped waves. A score of small fishing vessels, their famously knit nets only half-full of fish, set their bows for home. Old women shuffled along the bay in tight clusters, clutching their baskets filled with the catch of the day, engaging in the latest village gossip, while carefree children played in the little grassy park adjacent to the docks. Rows and rows of sardines, drizzled with oil and wine, lay out to dry in the sun along the perimeter of the park nearest the beach. The soldier who had peeked in at them earlier strolled along the water's edge, talking earnestly to a pretty, shy young girl in a bright, floral dress. Skulking near the piers, a gang of teenage boys huffed on cigarettes as they jeered menacingly at passers-by. Dr. Grassi knew them all. In fact, in his lifetime, the doctor had brought many of them into the world and buried many of their loved ones.

With the wisdom of a physician and the insight of a

prophet, Dr. Grassi knew who would be living a year from now and who would not. He knew that Mario, the grizzly owner of Siviano's largest fishing boat, would be dead of lung cancer before Christmas. He knew that the languid soldier talking the ear off the young Siviano maiden would never see the blossoms of next year's lemon trees. He knew that at least three of the six pubescent boys mocking the smitten soldier behind his back as he walked by them would disappear forever, never to be heard from again. And as sure as he knew that the sun would set that evening, he knew his own fate.

Dr. Grassi turned from the window. "Many people here have chosen their fates already, signora Sigali. Those who have cast their lots with the partisans are well aware of the price they will pay for their rebellion—as well as those who have sided with the Fascists, of course. It is, after all, civil war. You are different, signora. We know that you were coerced into coming here. It grieves me to think that you are caught in the middle of this mess."

Lara agreed. "We know where to hide, who to go to for help and how to fight the enemy among us, but you know nothing of Monte Isola. You are helpless."

"When the time comes," her father continued, "you must know that we will be here to help you."

Still unconvinced, Armida insisted there must be an ulterior motive. "What do you expect from me in return, dottore?" she demanded.

"Just tell us what you hear and see at the villa."

"You want me to *spy* for you!" Armida's voice cracked. "I thought you were concerned for my welfare."

"You would not be spying for *me*!" rebuked the doctor, cautioning Armida to lower her voice. "I do not need spies to know what the future holds for me."

He led her to the window and pointed to the children playing in the park and the old women who were now approaching his office. "You would be helping others, like those children who could be innocent victims in the days ahead, and those defenseless, old women. They certainly won't survive unless they have ample warning."

Before Armida could answer, the office door was flung open by Nurse Mueller. Glaring suspiciously at the trio, she announced that she had just received Elsa Kolbe's medication.

"*And*, Dr. Grassi," she fumed, "I cannot find an interpreter. I suggest you find one yourself."

Ignoring her, the doctor mumbled something under his breath before reaching out to shake Armida's hand. "It was pleasant chatting with you, signora Sigali. Now, please excuse us. I trust in time, under my care, your condition will improve. You will have to follow my instructions very carefully, however, if we are to see any progress."

Armida held his hand limply, a blank look on her face.

The doctor instructed Nurse Mueller to give Elsa's medication to Armida. Grudgingly, the nurse complied. Addressing his daughter, the doctor continued, "Lara, please make an appointment with signora Sigali before she leaves. I would like to see her regularly. Once a week."

"Yes, papa."

Dr. Leonardo Grassi cast a final, disparaging look at the nurse before stuffing some papers into his already bulging pockets. "You first, fräulein," he announced curtly, bowing his head and holding his hand out for her to go before him. Glowering, Nurse Mueller turned on her heels and stormed out of the room.

Before following her out, the doctor delivered one last instruction to his daughter. "Lara, I think Sundays would work best. Servants need a Sabbath, no? Have the signora meet us here early next Sunday. We will escort her to Mass. It is important for her mental health that she has more socialization. If there is a problem, I will have Dr. Schroeder speak with Herr Kolbe."

"Yes, papa."

Taking a piece of letterhead from her father's desk drawer, Lara quickly typed a brief note specifying that Armida was to spend each Sunday under the care of Dr. Grassi. She placed it in an envelope, scribbled Werner Kolbe's name on it and handed it to Armida to give to the commandant.

Armida hesitated before taking it. "What if I don't want to spend Sundays with you and your father?" she said.

Lara placed the envelope in Armida's hand and closed her fingers over it. "Trust me. You will."

chapter twenty-nine

GIVEN THE FACT that Armida's calloused overlords continued taking advantage of her, it was no small wonder that Sundays soon became her favorite day of the week. Armida owed her one and only day of emancipation to Dr. Schroeder, who intervened on Dr. Grassi's behalf and convinced Herr Kolbe that without a regular reprieve, she would surely suffer a nervous breakdown.

"What?" shrieked Elsa when she discovered Armida would not be at her disposal on Sundays any longer. "I can't be expected to do the cooking and cleaning!"

"You'll have to make do," Werner replied. "Either that or find a replacement."

"There are no replacements in this barbarous hole. Besides, no one else can cook like Armida. We simply can't let her have a day off."

"Dr. Schroeder said if she doesn't get at least one day of rest per week, exhaustion will render her incapable of performing any duties at all."

"Fine for Dr. Schroeder to say! What did you tell him?"

"I told him I'd agree to the arrangement as long as Armida prepared our Sunday meals in advance before she leaves in the morning."

"Did you tell him we expect to see an improvement in her

attitude as well? The woman carries herself like a baroness instead of the nobody that she is."

"He said weekly supervised retreats with Dr. Grassi will ultimately improve her disposition. 'If you gain a house-keeper who can produce more work in six days than she could in seven,' he said, 'and be a pleasant servant as well, you will find this arrangement to be more than profitable.' I have to take him at his word."

Werner hedged, as though hesitant to tell Elsa one last thing. "Dr. Schroeder also said the wife of Prince Borghese has heard of Armida's cooking and was asking him questions about her. He believes if she could, she would like to hire her as their cook."

Elsa gasped in disbelief.

"So, you see, Elsa, we have no choice if we want to keep Armida."

And so a new Sunday ritual began whereby Armida would leave the villa before dawn—while her wardens were yet sound asleep—and make her way down to Leonardo and Lara's apartment, situated above the doctor's office. Weather permitting, it was a brisk ten-minute walk. Most women would refuse to venture out at such a forbidding hour, but Armida burst forth from her imprisonment like a captive schoolgirl embarking on a long-awaited holiday. Anyone along her route unfortunate enough to be up at that hour could testify that Armida walked by with a bounce in her step, sometimes humming to herself, almost always pausing to inhale the pungent scents released by the nocturnal stir-rings of Lago d'Iseo wafting through Siviano's damp, vapor-ous lanes.

For her, at first, it was a day of denial; a day she put everything out of her mind but freedom. By the time she arrived at the Grassis' she was drunk with it. No Carditis to bully her, no high-handed insults from the Kolbes. Lara Grassi would customarily greet her with a cup of espresso, seating Armida at a table on a tiny wrought iron balcony overlooking the lake, where together they would savor the sunrise over the mountains and indulge in the simple, ancient pleasures of conversation.

Absent from these early Sunday morning routines was Leonardo, who typically slept like a baby in his bedroom awaiting the assigned poking and prodding of his daughter when she deemed it was time for him to wake up and get ready for church. As the only physician in Siviano, the luxury of sleeping in eluded him, except on Sunday mornings, when somehow, inexplicably, the typical urgent demands of his profession vanished. Emergencies stalled. Babies waiting to be born mysteriously delayed their arrival. Sickness and death were held at bay by an invisible hand, in effect giving the selfless doctor one night of blessed, uninterrupted sleep before rising to escort Lara and Armida to church. The miraculous cessation of medical crises most Sunday mornings was truly remarkable, and according to his devoted patients, an indisputable sign of God's personal favor toward their beloved doctor, bestowed on him for no other purpose than to prepare him for another week of sleepless nights.

Sunday or not, for Armida Sigali the Grassi residence was a refuge from the probing eyes and loose tongues of Siviano's gossips, a sanctuary of peace, a magical place where friends never left quite the same as they came. It didn't happen overnight, but over the course of several weeks—like a slab of marble—she succumbed to an invisible mallet. Her rough edges were sanded smooth by hours spent in an atmosphere of acceptance, by the many acts of kindness extended to her by the Grassis and by the long intimate conversations she had with Lara.

Then, one Sunday morning in early November, Armida arrived in a more somber mood.

"Ironic, isn't it?" observed Lara, over espresso and pane crostini on the balcony, after Armida confessed she had abandoned her children in America. "Why do we hurt the very ones who love us the most?"

"It was like I was a different person," Armida replied, tugging her knit cap down over her ears. "I turned on my children because I wanted to hurt Egisto, even though Egisto swore he loved me and no one else. Why wouldn't I believe him?"

"Because you couldn't believe anyone could really love you." Lara placed her hand over Armida's. "Not even your children."

Unable to speak, Armida nodded.

"Perhaps you thought you were unlovable because you failed other people's expectations of you. If so, you were wrong. People *can* love unconditionally, Armida. Look at children; they love their parents unconditionally."

Armida got up from the table and leaned over the balcony. "I've made a mess of my life, Lara. I've burned too many bridges." She tossed some breadcrumbs over the railing to a noisy throng of pigeons clamoring for food in the street below. "What's the use? It's too late. I was so hateful to Silverio and Violenza. They will never forgive me."

"Don't *expect* them to forgive you," cautioned Lara. "Expectations often end in disappointment. Take your children as they are, whether they've forgiven you or not. Forgiveness will come at the right time for them."

Armida stared at the greedy birds fighting over the crumbs in the street. She brushed crumbs off her jacket and then raised her gaze to the iridescent lake unveiling its gold-tinged face to her. The soft, rhythmical lapping of waves on the pebble beach butting up to the street below did little to soothe her conscience.

"I can't expect you to understand, Lara." she mumbled. "I *abandoned* them. What kind of mother abandons her own children?"

"A mother who is sick. A mother who isn't thinking correctly."

"They will never forgive me," Armida repeated, squinting as she shielded her eyes from the sun's reflection off the water. "And I don't blame them."

"When God forgives us, we find forgiveness for ourselves."

"Ooofff!" Armida vibrated her lips together and then bit them hard to keep from saying things she would regret. Self-loathing rose like bile in her throat. *Fine for Lara to counsel me on what I should, or shouldn't do. What does she know of hate, shame, suicidal urges and all the wicked thoughts that have consumed my life? She's like Carilda and Bianca; too sweet and trusting to understand.*

Undaunted, Lara picked up their dirty plates and cups, and pausing before going into the house to wake up her father, she said, "No one knows who a person really is inside. Even we don't know ourselves sometimes. But God does. So don't worry so much about the past. You are a new person now and we will just pray that after the war the new Armida Sigali will prove that the old Armida Sigali no longer exists."

Something that Lara said hit Armida. *You are a new*

person . . . the old Armida Sigali no longer exists. She repeated it to herself over and over again as she helped Lara do the dishes. *I am a new person . . . the old me no longer exists.*

"I've never thought of it that way," she ventured, when they were done with dishes. "That I really could say good-bye to the old me. Maybe there's hope after all."

Lara pulled Armida into the foyer and handed her a wool scarf to put around her neck. "Of course you can leave the old you behind, Armida. I've done it. We all can."

"Really? Like what?"

"My mother died in childbirth when I was ten years old. Even though her labor was premature, unexpected, papa blamed himself. He'd been out delivering another woman's baby in the village at the time. I was home with mama and was terrified by her screams; by all the blood and the pain she was in. I left her to get papa—I was only gone a half-hour at the most—but when we got back she was cold as ice, her dead eyes staring at the door as though she'd been expecting us to walk in and save her at any moment. The baby, a girl, was dead as well."

"I blamed the mother in the village for mama's death. I blamed papa. I had believed he could do anything . . . save anybody. When he failed to save his own wife and child, I lost respect for him. We grew apart. We might as well have lived on different continents, we had so little to do with each other. Bitterness had become such a part of my identity, people here in Siviano called me la Limone, *The Lemon*."

"I can't imagine," said Armida. "You're nothing like that now and you're so close to your father."

"My point, exactly." Lara grinned. "One day signora Fuma-galli—the woman who comes to our Sunday meals—said to me, 'Lara, you're a grown woman now. You are no longer a child. Do you really want to become what people are calling you? A lemon? You will, you know, if you don't forgive your papa and everyone else you blame for your mama's death.'"

"Is that what you did? But, how?"

"I took to heart what she said—because I knew it was true—and started by forgiving God. He was the one I blamed the most. From there, I continued forgiving people as they came to my mind until finally one day I woke up and realized the sky was bluer than I had remembered, the flowers brighter, and my papa was my hero again. Do you know what signora Fumagalli said about you the other day, Armida?"

Armida knotted her scarf and tucked the loose ends into her jacket. "What?"

"She said, 'Armida reminds me of you when you were younger, Lara. She's starting to change like you did, too. I see it in the softness of her eyes and the way she takes more time with people. Little things. She's finally learning forgiveness, isn't she?'"

"She really said that?"

"Yes."

A lump in her throat caused Armida to swallow hard. *I'm trying to forgive. It's hard, but I'm trying. Maybe there's still hope for me after all.*

As Lara, Dr. Grassi, and Armida left the apartment to begin their arduous climb up the steep hill to the Sanctuary of the Madonna della Ceriola, Lara silently prayed for Armida. Traversing ancient olive orchards and vineyards, Dr. Grassi saved his prayers for Mass, recounting instead the very latest news of the war with theatrical flair, waving his walking stick as though it were a shepherd's staff.

Armida—worried sick about her sister, Argene—was a rapt audience.

"Have you heard any news from Monte di Ripa, doctor?" she asked.

"I don't know about your town," he sighed, wiping his brow with the back of his sleeve, even though it was still chilly. "But, I heard there was a terrible battle in Massa. It is close to Ripa, no? To my knowledge the entire area was bombed until almost nothing was left. I was told that only those who escaped before the bombing, survived."

When Armida pressed for more information, Lara said, "We heard that many people from your area fled to Valdicastello and Sant'Anna. The Germans accused the residents of Sant'Anna of harboring partisans. It was rumored that—as an example to others—they herded every person in the village into the church and killed them all: men, women, and children."

Both Lara and her father stopped and crossed themselves. "We do not doubt the truth of this report," Lara added. "It has happened in other villages near us!"

"What about Valdicastello?" Armida stepped gingerly around a flock of goats blocking their path. She knew Valdicastello would be the nearest city of refuge for those, like Argene, fleeing the bombing in Ripa.

"When the Germans left Sant'Anna, they descended on Valdicastello. That is all we know."

Prudently, Dr. Grassi changed the subject. "You appear to be a very healthy woman, signora. Nonetheless, as your doctor I feel I should ask you if you are having any physical problems."

"I'm fine."

Armida was, he could see, a healthy woman: not too thin, nor fat, never sick, and almost always robust and rosy-cheeked. She was remarkably young-looking, notwithstanding her age. There was not a hint of gray in her lustrous, black hair and the few wrinkles that had developed around her eyes were nearly imperceptible, appearing only when she smiled broadly, which was not often.

Leonardo ignored Armida's response and questioned her further, asking her how much fish she currently consumed in her diet and what her consumption of fish had been during her years in America. Surprised by his question, she admitted that while in Minnesota, her appetite for it had been impossible to satisfy.

Eagerly, he explained evolving medical theories regarding the thyroid gland and its influence on the human mind. More studies were verifying the link between thyroid disease and mental disorders. Inadequate iodine intake was thought to be a major culprit.

"Why are you telling *me* this?" she asked.

The doctor reddened, realizing he had betrayed a confidence. "Oh," he replied, "I seem to recall someone telling me that you suffered an episode of . . . distress . . . long ago, when you lived in America. I just thought you might be interested, that's all."

Armida shot an accusatory look in Lara's direction.

Oddly enough, Armida was not embarrassed or ashamed that the doctor knew of her mental history. At least, not like she once might have been. His subtle hints were nothing more than an awkward attempt to dispel any fears he thought Armida might harbor of having another nervous breakdown. Little did Dr. Grassi know how much his clumsy charm endeared him to her. Still, she feared that by reaching out to her Lara and Leonardo were putting their own lives at stake. The more they knew about her the more incriminating it could be for them.

"Well, child," shrugged the doctor. "Whatever iodine deficiencies you may have had in the past, you obviously do not have them now."

Arriving finally at the Sanctuary, the tired pilgrims were rewarded with a spectacular morning sky, a panoramic view of the lake, and a lively reception by the other islanders who had made the exhilarating hike up the mountain. Having long ago hardened her heart to religion, it surprised Armida that it now stimulated her like nothing else she had ever experienced. She sat transfixed through the long service, understanding little, and yet deep within her it stirred a well that had long ago been sealed up. She felt an alien sweetness invade her, as though she were a cup being filled with honey to overflowing.

I am a new person . . . the old me no longer exists.

A WEEKLY ROUTINE developed whereby, following Mass each Sunday, Armida would return to the village with the Grassis and several others invited to share a meal with them. Initially, Leonardo and Lara had a difficult time persuading anyone to their Sabbath dinners. Armida was a marked woman. Probably a Nazi sympathizer, a traitor, even a spy, said some. Eventually, however, the old, the poor, and the feeble-minded began accepting the Grassis' dinner invitations, which was fine as far as Lara and Leonardo were concerned. In Lara's own words, it was just too bad that the others could not overcome their prejudices to befriend a woman like Armida.

Each Sunday meal began the same way. Without fail, no sooner would they all sit down at the table to eat, but the dire supplications would begin. Telephone calls, frantic knocks at the door, desperate cries from the street.

"*Dottore! The baby is coming. Hurry!*"

"*Dottore! My husband needs you—his heart!*"

"*Dottore! Come quickly! Mama fell and can't get up!*"

Washing one or two bites of food down with a gulp of wine, the doctor would gallantly excuse himself, grabbing his overcoat and hat before racing out the door to answer the summons. Subsequently, Lara would excuse herself as well, announcing she must help her father.

"Oh! Armida," she would say as an afterthought. "Would you be a dear and please take over until I return? We can't leave our friends without a host."

Of course, Armida was used to serving and following instructions, not hosting or entertaining. But, because she had no other choice, she did as she was asked and as a result, she soon became conscious of another radical change within herself. The hours she spent directing Sunday afternoon conversations and activities in the Grassis' absence began to restore her self-confidence in ways she hadn't thought possible. It forced her to interact with strangers and perceive the needs of others. It also rekindled that lost sense of nurturing she had once experienced with her own children.

By early December, Lara was complimenting Armida on her progress. "Why, you're a *natural*, Armida!" she gushed. "After this war is over, I imagine you'll open up your own business. What will it be? A café . . . a bakery, a tailor shop?"

Blushing, Armida replied, "A dress shop. I would like that. Perhaps Carilda Bertozzi and I could go into business together. She is a great seamstress. So is her daughter, Bianca."

"You will go back to Ripa then, when the war is over?" A shadow passed over Lara's face.

"Argene is there. I must find her and then . . . " Armida stopped in mid-sentence and looked away. *I am a new person . . . the old me no longer exists.*

"We'll see," she said.

chapter thirty

❧

THERE ARE FACTORS that can affect the outcome of a war which are beyond anyone's control. The weather is one of them.

The winter of 1944–45 turned out to be one of the coldest on record. It roared into Lombardy from Switzerland late one Monday night in early December, following a particularly mild weekend, and remained solidly locked over the mountains, with no breaks, through March. Food shortages ensued, ravaging the flailing Salò Republic. Monte Isola's hunters scoured the frozen countryside for anything that moved, coming back empty-handed most of the time. Then the entire province ran out of salt, further weakening those already plagued by hunger. Christmas that year was celebrated with tightfisted meagerness and great trepidation.

That's what the locals told Danilo and me; the ones that survived and could still remember. They were tight-lipped with us, but some of them did say they had seen Armida on Christmas Day, helping Dr. Grassi distribute what little food he had to share with others. And by the end of January, when the island's supply of dry wood was depleted—forcing residents to burn anything ignitable to keep warm—they said they saw Armida and Lara Grassi going around to the houses of the old *and the poor, giving them blankets, or burlap sacks and old rugs, to keep them warm.*

Villagers also told us that the Germans, reeling from military losses on the western front, tightened their grip on the Republic of Salò in a last ditch effort to withstand the Allied juggernaut advancing from breaks in the Gothic Line to the south. On public buildings throughout the region notices were posted, spelling out the penalties for breaking curfew, aiding partisans, or for even removing the notices. All offenses were punishable by death.

For every German soldier killed or wounded by partisans, ten civilians selected at random were executed, their bodies left to hang in the piazza, or public square, for twelve hours afterward, as a deterrent to others. Rastrellamenti—unannounced sting operations in which Italians were snatched from their homes or businesses and shipped to Germany where they were press-ganged into forced labor—were intensified. Local partisan bands grew bolder and more savage, their ranks swelling with Communists and Allied agents and partisans from Italy's newly liberated south.

In short, we were told, by the spring of 1945 there was nowhere on earth as volatile and ripe for slaughter as the pristine mountain lakes of the Italian Socialist Republic.

❧

ARMIDA SIGALI FOUND herself becoming more dependent on the goodwill extended to her by the Grassis each Sunday. Tramping through crusty snowdrifts, biting winds burning her exposed skin, she found sustenance and consolation in their home, where they lavished her with love and acceptance. Never once did they ask her to reveal anything she witnessed or overheard at the villa. The realization that they accepted her unconditionally, in the face of such danger and such prejudice from the local townspeople, empowered her to face the long hours of grinding servitude and abuse at the hands of Bruno and Werner.

One early Sunday morning in late February, Lara Grassi opened the door of her apartment in response to Armida's knock. She immediately noticed something was terribly wrong. Shrouded in a moth-eaten blanket wound tightly about herself like an Egyptian mummy, Armida refused to enter when Lara invited her in.

"What is it? What's wrong?" asked Lara, alarmed.

Shivering uncontrollably, Armida said nothing. Her face was a shadow, buried deep within the folds of the blanket.

Lara placed her arm on the small of Armida's back and tried to maneuver her inside, but Armida would go no further than the darkened entryway, pushing against Lara so hard in protest that Lara finally gave up and pulled a chair into the hall, instructing Armida to sit down in it. Milo, aroused from his canine throne near the warm hearth in the sitting room, stretched and peeked around the corner. He growled at the strange intruder until Lara rebuked him.

"Stop it, Milo. Can't you see it's Armida?"

Returning to the kitchen, Lara lifted a small kerosene lamp from the counter, lit it, and held it up so that its penetrating glow illuminated the hallway. Armida recoiled, one hand shooting up to shield her face from the light. As she did, Lara noticed that her flaccid fingers were a sickening grey-green color, like the leaves of a geranium after a hard frost. Setting the lamp back down on the counter, Lara ran into the sitting room, grabbed a towel hanging near the wood-stove to dry and rushed back to massage Armida's hands.

"You are an angel, Lara," Armida whispered. "You still have wood to burn, eh?"

Vigorously, Lara rubbed Armida's ice-cold fingers. "Papa receives wood and food these days for pay, although I don't dare ask where his patients get it. I only pray they are not going without themselves." She stopped and stared hard at Armida, whose face—except for one, steely blue eye—was still completely covered by the blanket.

"Come near the fire," she ordered. "You may have frostbite!"

Reluctantly, Armida let Lara lead her into the sitting room where she pulled up a stool and lifted Armida's feet onto it, close to the woodstove. She took off Armida's shoes and then cautiously placed her hand on the edge of the blanket near her friend's face, gently pulling it away.

"My God!" Lara gasped in horror. "What happened to you?"

Milo tucked his tail between his legs, lowered his head, and let out a mournful howl. The right side of Armida's face was nearly unrecognizable. Her eye was swollen shut completely. Dried blood coursed a scarlet trail from her nose, along her mouth, and down onto her neck. A deep, oozing gash extended from the top of her cheekbone to the front of her ear and the blood from it was caked onto her hair, which lay matted flat against the side of her head.

Livid, Lara raced back to the kitchen, where she began wetting some cloths to make a poultice. "*Papa!* Come quick!" she shouted. "*Hurry!*"

Wide-eyed and disheveled, his bathrobe knotted loosely about his thick belly and his glasses half on his nose and half off, Dr. Grassi flew out of his bedroom. From the tone of his daughter's voice, he assumed their home was being raided and half-expected to find himself facing a firing squad. He blinked several times, adjusted his glasses, surveyed the room, and looked quizzically at Lara who was frantically assembling the poultice and wiping tears from her cheeks at the same time.

She nodded toward Armida. *Go, look at her,* her eyes said.

The doctor tip-toed into the sitting room. When he saw her disfigured face, he moaned, "God in Heaven! Lara, bring me those towels, quickly! And another blanket! And bring me the iodine!"

"Monsters!" he fumed, examining Armida closely. "Does it hurt here?" he asked, gently touching first her shoulder and then running his trained hands down her forearm, wrist and fingers.

Armida cried out.

"Hmm. How about here?" he asked, feeling along her spine.

She winced, but shook her head "no."

"Well," said Leonardo, relieved. "It doesn't appear anything is broken."

"Who did this to you?" pleaded Lara, daubing Armida's cuts and bruises. "Please, you must tell us what happened."

Wincing in pain, with great effort, Armida reached into the pocket of her jacket and withdrew a small pouch made of crimson velvet tied shut with a gold braided drawstring.

"It all started yesterday . . . with this," she said cryptically, mouthing the words with difficulty through her swollen lips. She tried to untie the pouch herself, but was too weak. Leonardo reached down and opened it for her. Inside the bag was a small crystal vial.

"Give it to me," said Armida, holding up the bruised palm of her left hand.

The doctor did as she asked, taking great care to help her curl her fingers around it. She held on to it as if it were a sacred relic guaranteeing its owner unmitigated healing and wholeness. "Inside are three seeds. . . ancient seeds from Franciacorta!" she whispered.

Lara and her father gaped at her in disbelief. *Grape seeds? From Franciacorta? How in the world had she come into the possession of such treasures?*

chapter thirty-one

AFTER WASHING AND bandaging Armida's face, making sure her extremities were free of frostbite, and forcing some more hot tea down her throat, the Grassis pulled two chairs up close to her and listened attentively as she explained the events leading up to the present.

"Yesterday morning," she began, "as I was serving breakfast at the villa, Elsa complained of having cabin fever and insisted Herr Kolbe take her away for a change of scenery. Bruno was home, so of course Chiara decided that she would also go crazy if Bruno did not take *her* somewhere as well. Werner, in a foul mood and desperate to appease Elsa, had originally planned to travel to Salò on Monday for some business, but decided to take Elsa and go yesterday instead, asking Bruno if there was somewhere between here and Lago Garda that she might find entertaining. Usually, Herr Kolbe does not consult with Bruno on anything. It would be beneath him, you know."

The Grassis bobbed their heads in agreement.

"Knowing full well that Werner loves wine, Bruno began bragging about the vineyards and wineries of Franciacorta, making himself indispensable by offering to go with them as a translator and expert on Italian wines. I assumed I would stay at the villa. Saturdays, as you know, are my busiest days because I have to have everything prepared in advance for them so I can spend my Sundays here."

A gurgling, slurping sound, like waves splashing gently over river stones, had crept into Armida's speech. She paused, swallowing the abundance of saliva pooled along the bottom and sides of her mouth, before pressing on.

"Bruno was adamant that I come along. When Werner asked him why it was necessary for me to accompany them, I was terrified that Bruno would admit he didn't trust me not to run away if I was left alone. Then the truth would come out about my children in America! But instead, Bruno said—half-jokingly—that they might need me to drive them home in the event they over-indulged in wine-tasting. Werner thought it a perfectly sensible idea and ordered me to get ready for the trip. What could I say? I do not dare cross Herr Kolbe!"

"Of course not!" exclaimed Lara.

"Never!" said the doctor.

"First we went to Salò," she continued. "The women went shopping while Bruno caroused with some friends and Werner met with some of his fellow officers. I was expected to carry all of the purchases for Chiara and Elsa."

"Bah!" Dr. Grassi slapped his hands on his knees. "People are starving and these inane women go *shopping?*"

"I saw Mussolini, himself," said Armida, ignoring the doctor's barb. "We saw him getting into a limousine with a woman. I am sure it was his mistress, not his wife. I could not believe my eyes."

The doctor and his daughter nearly choked on their tea. Though they despised what Mussolini had done to their country, he was, nevertheless, a national legend whom they could not imagine seeing in the flesh.

Armida looked up at the ceiling trying to recall where she was in her story. "Oh yes. Chiara, Elsa and I had just stepped out of a tailor's shop when we saw him. Chiara fell all over herself, as though she was fourteen instead of forty. She must have thought she had died and gone to heaven! Elsa, however, couldn't have cared less, although if it had been Hitler she would have behaved shamelessly. Chiara considered running over to him to get his autograph, but was too shocked and intimidated to move. She pulled a piece of paper and pen out of her purse and told me to go over and get his autograph for her. How could I? I was carrying all of their boxes, and since she wouldn't lower herself to take them from me, we just stood there and watched the limousine disappear. The truth be told, the Duce looked very old and haggard, nothing at all like I imagined him to be, although Chiara thought him still a handsome man. A short time later, after eating dinner, we drove back through Franciacorta. It was starting to get dark, but the roads were clear and Bruno assured Herr Kolbe that it was not too late to visit any winery he desired. After haggling over where to go, we ended up at the Cavalleri estate near Erbusco. That's when the trouble began."

Armida paused to drink the rest of her tea. It was a laborious process, recounting her story to the Grassis, what with her lips feeling so numb and some of her teeth loose, but as long as they were willing to bear with her, she was game to tell them everything, even if it took all day.

"Bruno," she finally continued, "bullied his way into the Cavalleri's foyer. At first their servant argued with him that he would not interrupt signore Cavalleri while he was dining, but when he saw Herr Kolbe get out of the car in his SS uniform, the blood rushed from his face and he immediately went into the dining room to announce our arrival.

Moments later, signore Cavalleri came out to greet us. It was very awkward, as you can imagine. Bruno made a fool of himself, throwing his inflated Fascist ego around. He introduced Herr Kolbe as though he were Caesar himself and commanded signore Cavalleri to give them a tour of his private wine cellar. Elsa began asking many stupid questions even a kindergartner would know, like: 'Do red grapes make red wine, and green grapes make white wine, signore Cavalleri?'"

Leonardo and Lara looked at each other and rolled their eyes.

"Werner was mortified and irritated with her, but clearly enamored with the Cavalleri's estate. Bruno played the expert, constantly interrupting and correcting signore Cavalleri as he was explaining his winemaking techniques. And Chiara, well she noted that the signore appreciated Elsa's beauty and competed for his attention by openly flirting with him.

"Eventually, we were escorted downstairs into a massive stone cellar with low arched ceilings and long, narrow rows of wine lining the walls. One of the maids—her name was Mariesole—gathered some chairs around a table beneath a beautiful crystal chandelier at the far end of the room. Of course, it was expected that the signore would freely offer Werner and Bruno his best wine, so while he proceeded to open a bottle, he instructed Mariesole to go upstairs to the kitchen and prepare some food, ordering me to go with her so that she would be sure to prepare some dishes that would please Werner."

Barely skipping a beat, Armida blurted, "You would not believe who Mariesole was! An Italian-American! From Chicago! She told me she was worried Bruno and Werner might detect her American accent, but I assured her they would not."

"Why is she here in Italy," asked Lara, "and not America?"

"She married an Italian longshoreman. They moved back here shortly before the war began. Not long afterwards, he was conscripted into the army but died in the Russian campaign. The Cavalleris, who knew Mariesole's parents, took her in after she was widowed. She told me that signore Cavalleri is a great man, a man of integrity and honor, but even so, like us, he is at the mercy of the Germans."

Armida picked up speed, her words tumbling over each other. "I told Mariesole I had children in Minnesota and I told her about Egisto. We talked as long as we dared about our fear of our American connections being discovered, and then we returned to the wine cellar. Although we had been gone only fifteen or twenty minutes, Elsa had already had too much to drink. She and Chiara were still vying for signore Cavalleri's attention."

"He must be a handsome man," observed Lara. "Were Bruno or Werner jealous?"

"At first I thought Werner might be jealous, but then I realized he is too deceived by his own importance to believe that another man's charm could eclipse his own. But you are correct about Bruno; he must be the center of attention at all times. He began to pout and to drink more, and the more he drank the uglier and more belligerent he became. Herr Kolbe, on the other hand, sat calmly in his chair, detached, sampling glass after glass of wine, observing everything as though he were watching a movie. All the while, signore Cavalleri was forced to oblige Bruno's demands to open even more bottles of wine and soon all of them were drunk.

"Then, out of the blue, Bruno asked signore Cavalleri if he had any grape seeds from the ancient days. 'Come now!' he yelled, when the signore hesitated. 'I know you have some. This is Franciacorta! I know history!'"

"The signore replied, 'You are a well-informed connoisseur, indeed.' He turned to Mariesole and instructed her to give his guests whatever they asked for. 'Our seeds are museum quality artifacts and highly valued, as you well know,' he said, 'and therefore they are under lock and key. I will be back in a moment.'"

"After signore Cavalleri excused himself, Herr Kolbe told Bruno he wanted the seeds to take back to Germany with him after the war. Bruno exploded. 'Italian seeds stay in Italy!' he shouted. 'You can take wine back home with you, but the seeds stay here!' I saw Werner's eyes narrow and the corner of his mouth twitch. 'I will take what I want, when I want it,' he growled."

"How did Chiara and Elsa react?" asked Lara.

"They each took up their husband's cause as though the war were being fought in Cavalleri's cellar. Bruno would have leaped over the table and strangled Werner if signore Cavalleri had not returned holding a scarlet pouch with the crystal vial inside it containing these three seeds."

Reverently, Armida stroked the clear glass vial she still cradled in her hands.

"When the signore realized that one way or another he was going to have to part with his seeds, he ventured a solution. 'Shall we make a wager?' he asked. Everyone thought it a great idea and ordered Mariesole to bring them a deck of cards. 'Everyone must play,' the signore teased, exempting himself and Marie. 'It is a special Franciacorta game. I will teach you.' Bruno and Werner looked at me; I did not know what to say. I do not gamble or play cards, so I am sure they assumed it would be harmless, not to mention humorous, to add me to the game.

"We played cards for well over an hour," she continued. "With each passing round they got more inebriated until the Carditis and Kolbes were in a stupor. When the last card was played, signore Cavalleri announced that I had won! He handed the purse to me, and kissing me as he did, he whispered in my ear, 'Hide these in a safe place. They may buy your freedom.'

"Bruno yelled, 'Impossible!' and tackled signore Cavalleri from behind, throwing him against the wall. Werner, in turn, knocked the table over and attacked Bruno, shouting, 'Cheating Italian bastard!' All of the pent-up hatred between them was unleashed in poor signore Cavalleri's wine cellar! Finally, the signore went upstairs and came back down with a cold bucket of water, throwing it over them like they were two dogs fighting over a piece of meat. Bruno and Werner were so drunk, and so exhausted from fighting, they didn't know what happened to them, and signore Cavalleri—realizing they were incapable of retaliating—commanded them to vacate his house."

Armida smiled at the irony. "Chiara and Elsa could not walk a straight line, so signore Cavalleri helped them with their coats and hats and carried them out to the car. Bruno staggered out of the house unaided, forcing himself between the women in the backseat, and then passed out on them, his head in Chiara's lap and his muddy boots on Elsa's spotless new white wool coat. The signore then helped Werner into the front passenger side of the car and ushered me around to the driver's seat. Before he opened the door for me, I reached into my pocket, pulled out the pouch containing the vial and handed it to him.

"'Here,' I said, explaining that Werner and Bruno would probably wake up in the morning and remember nothing about the card game. He pushed my hand away. 'No, signora,' he said. 'There is no such thing as coincidence. There is a reason you have the seeds now! Hide them immediately. If they remember this evening, they will each try to force you to give them the seeds. Tell them you lost them. Tell them you can't remember where you put them. Tell them anything, but do not, under any circumstances, give them the seeds. If disaster comes, you may use my name as someone who will purchase these seeds to buy your life or your freedom. But, if you escape the storm that is coming, the seeds are yours to do with as you please. May God protect you, signora!' With that, he helped me into my seat, walked back to the villa and watched and waved from his door as we drove away."

The doctor and his daughter were silent for a long time before Lara reached out, touched Armida's cheek, and said, "You still haven't told us who did this to you."

Terrified to say the name out loud, Armida mouthed the word, "Alessandro."

"I knew it!" Dr. Grassi roared, pounding his fist on the arm of his chair.

Armida kept her voice low, forcing Lara and her father to lean close to hear.

"It was about one o'clock in the morning," she said, "by the time the military ferry from Iseo transported us back here to the island and we arrived at the villa. Each of them had slept the entire way home. Usually Alessandro is out all night on Saturdays, but when I pulled up to the villa there was a light

on so I knew he must be home. Because I couldn't get anyone in the car to wake up, and wouldn't have been able to get
them all into the house by myself anyway, I had to ask Alessandro to help me. He was furious."

"Why?" asked Leonardo.

Armida coughed—so hard and deep, she doubled over
in pain—before explaining, "Who knows? Perhaps he was
angry because he was not included in our outing. Perhaps
he simply did not want to be bothered helping me carry his
parents and the Kolbes into the villa. Alessandro is always
angry. He doesn't need an excuse."

"Anyway," she continued weakly, "as Alessandro was dragging his father into the house, Bruno woke up. Drunkenly,
he told his son that I had stolen a treasure from him and that
if he had to, he would kill me to get it back. Meanwhile, I
was putting Chiara and Elsa to bed and Werner was still out
in the car. Alessandro asked me what Bruno had meant by
stealing his father's 'treasure.' I said, 'Your father is drunk,
Alessandro.' But he was suspicious, and didn't believe me."

"'I am going out to get Herr Kolbe,' he said. 'When I
come back, Armida, you had better tell me the truth or there
will be hell to pay.' I panicked. I hadn't thought of what to
do or say yet. I had borne the brunt of Alessandro's temper
before, but never like this. When Alessandro returned with
Werner, he was in a rage. He flung Herr Kolbe on his bed
and confronted me again. 'Kolbe tells me the same thing!' he
shouted. 'He mumbled something about you having robbed
him of what is rightfully his.' Again, I denied knowing
anything."

Armida started shaking uncontrollably again, violent
spasms jerking her body, making Dr. Grassi wonder if she
was still in shock. Lara poured another round of tea while

Leonardo pulled the blanket tighter around Armida's shoulders.

Armida was determined to finish her story. "Suddenly Alessandro's hands were around my neck," she said. "He was screaming, 'Liar! You'll steal us blind. I should have killed you long ago!' I tried to pry myself away from him but the more I struggled the more savage he became. I tried to talk, but every time I opened my mouth he slapped me and when I started crying and calling for help he punched me in the stomach so hard I nearly passed out. Finally, he threw me to the ground, like I was piece of rotten garbage. I crawled on my hands and knees toward the kitchen door thinking he was finished with me, but he followed me, laughing as he kicked me in the back and my head. At that moment, truly, I thought I was going to die."

Lara stifled a sob.

Taking a deep breath, her tremors subsiding, Armida resumed. "After awhile, he must have tired of his sport because suddenly he stopped. I couldn't move. I couldn't lift my face out of the pool of blood that was collecting on the floor all around me. Out of my left ear I heard him light a match. Then I heard Elsa's voice; it was slurred. She was still drunk. She said, 'Alessandro! Werner is passed out cold. He won't wake up for hours.'

"I lay on the floor a long time, trying to block out everything I heard after that. It seemed like hours had gone by; I guessed that it must be 5:00 in the morning, or close to it. Finally, I heard Elsa go back to her room. A short time later I heard Alessandro begin to snore. At first, I thought I was paralyzed. I prayed, *God, help me move!*

"No sooner had the words left my tongue, but I felt a

surge of courage. Slowly, I dragged myself out of the house and down to the car. There was a blanket in the back seat. Even with my coat on, it was so cold I decided to wrap it around myself to keep from freezing. Then, I remembered it was Sunday and that you would be here waiting for me. *I can either hide in the car and freeze to death*, I told myself, *or drag myself to the Grassis and get help.* At first I did not think I could make it here. It was very slow and painful at first, but the further I got away from the villa, and the closer I got here, the stronger my legs felt."

Exhausted from speaking, Armida let her head fall onto the back of the chair. She closed her eyes, her fingers still clenched triumphantly around the vial of seeds.

The Grassis let her rest, waiting for her to get a second wind, their minds racing. They understood only too well what a dangerous predicament Armida was in. When the Carditis and the Kolbes woke up would they remember their evening in Franciacorta? Would they recollect gambling for the priceless seeds, recall Armida winning them? Even if they didn't, would Alessandro continue to make an issue of it?

Ten minutes later, when Armida finally opened her eyes again, Dr. Grassi warned, "You must do something with those seeds, Armida."

Lara agreed.

"Where could I hide them?"

Noticing a metallic glint just below the base of Armida's throat, Leonardo leaned over and lifted it up, away from her neck. "What is this?"

"My mother's watch," she replied, setting the vial cautiously on her lap and reaching up to pull the silver-encased timepiece out of the doctor's hands. "It was a gift from my father when they were married. Argene thinks everything is a sign; perhaps this is one?"

"Yes, and a timely one at that!" exclaimed Lara, jumping up. She brought out her sewing basket from a cupboard in the dining room and began rummaging through it. "There's no time to lose. I'll use a small piece of strong linen and stitch a tiny compartment for each seed. Papa, you take the watch and open the back of it so we can hide the packet of seeds in it. No one will ever guess."

While his daughter bustled about, the doctor took the timepiece from Armida and did as he was told, asking Armida what she thought they should do with the crystal vial and the pouch it had come in.

"Break the glass," she replied, "then put the broken pieces back in the bag and give it to me."

But Leonardo insisted she allow him to dispose of it. Why in the world, he asked, would she want to keep the evidence on her?

"If Bruno and Werner *do* remember what happened last night," she explained, "and I have destroyed the evidence, they will have more cause to believe I am lying and will ransack everything I own to find it. This way, I can show them the broken vial and say I don't know what happened to the seeds. Or, I can say that Bruno grabbed them from me while he was drunk and broke the vial himself. I can even pretend that I do not understand its importance and let them find the bag among my belongings and assume what they want."

"Yes, yes. I see," the doctor conceded.

Pausing from her stitching, Lara said, "Surely you are not going back to the villa, Armida? It would be suicide!"

Dr. Grassi agreed and began discussing an escape plan

that he had been devising for quite some time. He had spoken to a local fisherman—it was too dangerous to name him yet—who could transport her safely to Isola. From there, he knew of a connection who could sneak her into Milan, and from Milan—well, he was still working on that part of his scheme.

Armida would have none of it. "It is not time for me to leave the island."

"Well then," countered the doctor, "Instead of treating you for your wounds here in my office, I'll just admit you to the hospital in Iseo for treatment, that's what I'll do. And," he added, emphasizing his intent with a wagging finger, "I won't release you until you are completely healed, which I will make sure is not until after the war is over. If you think for one minute that I will allow you back into the hands of those fiends, then you do not know Leonardo Grassi."

"If *you* think," retorted Armida, "that I am so cowardly that I would do as you suggest, then you do not know Armida Sigali. There are no guarantees that if I try to escape now, I will survive, are there?"

He had to admit there were not.

"As I said, I am not ready to leave Monte Isola, nor the friends who have come to mean so much to me. I have unfinished work to do here."

Leonardo looked surprised. "What, pray tell, would that be?"

"To give you the information you asked for when I first met you."

One could have heard a pin drop. Even Milo stopped chewing on his strip of old ribbed boot leather, raising his head and tilting his ear toward Armida as though he, too, could not believe what she had just said. Lara let her sewing fall onto her lap.

Gravely, Dr. Grassi whispered, "Armida, you don't have to do this."

"I have nothing to lose, do I?"

"Blast your reasoning!"

"You know I'm right; nothing you can say will change my mind."

After what seemed like an eternity, he relented. "How much do you already know?"

"I know whose houses will be raided next. I know which villagers Bruno and Alessandro suspect are partisans." She frowned and added, "My fear has always been that your names would be brought up. Just last night, although he was drunk, Werner mentioned he was beginning to suspect Dr. Schroeder of sedition."

"Nurse Mueller!" Leonardo spit out her name as though it were snake venom. "I knew she could not be trusted. That cold-blooded, odious woman!"

Even though the doctor brushed aside Armida's protests, saying they would talk about it later, a rush of desperation descended upon all three of them as they each began mentally processing what they must do. Lara hurriedly positioned the finished linen packet holding the three seeds behind the face of the watch, while Leonardo stormed into his bedroom to change his clothes and retrieve some papers.

"Tell me," Lara asked, "what will you do with these seeds, Armida? They are ancient. Their value, other than being heirlooms, is simply scientific, you know."

"If I live, I would like to plant them in the Bertozzi vineyard in Ripa," Armida replied, sounding as eerie as she looked. "I will plant one seed for my son, Silverio, one seed for my daughter, Violenza, and one seed for my sister, Argene. Perhaps they will sprout. Miracles can happen, no?"

"You should be thinking of how you can use them to buy your freedom, as signore Cavalleri suggested."

"Except for you and your father, I trust no one with my freedom, and I doubt you would take a bribe from me." Armida said it teasingly, but Lara did not find it funny.

"Your safety isn't a joke," snapped Lara. "Although papa and I would do anything to help you, others involved in helping you flee would not be so generous."

Armida shrugged.

"Anyway," Lara added, "if your children were here they would tell you the same thing. They would not agree with you planting the seeds in a vineyard as a symbolic gesture for them."

Armida disagreed. "Covering these seeds with the earth of my husband's vineyard is not symbolism. It is closing the breach between us all, in Ripa, where it all began, where all the cracks started. And it would be a testimony too, a sign that I am willing, for once, to sacrifice my life for someone else. I have never known anything bigger than myself. But now, finally, I have an opportunity to prove I have really changed; to myself and everyone else. I am going to reclaim my soul."

"You talk as though your life is over, Armida," ventured Lara softly. "It's not too late, you know."

"Too late for what?"

"To marry again; even to reconcile with Egisto. You are still a young woman with so much to live for."

A smile tugged at the upper corners of Armida's mangled lips. "If I survive the war, I will give myself to the service of God."

"The service of . . . " stammered Lara in disbelief. "You would enter the *convent*? Since when did you decide this?"

Armida laughed—actually *laughed*. "No, I am not suited for the life of a nun. Remember when I told you I thought I wanted to settle down in Ripa again and start my own business?

Lara nodded.

"Well, I changed my mind. I've decided I would try living here for awhile, near the lakes. I want Argene to meet you and your father and see this beautiful island. I want her to sail on Lago d'Iseo. I could take her to Franciacorta, to a monastery I saw near Erbusco, close to the Cavalleri Estate, and offer them my services. I could cook or clean for the monks there; I could tend the vineyards, or help make the wine for the monastery. I would work for nothing if Argene and I could have free room and board. Think of it! I could work in peace with the satisfaction of serving those who love God and their fellow men, instead of themselves." She glanced toward Dr. Grassi's bedroom door to make sure he couldn't hear her. "I meant what I said, Lara, about revealing what I've heard at the villa."

Lara shook her head. "If you do tell us everything you know it will become obvious to Herr Kolbe and Bruno that there is a conspirator in their home. I tell you, it is too dangerous for you to stay here! Signore Cavalleri was right; you should not hesitate to use the seeds he gave you to buy your freedom. With the money, we could easily bribe someone to take you away immediately or find a hiding place for you until it is safe to leave. You cannot go back to the villa, Armida. It is simply too big a risk. It is suicide. I won't allow it."

"My dear, dear friend." Armida reached for Lara's hand. "I could not give you the information you need to save innocent lives if I was no longer living in the villa with the Kolbes and Carditis. They would not waste a moment in hunting me down if suddenly I disappeared. You and your father would be Bruno's first suspects. It is a far greater danger to all of us if I do *not* go back to the villa today."

Though Lara knew it was true, she refused to give in. "But . . ."

"Lara," said Armida, her voice even and clear. "I am a new person. The old me no longer exists. Remember? My pride has been stripped away from me. My life has never meant so little to me, yet so much! The voices in my head aren't condemning me anymore. They're not shouting at me to run away every time I feel threatened. They're not accusing me of being crazy, or worthless, or unlovable, or an unfit mother. They're not telling me that the people who really love me, hate me. I have made up my mind and nothing will change it," she concluded. "When these seeds are buried in Ripa, it will be a sign that I am finally free, forgiven and reconciled. I will not be forgotten. These seeds, Lara, are life. They are me."

chapter thirty-two

SPRING'S ARRIVAL IN 1945 was welcomed with giddy awe by the residents of St. Paul, Minnesota, as though they were witnessing the birth of an overdue baby after a long, harrowing labor. It was celebrated accordingly, along with a rush of community artistic endeavors meant to counteract the mind-numbing effects of the war. The communion of the two life-giving auguries, a warming earth and creative initiative, spelled relief to Egisto Bertozzi, who embraced his heavy workload as therapy for his insomnia and over-active imagination. Simply put, he was now too busy to think about Armida during the day and far too tired to stay awake at night worrying about her. There were nights he collapsed into bed covered in marble dust, with every intention of showering first, only to wake up in the morning fully clothed, his pillow and bedspread gritty with the detritus of his previous day's labor.

On Saturday afternoon, April 29, Egisto was in his studio again. The window was open and he was humming along with the radio as he worked, even though his muscles ached and his nasal passages burned from working seven days a week, twelve and fourteen hours a day for the last month. St. James Lutheran Church had commissioned him to carve twelve medallions representing the twelve disciples of Christ.

The church board had requested the medallions be finished no later than June.

As he took measurements for one of the medallions, the radio station played "After You've Gone." The song took him back to 1918, the year after Babe was born. He continued working, unable to stop his mind from reeling in memories of that time. It seemed like yesterday that he and Armida had emigrated to America; like yesterday they had rejoiced at having a baby girl. He remembered how hard it was for Armida to get back on her feet after the delivery, how colicky Babe was, how difficult she was to raise compared to Siv. For the millionth time, he kicked himself for not having burned the letter to Marietta.

Letters. After a three-year embargo, he had finally received his first letter from home. His mother, brothers and sister, and all of their children, were still alive; destitute and broken, but alive. No one knew exactly where Armida was; only that she might be somewhere in the lake region. The son of Julia's friend had died in the war having never found her.

Egisto finished his measurements and tried to force his mind to focus on the task at hand, but Armida lurked beneath the layers of his busyness. A tap on his shoulder startled him. He'd been so preoccupied thinking of Armida he hadn't heard anyone walk in.

A strange man tipped his hat respectfully to him. "Uh, sir, are you Egisto Bertozzi?"

"I am he. Can I help you?"

"T. J. Strasser. Photographer, *Pioneer Press*. Sorry for coming over on a Saturday, but I was told you'd be here today. We're swamped at the *Press* too. Been working seven days a week lately myself."

Surveying the cluttered studio, Strasser noticed the radio perched on the ledge above Egisto's workstation. "Wow! A Crosley 6H2 Tombstone!" he cried, rubbing his hand along the marbled wood. "I love these radios. Art Deco. 1934?"

Egisto nodded. He turned the circular knob to dial in a station that played more contemporary music, stopping when the lyrics of a popular song began to play:

"You've got to accentuate the positive . . . Eliminate the negative and latch on to the affirmative . . . "

"Johnny Mercer!" T. J. snapped his fingers. 'Accentuate the Positive'—great song!" After swaying with the music for a few measures, he tore himself away from the radio and instructed Egisto to stand in front of a wall displaying several of the completed medallions he had been working on. "I suppose we better get down to business, Mr. Bertozzi. Could you hold your drill up near that . . . uh, whatchamacallit?"

"Medallion," Egisto replied, raising his pneumatic drill toward a circular stone with the words 'St. Bartholomew' engraved along the bottom edge.

"Yeah, medallion . . . there you go. Did you hear the news last night?" The light on T. J.'s camera flashed, causing Egisto to blink. "You know how we broke through the Veneto Line up in northern Italy? Well, they say the Germans are turning tail now, beating it back to Berlin."

Had Mr. Strasser noticed the expression on Egisto's face, he would have dropped the subject, but he was distracted, rummaging through Egisto's tools with his free hand. Chisels, droves, fraises, bash hammers and cutters scuttled across the surface of the table, until he zeroed in on a long shiny instrument. "I figured you being Italian and all, you'd be interested." Holding up a metal pick, he looked at Egisto and added, "What do you say we get you showing off this . . . um?"

"Subbia. It is a cutting point."

"Right. Just sit here in this chair and hold it up toward me like you're giving me a demonstration, okay?" As he was focusing his lens, the tranquilizing voice of Perry Como floated out of the Tombstone.

"Till the end of time, long as stars are in the blue . . . "

"Man," sighed T. J. lowering his camera. "My wife goes crazy over this song. If she were here right now, she'd make me stop what I was doing and dance with her. She wouldn't care one bit where we were or who was watching either." Raising his camera back up to his cheek, he laughed. "I'll bet your wife's the same way. Perry Como's got that effect on all the women, doesn't he?"

Egisto wasn't about to tell his exuberant interloper that not only did he no longer have a wife, but he had no idea where the mother of his children was at that moment. "So I've heard."

Snap! The camera light flashed again. Egisto pressed his thumbs into the inner corners of his eyes and rubbed, hoping that it was the last picture the photographer would take.

"One more, Mr. Bertozzi," said T. J., "and I think we'll be done. Let's see . . . "

Egisto counted to ten and opened his eyes. It occurred to him that he could speed up the process if he helped the young man out.

"Mr. Strasser?"

"Yeah?"

"The stone I am using for these medallions is exquisite. I don't know if you've noticed." He held up a small, uncut slab of Kasota limestone for T. J. to inspect.

The photographer looked blankly at the stone as though it

were a common chunk of cement. "Nice," he said. "Hey, wait a minute! I've got a great idea."

Using his hands to indicate how he wanted Egisto to display the stone for the camera, he prepared to take the last shot. "Smile!" he commanded, clicking the shutter at just the right moment. "Perfect!"

Slinging his camera over his shoulder, he held out his hand. "Thanks for your time, Mr. Bertozzi. I have to admit, I don't know much about stonework and all that stuff, but my boss says you're pretty famous, and you seem like an alright guy, so it's been a real pleasure. Well, so long . . . "

Just as Mr. Strasser turned to go, a deep voice boomed from the radio: "We interrupt this regularly scheduled program to bring you a late-breaking report from Milan, Italy."

"Hey!" shouted T. J. "That sounds like James Arness!"

Egisto strained to hear what the announcer on the news bulletin was saying. "Who?"

"James Arness! He's one of us, from Minnesota. You know; Bronze star, Purple Heart, one of the first guys to hit the beach at Anzio. Wait a minute . . . that's your neck of the woods, right? Got himself a leg full of bullets over there. A year in the hospital, and he still limps. You should see him. Big fella; six-foot-seven and a forty-eight-inch chest! Imagine him, single-handedly walking up and pitching a grenade into a Nazi machine gun nest. Wow."

Egisto held his index finger to his lips. "Ssh!"

"Sorry." T. J. plopped down on the nearest bench and scratched his ear. "Mind if I stay and listen?"

Without responding, Egisto turned the volume up on the radio. Arness's voice thundered over the airwaves. "Flash! April 29—Milan, Italy—Mussolini is dead! Repeat! Allied forces advancing north through crumbling enemy defenses report that a Nazi motorcade smuggling Fascist dictator, Benito Mussolini, was ambushed yesterday forty-five miles from the Austrian border. Disguised as a German soldier, Mussolini was killed along with his mistress, Claretta Petacci. Sources in Italy report they were gunned down by communist partisans on the western shores of Lake Como near the town of Dongo. He was . . . what? What's that?" Arness paused in mid-sentence.

Stunned, Egisto collapsed onto a stool.

"Ladies and gentlemen!" the announcer continued, apologizing for the disruption. "I've just received this breaking news alert! According to reliable sources, the bodies of Benito Mussolini and Claretta Petacci were found this morning, dumped in front of an abandoned garage in Milan's Piazzale Loreto. You may remember that it was at the Piazzale Loreto—less than two years ago—that the mutilated remains of fifteen suspected partisans were thrown into a bloody heap for public display as an example of what the Nazis would do to rebel sympathizers. Reports at that time claimed Fascist guards dubbed the martyred freedom fighters a 'pile of rubbish.' Since that fateful day, partisans, seeking revenge, have vowed they would hang Mussolini, dead or alive, from the rafters of this garage in Milan. Now, shocking pictures pouring out of Italy today—and folks, they are truly shocking—show just that. Mussolini and Petacci, along with the body of at least one other Fascist, are, as I speak, hanging from meat hooks, upside down . . . from the roof of a garage . . . an Esso garage . . . in Milan's Piazzale Loreto. Eyewitnesses to the grisly scene report that hundreds, possibly thousands, of enraged Milanese, in violent retribution for years of oppression, are wreaking vengeance on the dead remains of what once was their beloved duce."

T. J. whistled. "Sounds pretty bad, eh?"

Egisto sat motionless, staring blankly out of the studio's wide clerestory window. At a loss for words, Mr. Strasser bowed his head and waited a few moments. Shouldering his camera, he finally rose and placed his hand on Egisto's shoulder. "Sorry, pal," he whispered.

Not knowing what else to say, he let himself out of the studio, shaking his head and muttering under his breath, "Poor guy. Wonder what's eating him?"

Egisto lowered his head between his knees. Two entirely conflicting voices in his head wrestled for supremacy.

The voice of Hope hovering over him said, *The war is finally over. Armida is still alive.*

The voice of Doom howled, *She's dead. Don't fool yourself.*

No, replied Hope. *She may have tried to kill herself when she was in America, but her letters didn't indicate she was still depressed. If she's in her right mind she has fight in her.*

She probably died months ago, Doom retorted. *Her body could be buried under tons of debris somewhere. She'll never be found.*

Egisto ran his fingers through his hair, giving ear to Hope again. *No, she's hiding. She's safe somewhere, just waiting for things to settle down.*

Doom snickered. *What are you thinking? Anyone living near Salò who was associated with the Fascists and Nazis will be killed by partisans.*

You don't know exactly where Armida is for sure, whispered Hope. *She may be far away from Salò.*

A third voice, the voice of Reason, interrupted his internal dialogue, coming cold and hard from outside of himself. *You don't know exactly where Armida fled, but you know it was in the Lake District. Francesco told you.*

Images of Mussolini and his mistress, their defiled corpses exposed for all the world to see, paraded across his mind's stage. He cradled his head in his hands and moaned. "It can't end like this."

Suddenly, as if the Little Nipper were reading his thoughts, the lilting melody of Les Brown's "Sentimental Journey" drifted softly across the room to him:

"Gonna take a sentimental journey . . . Gonna set my heart at ease . . . "

An invisible hand seemed to lift Egisto's chin and pull his shoulders back. With the refrain, *"Gonna take that sentimental journey home,"* playing over and over in his mind like a broken record, Egisto resolved to do whatever it took to find Armida . . . even if it meant going back to Italy to find her.

No matter what, I owe it to her, he thought. *I owe it to Silverio and Violenza.*

⁂

WHEN ALLIED TROOPS *seized Milan, we cried, we screamed, we celebrated. Our joy, however, was tempered by the bloodletting in the war's aftermath. It was, arguably, most vicious along the shores of Lago d'Iseo where whole villages were decimated. Wedged between Lake Garda, home of the Saló Republic, and Lake Como, where Mussolini was captured, the residents of Lago d'Iseo were surrounded and inundated with partisans and Nazis seeking revenge on each other.*

Siviano was racked with violence. Partisans clogged the narrow streets, breaking into homes and dragging out those they believed were traitors or Fascist sympathizers. Bodies hung from nooses thrown over trees, balconies and bridges. People were shot point blank in the streets and left for the dogs to play with. Others were tied with rocks and thrown into the lake.

Imagining Armida there, in the midst of all that pent up hate and revenge, the insanity that possessed the survivors, was, well, something I could never bring myself to do.

❧

PART VI

1946

Finchè c'è vita c'è speranza

"Where there's life, there's hope"

chapter thirty-three

His bladder ready to burst, Francesco pulled over to the side of the road beneath the shadow of Mount Altissimo and relieved himself.

"Damn," he muttered tersely. "How did I ever get roped into this bloody mess?"

No sooner had he asked the question, than a red Turismo Super Sport came screaming around a hairpin bend in the serpentine mountain road above him. The flushed driver, flailing his arm out the window and shouting as he drew nearer, screeched almost to a stop as he passed so that Francesco would be sure to hear him. "Get out of the way, idiot! You're blocking the road!"

The angry motorist gunned his engine and peeled away, his tires skidding along the gravel at an angle deliberately designed to cloak Francesco in a cloud of choking griege-colored dust. Placing his right hand over his left bicep, Francesco jerked his fist into the air and yelled after him, "Same to you!"

Once the dust dissipated, he shook himself soundly and retrieved an unfiltered Russian papirosi cigarette from his shirt pocket. Squashing the cardboard tip between his fingers, he lit it, glowering enviously at the ruby sedan now racing down the twisted curves far below him. What he wouldn't give, he thought morosely, to be behind the wheel of a fancy Turismo himself.

"How could anyone be that rich?" he wondered out loud, throwing his match onto the urine-soaked rocks near his feet. Why, it was little more than a year since the fall of the Salò Republic and still, neither he nor his friends could afford new clothes or shoes, let alone the extravagance of a big, flashy car. Edging his way around the hood of his rickety, old Topolino pickup truck, he had to reluctantly admit that he was luckier than most. At least—because his house and business had not been completely destroyed during the war—he didn't have to start life over from scratch like his mother and Carilda and so many others he knew.

Well, he shrugged, brushing away the thought as one would lint on a dark shirt, *that's life.*

With a wife and three children, he had his own affairs to worry about. And now this with Egisto; this inconvenience, this untimely, frivolous family duty. He kicked the bald front tire on the Topolino and inspected the equally bald tires on the back of the truck. Then, he double-checked the bed of the truck to make sure his cargo was secure and lashed down tightly. Everything appeared to be in order. He returned to the driver's seat, resigning himself to the task at hand. The engine sputtered to life, Francesco checked the address scribbled in the margins of his map one last time and off he went, lumbering down the last stretch of chewed up road, past the hushed, spectral villages of Azzano and Fabbiano, toward Seravezza and Ripa and then finally, after that, home to Querceta.

Granite and limestone outcroppings studded the landscape along the steep descent, conjuring up distant memories of when he and his brothers had labored in the Alpi Apuane marble quarries long, long ago. Such young, ignorant apprentices they had been then! They had loved working outdoors; loved the isolated mountain villages with their peculiar people and the close-knit fraternity of stone laborers. They had worn the dangers and challenges of their profession like a badge of honor. Now, sniffed Francesco, the marble industry was modernized. But, back when he and his brothers cut and hauled stone from the quarries, it was backbreaking, deadly work. Flicking the remains of his cigarette out the window, he was vaguely cognizant of the fact that he was lapsing into his old habit of comparing the past with the present, something his wife, Pia, scolded him about constantly.

Francesco, you're at it again! he could imagine her saying if she were there with him in the truck. *Do you think you are the only one to suffer during the war? Be thankful we are alive! The old days were good, but they weren't perfect, you know.*

Pia's harangues were even worse when he remonstrated about his brother Egisto; how Egisto was lucky because he had escaped all the horrors of war in America. He had even become prosperous during it, while they were reduced to bankruptcy. "It should have been me that went to America, not Egisto," Francesco had once complained bitterly to his wife.

Her response had been: "Oh, Egisto this, and Egisto that! You still haven't gotten over the fact that you, the eldest, were expected to stay in Italy? What is wrong with you? You would think you were the poorest of the poor instead of a very lucky man who still has his family and his business. *Boh!*"

Francesco always balked when Pia spoke to him like that, but he knew she was right, even though he found it next to impossible to rid his mind of such regrets. The truth be told, Francesco was anxious about Egisto, and for good reason.

His brother, whom he hadn't seen in over thirty years, would be home in less than a month and his family's preoccupation with his homecoming was vexing him to no end. His mother Carmela, in her nineties and frail, was so overjoyed at the prospect of seeing Egisto again that she walked about in a perpetual daze, while his sister Carilda and everyone else could think of nothing else but the monumental reception they planned on hosting in Egisto's honor.

It wasn't that Francesco didn't share in their excitement. He was just, well, apprehensive. After all, thirty years—even though he and Egisto had stayed in touch—was a long time. Just how does a sibling behave when reunited after such a long separation? And what in the world would Egisto's reaction to *them* be? Once, he and Egisto had shared many things in common; politics, philosophies, youth. But now? Like it or not, the war had changed everything and everybody, and Pia's sermonizing, Francesco concluded indignantly, couldn't change that fact.

Roused from his malaise, Francesco suddenly down-shifted, pitching the truck into fitful, lurching spurts past a deserted stone quarry. The engine quit, his truck resting haphazardly at the base of the pit. He looked to his left and noticed a huge mound of rock and debris, along with the van-dalized remains of several *mambrucche*—long, narrow carts used to transport slabs of marble. Something about the place sent chills up his spine. With a jolt, he realized the road he was on, until recently, had delineated a significant section of the infamous Gothic Line.

A violent blast of air, caused by the peculiar downdrafts created within that particular quarry, kicked up a swirling funnel of marbled powder that spun across the road directly in front of him. Though normally not a superstitious man,

Francesco was so spooked he flooded the engine trying to start it too quickly. The whirlwind paused menacingly, directly in his path, several feet from the hood of the truck, as though daring him to turn around and go back. Then the dust devil turned and melted into the side of the mountain, extinguished in a single breath.

Unnerved, Francesco's imagination went wild. Was this the site of some German atrocity, some horrific war crime? Had the quarry been a cover for desperate partisans planning retribution or defending their lives from snipers? Were the abandoned carts used by the Nazis to haul the hapless victims to God-knows-where? There had been so much bloodletting and butchery in these mountains during the war, it made his head swim to think of it. Better not think of it, he reasoned. He pumped the accelerator gradually this time, cajoling the engine to back to life. It was better to forget. Better to pretend, at least for the moment, that the war had never happened.

The monotonous drive, the whole weird trip, was getting to him. He could feel it in the sharp rumblings clawing inside his stomach, in his stiff neck, his tight jaw. He resisted the urge to stop at the next village and rest. If he could just concentrate on something positive—his family, his business, his dreams of the future—perhaps he could shake the sense of dread that nipped at his heels and hounded his waking hours.

The thought of Ario and Aladino, and his daughter Lola, came first to his rescue. His two sons showed great promise as the future owners of the Bertozzi Marble Company. Francesco found solace thinking about his sons inheriting the business. Then he frowned. No matter how hard he tried to ignore it, in every scenario involving his future and his prosperity, Egisto came into the equation. Complicating matters was the unspoken understanding that income generated by Francesco's marble business, vis-à-vis Egisto's money from America, was supposed to help support his mother and his brother and sister as much as possible, which wasn't much since the war.

The self-admission made him cringe. The resumption of Egisto's monthly checks had been a crucial element in the ability of the Bertozzis getting back on their feet financially after the war. But since all of Egisto's checks were sent to Francesco, the real problem—in his estimation—was that his mother and siblings expected him to delegate money to them according to their own specific needs and there simply wasn't enough money to cover everyone's demands. Were he to dole out his limited resources in equal proportions to all the family members, the business would never take off.

Because no one understood or appreciated the burden of responsibility Francesco bore as the titular "head of the family," and since it was impossible to please everyone, he had distanced himself from his mother and siblings over time for the sake of self-protection. It was very un-Italian, and he knew it. Still, he consoled himself with the thought: *Let my family walk in my shoes for awhile and see how well they would do. I have done my best.*

Moments later, the suffocating August heat rising up from the approaching coastal plain displaced the cooler mountain air; a sure sign he was almost to his destination. Starting to perspire profusely, he nervously lit his last papirosi while navigating his truck through Seravezza's empty streets. He crossed the landmark ancient bridge that shot him across the main road and into the outskirts of Ripa, spread out before him like a worn and damaged, yet still grossly rich, medieval tapestry. He smelled the sea moments before he saw the ribboned white beaches and shimmering azure surf in the distance.

God! Why did he have to make this last stop?

Scowling, he drove slowly down several streets still cluttered with piles of rubble from the war, until he saw the address that matched his instructions. He turned off the engine and waited, an ominous, acidic dread crawling up his throat. The row of ramshackle tenements facing him reinforced Pia's contention that he should, indeed, consider himself a lucky man. He wondered how some people would ever be able to rebuild their lives from such squalor. Ragged children played in the street like zombies, their big, round eyes riveted on the handsome, self-possessed stranger sitting in the Topolino pickup.

Being that it was Sunday, Francesco assumed parents were somewhere nearby, but no adult was in sight. He had hoped that someone would be waiting for him, that someone would approach him when they saw him pull up and simply take over so that he would have to do nothing but tip his hat, say "*buon giorno, prego, and ciao*" and drive away. But other than the silent, spectral street urchins, it was as though he were alone in a lifeless moonscape. Finally gathering courage, Francesco stepped out of the truck, dropped his cigarette butt onto the sidewalk, crushed it beneath the toe of his boot, and with a ponderous gait marched up to one of the doors and knocked.

The voices drifting out of the open windows assured Francesco that someone was in the apartment, although it took several moments before the door opened. When it did, a small but proud looking man stood before him, a stained napkin tucked into the collar of his shabby, poorly fitted shirt. Bewildered, he asked, "Posso?"

Francesco had rehearsed this moment a million times it seemed, but now, when it came right down to it, he couldn't even open his mouth. He looked wordlessly at the inquiring face before him.

"Can I help you, signore?" the man asked, inspecting Francesco's face carefully, in the event he might possibly recognize some old, forgotten friend.

Francesco coughed. "Orlando?"

"Si." The man's eyebrows shot up. His hand went instinctively to the napkin at his throat. In the background, a woman's voice asked who was at the door.

"Sigali?" asked Francesco. "Orlando Sigali?"

Ignoring his wife's demands to know whom he was talking to, Orlando replied, "Si."

"I am Francesco Bertozzi."

Orlando cocked his head slightly to the left, looked over Francesco's shoulder, and seeing a gleaming white casket in the back of the Topolino pickup parked outside his home, he uttered something unintelligible.

Francesco licked his cracked lips. "Egisto sent instructions for you. I'm so sorry."

"Yes, it's a nasty business, I know," muttered Orlando. Turning, he called out to his wife, "Mama! It's Armida's brother-in-law. He's brought Armida home."

To SAY THAT bringing Armida's body back all the way from Lago d'Iseo was "nasty business" was a gross understatement in Francesco's opinion. It had been a loathsome undertaking, not to mention a colossal bother. Helping Orlando carry her coffin into the Sigali's oppressively hot, tiny crowded apartment was not something he had planned on doing. Orlando's wife, noticing Francesco looked deathly pale, had offered him a glass of wine, but he declined graciously. The very thought made him want to retch. He just wanted out of the close surroundings, the smell of spaghetti, dirty diapers and garbage in the streets, away from everything related to Armida Sigali. More than anything, he just wanted to get back home.

A half-hour later, heading down the straight, civilized via Provinciale toward Querceta, he breathed a sigh of relief. *I have spent the last year helping Egisto find his wife,* he thought. *Now, maybe Egisto can help me.*

Egisto had already sent a large sum of money to Francesco to cover all of the estimated expenses of bringing Armida's body back to Ripa. Francesco was confident his brother would reimburse him for the extra unexpected bills incurred during his trip to Lago d'Iseo, where anything that could have gone wrong, did. The detective whom Egisto had hired to find Armida had met Francesco in Siviano as planned, but had failed to have her body ready for transport like he had promised. Subsequently, it had taken another two full days before Francesco was able to return home. Two days of hotel and food bills. Two days of disturbing conversations with the locals. Two days of details of Armida's death he would rather have not known.

There was no way Francesco was going to tell Egisto the sordid rumors he had heard in Siviano regarding Armida: that she had turned people in and bedded German officers to survive, that she had run off with Bruno Carditi and he had killed her after deciding to escape to Germany. Others told him entirely different stories; that she was a heroine. That she had died saving someone else. He didn't believe it. Not

Armida Sigali. Not the woman he had known. He would wash his hands of the entire ordeal and let the detective spell it all out in the final report he was supposedly sending Egisto soon. If his brother wanted to know more, he would have to go to Siviano himself.

Francesco shook his head at the amount of money he knew his brother had spent to find Armida. *What kind of man spends a small fortune to track down a woman who has continually rejected him, and not only that, but bring her body all the way back to her birthplace for a decent burial?* Egisto baffled him. *Armida made her bed with the Fascists. I would have let her lie with them.*

In the distance he saw the broken tiled roof of the Bertozzi Marble Company and his much-in-need-of-repair home nestled alongside it, and before he knew it he was pulling into the driveway in front of the sign that read, *"Francesco Bertozzi—marmi d'arte e funerari."*

Pia nodded to him from the kitchen's beaded doorway while Ario, working in the courtyard, smiled and waved his cap.

Well, it's Egisto's life, concluded Francesco to himself, turning off the ignition. *He can do what he wants with his money, as long as he doesn't forget about us. Maybe he'll realize how rich he really is when he gets here and sees how we're living. Then, I won't have to suggest that he gives his inheritance to me when mama dies. He'll just know it's the right thing to do.*

chapter thirty-four

I wish Siv and Babe would have come with me, thought
Egisto, punching his pillow into the shape of a jelly roll and
shoving it under his neck. *But then, how could I expect them
to leave their children and be gone for this long? Someday I must
bring them back so they understand. So they understand me. So
they understand their mother . . .*

Egisto couldn't sleep. Being jet-lagged, he knew it was
futile to even try, so he rose from his bed and stole quietly
out onto Francesco's terrazzo patio at the back of the villa.
Standing beneath a trellis of luxuriant grapevines, he sniffed
the corpulent clusters of plum-black grapes, like giant ame-
thysts dangling above his head, and watched the billowing
sheets on Pia's clothesline flapping erratically on midnight's
maritime breezes, translucent in the moonlight. He soft-
ened to the melancholic chanting of cicadas and the rustling
of leaves that rippled through the neighbor's olive orchard.
He had forgotten just how silvery and coarsely delicate olive
leaves were, and the otherworldliness of his surroundings
made him wish that all of Italy was as unspoiled and pregnant with life as Francesco and Pia's courtyard.

But it wasn't.

Franceso had forewarned his brother that Italy was not
what it once was. He was right. The devastation Egisto witnessed from Milan to Monte di Ripa was shocking. Yet,

ironically, standing there in the middle of the night in the courtyard separating Francesco's stucco villa and the Bertozzi Marble Company, a surge of elation possessed him. He was caught in a current, the past, present, and future converging into one enormous, symbiotic stream. At once both rapturous and dreadful, the sensory overload of being home again nearly swept him off his feet. He closed his eyes and rubbed his temples as a dull pain began to crawl its way, spider-like, along the base of his neck and up along both sides of his skull. The fact of the matter was, in the last twenty-four hours Egisto had been inundated with far too many experiences for any human being to adequately process.

Still, he was determined to give it a try. He had to. Rehashing his trip until he couldn't keep his eyes open any longer was preferable to falling asleep only to be tormented with nightmares—like the ones he had been having since the war ended, and his search for Armida began. Reaching up, he plucked several fat grapes from the arbor, settled down onto a granite bench next to the shed facing Pia's overgrown vegetable garden, and let the events of the day replay in his mind.

Leaving Minnesota certainly hadn't been as easy as he had imagined. Having hired a private investigator in Italy to find Armida, the timing of his trip was contingent upon the results of the investigation. When Armida's body was suddenly and unexpectedly found, Egisto not only had to rush to fulfill his commitments at Drake, book a flight, and get his personal life in order so that he could be gone for an extended period of time, but he also had to make arrangements for Armida's body to be transferred to Ripa for a proper burial in the family cemetery. Francesco had proved invaluable in locating one of Armida's brothers, and had even gone up to Lago d'Iseo himself to transport her body back. Egisto felt guilty he wasn't able to do it himself, but he intended to make it up to Francesco.

The actual flight, since he had never flown before, was another matter altogether. It was the thrill of a lifetime for Egisto, from the loud, cumbersome, twin-engine commute from Minneapolis to New York, to the ultra-modern TWA flight from New York to Paris on the celebrated Lockheed "Connie"—the fastest, most impressive commercial plane in existence. Recalling the speed and elevation at which the four-engine Constellation had carried him effortlessly above the Atlantic gave him goosebumps all over again. Popping a juicy grape into his mouth, Egisto allowed the exquisite flavor to saturate his taste buds in sync with the delicious memory of flying on the sleek aircraft, especially as he relived seeing Italy for the first time by air. It was wonderful, until the pilot pointed out the mountain lakes glistening on the northeast horizon before landing in the burned out ruins of what had once been the glorious city of Milan.

He willed his memory forward to the last leg of his journey where he caught a commuter flight from Milan to Pisa, finally collapsing into the collective arms of his family. They all wept openly, his mother clinging to him, refusing to let him go. In fact, it wasn't until they all arrived at Francesco's house for dinner that Carilda was finally able to tear her mother away from Egisto.

Ah, Carilda. She was still, after all these years, sunshine in the flesh. Egisto leaned back against the shed and stared at the fatted moon; an all-knowing, unblinking celestial eye gazing back at him. Carilda's four daughters, along with their husbands and children, met up with them at Francesco's house. The dinner celebration had lasted hours. Egisto rubbed his belly and smiled.

Before leaving to go home Bianca had said, "Zio Egisto, please come to Bientina and stay with Danilo and me for a few days!"

"It would be an honor," he had replied. And he meant it.

Egisto shook himself back to the present. It was almost 3:00 in the morning and though he was utterly spent, he continued to fight the need to sleep . . . the fear of it. It was a fear he could trace back to weeks ago, the day he had received the detective's report detailing Armida's death. Ever since then, sleep had offered him nothing but a steady stream of nightmares.

It had taken the detective, a bellicose man by the name of signore Rizzo, a long time just to discover exactly where Armida had ended up after fleeing Forte dei Marmi with the Carditis. Once he was able to pinpoint her whereabouts in Lago d'Iseo, he quickly refined his search to Monte Isola, and then ultimately, Siviano. The locals refused to cooperate with him at first. After all, the detective noted in his report, "We Italians have been suspicious of each other for the last ten years."

Siviano had lost some of their best citizens in the final, gruesome moments of Salò's fall, he claimed, and the last thing the survivors wanted to do was embark on yet another investigation of an unsolved death; especially the death of an outsider like Armida Sigali. Rizzo—in no small part spurred on by Egisto's willingness to pay whatever it cost to find Armida—prevailed by spying, lying and bribing his way through the village until at last he found some people willing to talk.

Signore Ponte, the clerk at one of the hotels near Siviano's busy pier, where scores of German officers had been billeted, claimed one of them had kept a woman captive in his room.

Allegedly, the maids heard her wailing and scratching from inside the closet door when they cleaned the room, but didn't dare go to the police. The clerk swore he remembered one of the maids saying she thought she heard the woman trying to tell her that her name was Armida, but when Rizzo interrogated them, they denied knowing anything about it. Other leads surfaced, the detective only briefly touching on them. One rather unreliable source told Rizzo that Armida had been close friends with the town's elderly doctor and his daughter, but he later discovered that the doctor had been found slumped over his blood-spattered desk, shot point blank through his left temple—supposedly for treason.

"Apparently," Rizzo wrote in his report, "the doctor had befriended one too many partisans."

When the persistent sleuth tried to hunt down the doctor's daughter, one Lara Grassi, he learned that her body had been found hanging from the rafters of a barn on the outskirts of town. Only twenty-four hours earlier, her father had been shot while trying to set the leg of a wounded partisan. A few informants claimed that, despondent over her father's murder, Lara had taken her own life, but the general consensus was that the same German commandant who had supposedly ordered her father's death, had ordered hers as well. It was unclear why she had been killed, but reports that she and her father were high-level underground partisans were rampant. He had spoken to some who said Dr. Grassi and his daughter were killed because they had found out, through Armida, information that would indict high-ranking Fascist and Nazi officials if they were captured by the Allies.

The commandant, noted Rizzo, an SS officer by the name of Werner Kolbe, was believed to have successfully fled over the border and might still be alive in Germany, although who could know? Quite surprising, marked the detective, was the fact that Kolbe's wife, Elsa, and Alessandro Carditi were intercepted by partisans as they tried boarding a freighter near Venice bound for North Africa. Like Mussolini and his mistress, they, too, were stood up against a wall and summarily executed.

As for Bruno Carditi and his wife Chiara? Signore Rizzo spared Egisto the details, but wrote, "Suffice to say, they are no more."

It wasn't until detective Rizzo stumbled across a local fisherman that the mystery began to unravel. He claimed to have found a woman's body the same day Mussolini was assassinated, submerged in the waters off San Paolo Island, just 500 meters offshore Monte Isola. A trip to the police station, a permit to exhume the body from an unmarked grave, a comparison of the remains with dental records shipped from Minnesota, and a coroner's examination closed the case.

Egisto jerked his head, as though slapped by an invisible hand, sleep deprivation having finally drugged him into a semi-conscious state. With great effort, he stood up and staggered back into the house, feeling his way to the bed where he slipped between the sheets, no longer able to keep his eyes open. The last thoughts circulating through his tired brain were the final words of detective Rizzo's report.

Armida Sigali's death certificate officially states that she died by drowning. However, the coroner noted distinct bruises on your wife's neck, and concedes that it is possible she was strangled before succumbing to the water, although strangulation was not the cause of her death. The coroner noted other mysterious markings on signora Sigali's body, such as long wooden slivers imbedded beneath her fingernails. The slivers, he said, indicated your wife had scratched deeply on wood. In self-defense, perhaps? It would verify the testimonies of the hotel maids who claimed she had been kept captive in a closet. A police investigation—if you choose to go that route, signore Bertozzi—is certainly possible. You must consider the state of affairs in Italy at the time of your wife's death and realize that whether she died by her own hand, or at the hands of the Germans, the Fascists, or the partisans, it is all rather moot at this point.

Most interesting were reports that shortly before her death, Bruno Carditi was forced to give Armida to Prince Borghese and his family. The Borghese housekeeper and cook had apparently fled in fear of their lives, and—as your wife's cooking had become legendary among the Fascists in Siviano—signora Borghese insisted on bringing Armida to live with them. Time did not allow me to pursue this lead. However, for a price, I would be more than happy to investigate further, should you find it a desirable pursuit. It would explain the location of your wife's body near the Borghese's palace on San Paolo Island.

As far as personal items, her body was partially clothed when exhumed. I received your instructions for the preparation of her remains and duly communicated them to the local mortician, especially that he dress the corpse in clothing befitting the honor due your wife. I confess I was remiss in one thing. I failed to notify you of a single piece of jewelry found on Armida's person: that of a timepiece made into a necklace. It had been concealed in an inner pocket of the blouse she was wearing when her body was found. Considering the looting that was occurring during the time of her death, it's a miracle the piece remained on her, but then, the man I hired to exhume her body seemed to be an honest soul.

Forced into making an executive decision in the matter, I permitted your wife to be buried with said timepiece. I hope you find my decision prudent and in keeping with what your wishes would have been. That concludes my investigation, signore Bertozzi, unless you have other assignments for me, in which case I remain respectfully at your service.

—Detective R. A. Rizzo

When Francesco, covered in marble dust, slipped into his house the following afternoon to eat lunch, he peeked into the guest bedroom only to find his brother gone.

"Where is Egisto?" he asked his wife, washing his hands in the sink. "I thought he would have slept at least until dinnertime."

Pia brought a platter of prosciutto and cheese over to the table, motioning for her husband to sit down. "When I came back from Mass this morning he was gone," she said. "He left this note saying he was walking to Monte di Ripa to visit Armida's grave and then he wanted to inspect Gigi's vineyard." She pulled a slip of paper out of her apron and placed it on the table next to Francesco.

Francesco scanned the note. "The cemetery is at least two miles away. On a hot day like this? He should have come and told me. I would have driven him there. What is he thinking?"

"Since when is walking two miles a crime?" Pia retorted. "What is it, Francesco? Why do you care what your brother does?"

Shoving his plate away, Francesco crossed his arms. "I'm not hungry."

"Fine!" Pia seized his plate. "Go ahead and pout, Francesco. You just don't like the fact that your brother doesn't need you to supervise everything he does. Do you think that he can't live without you? Egisto is a grown man and can take care of himself. Or maybe you don't like the fact that Egisto honors his wife, God bless her soul, by doing the right thing. I suppose if I died, you would never come visit my grave!"

Pia's lower lip quivered ever so slightly as she waited for her husband to acknowledge her wounded feelings. When she received no such recognition, she turned on her heels, stalked out through the beaded kitchen door, and dumped his lunch in her vegetable garden.

Perhaps she should have waited a few seconds longer, for following behind her, his arms outstretched in belated appeasement, Francesco was apologizing profusely.

"Forgive me, Pia," he said. "I don't know what's come over me."

"I can tell you," she replied. "Egisto is only here for a few weeks and you have to tell him what you plan to do with his inheritance before he leaves."

❧

MAMA AND I *decided to stay in Monte di Ripa for four or five days while Danilo and Bice took the children and nonna back to Pontedera. Mama's home, which had been gutted during the war, had been repaired enough that we could spend the night in the makeshift bedroom and use a part of the kitchen. When Danilo retired, the plan was for us to move back and finish mama's house so we could all live there together. Something about Egisto being home again and being close to nonno's vineyard made us feel as though we had won a war ourselves; that we were going to be a family again.*

Mama and I were at the Vellechia cemetery putting flowers on Armida's grave when zio Egisto unexpectedly turned up. It was his first morning in Italy and he still looked shell-shocked. He had cried tears of joy the previous night when he arrived at the airport, but when he saw Armida's grave he broke down and wept. After he paid his respects to her, he and mama had several conversations that, at times, made me feel like an intruder listening in on secrets not meant for me to hear.

"Do you still miss Barlaam?" Egisto asked her, as we visited other graves in the cemetery.

"Every day," replied mama.

"Was he a good husband? What do you miss about him?"

"He wasn't perfect, but we had become part of each other. I miss his companionship and having him here to be a father to our children. I miss so many things about him." Mama

touched Egisto's forearm. "I'm sure you feel the same way about Armida."

"We were happy before she had her breakdown," agreed Egisto. "Afterwards, I was willing to do anything to get her back." He choked up. Straining to recover, he rubbed his eyes and said, "Now, I would do anything to bring her back to life."

Mama knew about the letter to Marietta and guessed that zio Egisto was blaming himself for everything that had happened.

"It's not your fault Armida died," mama said.

"What if I had have never left Italy? She might still be alive."

"Had you not gone to America, you and Marietta may have reconciled and then you would have never known Armida as your wife."

Bluntly, as though offended at the thought, he replied, "Marietta and I were not meant to be."

It was then I knew zio Egisto had changed. Mama knew it too. She told me later that he was no longer a young man who didn't believe in anything. He had experienced life, love, and loss and now believed in something greater than himself.

Before we left to go to mama's house, Egisto stopped at a tombstone marked "Pavone" and bent down to inspect the stonework. Mama whispered to me that it was the grave of a woman who had been known as "Widow Pavone" in her day and that zio Egisto had sculpted her headstone before going to America. Neither of us understood why he peered so closely at a carved cluster of grapes on it, or why he touched one of them and smiled, muttering "Mercy triumphs over Justice."

Later that morning, around 11:30, we packed a lunch at mama's house, crossed via Strettoia and climbed up Monte di

Ripa to mama and Egisto's childhood home. It, too, had been bombed. Everywhere we looked, there were shattered buildings and torn- up olive orchards and vineyards, waiting for someone to nurture back to life. Mama and Egisto walked through the debris, their heads together, reminiscing. Once in a while, one of them would bend down and pick something up. Mama found an old key. It had opened the art studio behind the house.

"I've been up here so many times since the war ended, digging through the rubble," she said, a look of amazement on her face. "How did I miss this?"

Egisto found a large pottery shard. He recognized it as being from the pitcher that had been in Carilda's old bedroom . . . the one he and Armida had stayed in the night they were married.

I kept my distance from them, from the house. I wanted them to experience this homecoming alone, as brother and sister. It was the vineyard that was drawing me, calling my name.

A short time later, that's where we were, sitting amidst the charred remnants of the vineyard, a checkered tablecloth spread out between us. We tore off big chunks of bread and zio Egisto used his pocketknife to cut thick slices of cheese. I chewed my bread slowly, remembering nonno. Mama opened the last bottle of wine we had saved from before the bombing. I noticed Egisto savored his and I wondered if he was having communion; if he was remembering Armida.

When we were done eating, mama pointed to her villa below us. "It will take time to rebuild my house, Egisto, but eventually it will be done."

Egisto nodded. I could tell he understood the metaphor for her life—and his.

Then she swept her hands to encompass the vineyard. "And

Bianca has agreed to help me replant papa's vineyard. Some of the vines are healthy, others are dead."

When I told mama I thought I had found Ferruccio's grape vines, still alive, she closed her eyes and smiled.

Zio Egisto promised he would come back again and said he would help rebuild the vineyard if it was needed. "I'm not an expert, but I can try my hand at grafting," he said.

Then he took his hand and dug a shallow hole in the dirt near the base of a brittle-looking plant next to him. The roots were dead. He got up and walked over to another vine bearing a few puny clusters of grapes, plucked them off, and returned to us. He handed us each some grapes, saving a cluster for himself. Sitting back down, he placed his cluster in the hole he had dug and covered it up.

"There," he said, brushing his hands on his trousers. "Let's see what happens to these seeds next spring. Who knows? Perhaps we will see a miracle."

❧

chapter thirty-five

"Where has the time gone?" fretted Carilda, bussing the breakfast table. Her granddaughter, Lucia, sat across from Egisto, staring at him with wide-eyed fascination, her chin barely cresting the top of the table.

From outside the open kitchen window at the Corrottis' house in Bientina, Bianca's voice floated up from the patio. "Mama, I'm hanging some clothes on the line. I'll be right in to help with dishes. Send Lucia out, would you?"

Carilda nodded to Lucia. "Did you hear your mama?"

"Si." Lucia shoved her chair back, and dancing around the table, she gave Egisto a long, furtive hug before skipping outside.

Observing the exchange, Carilda remarked, "Lucia reminds me of Bianca when she was a little girl. Her eyes light up when she looks at you, just like Bianca's did whenever papa came to visit. You should have seen them together; they were inseparable!" Teasingly, she added, "No doubt if you lived here, Egisto, you would spoil Lucia rotten, just like papa spoiled Bianca."

"But, of course. I have to make up for lost time, don't I?"

"Well," Carilda countered, "you've done enough spoiling for one trip. You must bring your children and grandchildren with you someday so that we can spoil them."

Egisto wiped his mouth, pulled the napkin from his collar

and placed it on top of his plate. "It's a promise. Breakfast was delicious, Carilda. Grazie."

"I wish you didn't have to leave!" she smiled, taking his plate from him. "I'm going to miss you, Egisto. Now go say good-bye to mama while I clean up."

Obediently, and with no small amount of trepidation, Egisto entered his mother's room. Carmela's depression had returned, on cue, as soon as Egisto had begun packing his bags to return to America. She was bedridden because of it. When Egisto approached her to say good-bye, she grabbed his hand and wouldn't let go.

"I'll be back, mama."

"When? In another thirty years? I'm eighty-eight years old! You may come back, but I will never see you again." She pulled his hand next to her frail chest. "I know it in here."

Egisto made light of her fears. "We will see each other again."

"What will happen when I die, Egisto? What will happen to the home your father and I shared—and the land? What about Carilda?"

"Francesco will see that the family is taken care of."

"Oh, Francesco! He has himself to think of, just like Alberto and Danilo and Bianca and everyone else must think of themselves. For Francesco, I think, everything is about the Bertozzi marble business. No one cares about me."

"That's not true."

"Yes, it is."

Egisto sighed. It was useless to argue with her.

"Your father would never have let this happen," she continued, throwing her arms in the air, her voice trembling like a child's. "Are you aware that papa left the vineyard to Carilda?"

"He did?"

Carmela lifted herself up on one of her elbows, lowering her voice and motioning for Egisto to move closer. "You wouldn't expect Carilda to go around telling everyone, would you? Your sister is far too humble to bring it up, but she was with your father when he died, and so was Bianca. They are witnesses, though some would discredit them as being illegitimate ones! They both heard your father say he wanted her to inherit the vineyard. Papa warned her it wouldn't be easy. After all, it's a man's world, isn't it Egisto?"

"Poor Carilda!" she wailed. "She took care of me during the war, and both of us widows! You can't imagine what we went through, Egisto! Awful! Terrible!"

"Mama," he said, "Francesco will be here soon. You know I must return to America this afternoon. Please, tell me what it is you want."

Pulling Egisto down so that his ear was near her mouth, she whispered hoarsely, "Tell Francesco that the vineyard belongs to Carilda. Tell him papa said so."

"Why haven't you told him yourself?"

"Who could talk of such things during the war? No one knew who would live and who would die. And now? Everyone is busy rebuilding. No one wants to take the time to talk about *my* wishes. My children act like I will live forever; they talk as though I will live to be one hundred! It makes it easier for them to brush my concerns aside. Besides, Francesco knows only the ways of Italy. But you, Egisto, you are an American now. You are different. I've seen the change in you."

"Being an American hasn't changed me, mama. I am the same person I always was."

"Being *in* America has changed you! Bianca and Danilo have told me all about America. They say women there can vote! Here, women have nothing unless their husbands give it to them."

"Yes, it *is* different in America," Egisto admitted. "Better for women, that is true. But it will change in Italy soon. You will see."

"It won't change soon enough for me. I can't wait, Egisto!"

"Francesco . . ."

Nearly hysterical, Carmela hissed, "I tell you, Francesco doesn't understand! Carilda deserves more than this. You and your brothers had an education. She had nothing. Why? She is a Bertozzi too, is she not? Promise it, Egisto! You are the only one who can intercede for me!"

The sound of an engine backfiring outside the house announced Francesco's arrival. Carmela clung to Egisto, begging him not to go until he promised he would speak to Francesco about the vineyard. If Carilda inherited the vineyard, she would have all of her daughters nearby to help replant and maintain it. But if Francesco inherited the vineyard and the old homestead, Egisto wasn't sure what he would do with it.

He would probably sell it, thought Egisto. It would be tempting, and certainly make sense, to take the money and put it into the family business. *But, why did papa want Carilda to have the vineyard? There must be a reason.*

His mother was right. While his brothers were struggling to keep their own families alive, the burden had fallen on Carilda to protect and care for their mother. With a depth of remorse bordering on shame, Egisto realized he and his brothers owed Carilda a debt of gratitude that could never be repaid. Certainly, the family vineyard was the very least his sister deserved.

"I'll tell Francesco today before I leave," said Egisto finally. "I promise."

Carmela let out a sob, kissed Egisto's hand and held it to her cheek. Not trusting herself to speak, she let his hand linger on her face as he kissed her forehead.

"Good-bye, mama."

Wordlessly, Carmela turned her face to the wall. Egisto rose, hesitated a moment, and then walked out of his mother's bedroom, carefully closing the door behind him. Francesco was waiting for him in the kitchen, having arrived with a bottle of homemade wine under each arm. Gathered around him were Bianca, Danilo and Carilda, laughing at his jokes. Lucia and her brother sat next to each other at the table, imitating their parents' gestures with loud guffaws, their mouths smeared with the chocolates uncle Francesco had brought them.

"Brother!" Francesco beamed, as Egisto entered the room. Magnanimously, he offered his sibling a bottle of wine to take back to America. "We were lucky. Our vines weren't destroyed in the war. Next year we will have a better harvest."

Egisto thanked him, placing the wine carefully in his suitcase. Then, following a round of tearful embraces, the Bertozzis followed the brothers outside and waved a final farewell as Francesco and Egisto pulled out of the driveway and disappeared out of sight.

"Well," said Francesco, merging his pickup on to the highway, "I hope you had a good trip, Egisto, although I must say it's gone by far too fast. I will miss you."

"I will miss you, too." Swallowing hard, Egisto added, "I can't thank you enough for all you've done for me, Francesco."

Francesco clicked his tongue. "It was nothing."

"Every time I needed you, you were there for me. You brought Armida back from Lago d'Iseo. You and Pia fed me and let me stay with you for most of my stay. You drove me anywhere I needed to go. I wish you could come to America so I could return your hospitality."

"We're family, Egisto."

"Still, you made me feel like I was more than an obligation."

Uncharacteristically, Francesco had no reply. He simply shrugged.

"We need to talk."

Francesco glanced sideways at his brother. "About what?"

"Mama."

"Oh!" Francesco laughed. "Let me guess. She wants to know what will happen when she dies."

"How did you know?"

"Every time I see her she asks me the same question."

"What do you tell her?"

"I tell her not to worry. I will take care of everything."

Egisto fumbled with his billfold, double-checking his ticket. "What does she say when you tell her that?"

"I don't know," Francesco answered, rolling his eyes. "She rants and raves for awhile. You know how she is."

"She has never mentioned to you what papa said before he died?"

Francesco grimaced. "What papa said?"

"Before he died, he had a request. Mama never told you?"

Francesco bit his lower lip as though trying very hard to remember. So much had happened, in such quick succession over the last several years, it had become one big blur. "Mama is always worried about Carilda," he said. "She rambles on and on about her deserving more than what life has dealt her. I don't know why. Bianca and Danilo take good care of them. What more could she ask for?"

"The vineyard."

Francesco downshifted in anticipation of an upcoming stop sign, and turned to look at his brother. "What?"

"The vineyard," repeated Egisto.

"The *family* vineyard?"

"Yes! Mama swears that papa, before he died, in the presence of Carilda and Bianca, demanded that Carilda have it as her inheritance when mama passes away."

Pressing on the accelerator a little too quickly, and with a little too much force, Francesco bellowed, "I don't believe it."

"I do," countered Egisto, the truck lurching onto the main highway to Pisa. Grabbing the safety bar on the door panel to steady himself, he added, "Do you really care? I don't."

Francesco's blanched face said it all. *He hadn't expected this. Of course, he knew their mother would die someday. He had allowed himself to occasionally fantasize about how he would manage the Bertozzi estate; at least, what was left of it. But this was never even remotely in the picture.*

"Are you telling me you don't care if your inheritance is less?" he growled. "Because it will be if we give Carilda the vineyard, you know."

"Money is not a problem for me, Francesco. I have enough. When mama dies, I want my share of the inheritance to go to Carilda anyway."

Francesco could not have looked more shocked if his brother had told him he was giving his inheritance away to a complete stranger. "You can't mean it."

"I do."

Francesco almost slammed into the car ahead of him. Angrily, he blustered, "This is outrageous. We'll have to write each other when you get back to America, Egisto. There is no time to talk about it now. Your flight leaves in half an hour and we're almost to the airport."

"I promised mama, Francesco. I can't leave here with a clear conscience unless we talk about it."

"I have the business to think of. Bills to be paid. It's preposterous to even think about it."

"You told me the future looks promising for the business."

"The future is conditional, Egisto, as you well know."

"As long as I am working, Francesco, I will continue to send you money. You have nothing to worry about on that count. But I'm curious. Just how successful does the business have to be for you to be able to support all of the family, including Carilda?"

Francesco's jaw twitched. "Are you insinuating I'm not doing my part in taking care of the family?"

"Of course not. Everyone knows you are doing your part."

"Do they?"

"Francesco, what if something happened to Bianca and Danilo? Who would take care of Carilda when *she* is old?"

"What if something happened to me and I couldn't work any longer? Who will take care of me and *my* family?" argued Francesco.

Egisto leaned his elbow on the door, resting his chin in his hand. "You have two fine sons. They will take care of you. It's different with Carilda. She has no sons."

"This is about something else, isn't it?" Francesco shot back.

"Like what?"

Francesco wouldn't answer.

"It's what papa wanted."

"You don't know that."

"I believe Carilda and mama. Even if papa hadn't made such a request, I would propose it myself."

Francesco ground his teeth in utter disbelief. They were

almost to the airport. "This is crazy. You can't expect me to give you an answer today."

"No, but the day will come when mama is gone and you will have to make those decisions." Egisto, gazing at the marbled mountains in the distance, near Monte di Ripa, started to daydream. He remembered staring at the same mountains with Armida years ago when they were leaving for America. The world had seemed so promising then; so full of adventure and hope.

"You have changed, Egisto."

Egisto continued staring silently at the mountains.

"Are you listening to me?" Francesco could not believe his brother had initiated such a serious subject, only to start daydreaming. "America has changed you, Egisto. You are not the same."

Pulling into the parking lot of the airport, Francesco found a parking spot, turned off the engine and lit a cigarette. Egisto was still lost in thought.

"You're not the same," Francesco repeated. "America has changed you. You are full of ridiculous ideas that don't work here."

"Perhaps I have changed."

Francesco nodded in affirmation, relieved his brother had come back to his senses. Confident the issue was behind them, he got out of the truck and helped Egisto with his luggage. Silently, they made their way into the terminal. When the announcement was made for boarding, the brothers kissed each other on the cheek and said good-bye.

Egisto joined the queue making their way to the departing gate and Francesco followed alongside, pausing with him as the person ahead of Egisto had his passport checked and stamped. Egisto, who would be next, had his American passport ready. He looked at it, turned to his brother, and with a strange glint in his eyes, smiled and said, "You have changed too, Francesco, though perhaps you don't realize it. The war—life—has changed us all. You're a good man. I know you will give the vineyard to Carilda when mama dies."

Not waiting for a response, Egisto stepped forward, was cleared for boarding and walked out onto the tarmac.

Moments later, watching the massive, sleek, Lockheed Constellation lift off the runway carrying his brother back to America, Francesco began to laugh uproariously. Fellow onlookers, gathered together on the observation deck, gawked at him. He didn't care. He stretched out his hand toward the vanishing plane and loud enough for all to hear, he declared, "Egisto Bertozzi, what an enigma!"

epilogue

IT WAS THE Americans' last night in Italy. At Bianca's house an ebullient horde of Bertozzis milled about on the deck, eating, drinking wine, and reminiscing. Their merriment produced a din that escalated to giddy proportions as the evening progressed. Time literally slipped away. The sun set over the sea. The temperature dropped, candles were lit, dessert was served, and a nostalgic ambiance permeated the magnetic night air. Lucia's husband, Carlo, translated responses to some of David's questions.

When did Carmela die?

Carlo explained that she had died in 1950. "Right here, in this very house," he said. "She was living with Carilda. Bianca and Danilo moved in shortly afterward."

Bianca whispered something in Carlo's ear. He lowered his voice and added, "Bianca wants you to know about the inheritance. She says that after Carmela died, Egisto wanted Carilda to receive his full share of the family inheritance, but it did not happen."

Carlo raised the flats of his hands parallel with each other and shrugged. "That is how things were done then."

"What happened with my grandfather's share of the inheritance?" asked David.

Carlo shrugged again. "It probably went into the family business. Who knows?"

"Did it cause hard feelings with Carilda?" David asked.

"Carilda was content in life without Egisto's money."

"What about Francesco and Alberto? Carilda didn't hold anything against them?"

"Alberto was an easygoing man and not the oldest," Carlo explained, "so he was neither one way nor the other when it came to money. But, Francesco had many responsibilities and it is possible that later in life he wished Carilda would have received Egisto's inheritance. I do not know. It is only speculation."

Carlo lowered his voice even more. "It could explain what happened after Egisto died . . . why we lost touch with your family. Bianca and her sisters wrote letters to America, but they all came back with 'Undeliverable' marked on them. Many times we tried to locate Violenza and Silverio, but we did not have any up-to-date information. And, of course, there is always the language barrier. Francesco's family said they could not find the correct addresses either." His voice reduced to a whisper, Carlo added, "Perhaps Francesco was afraid that Egisto's children—or grandchildren—would come back someday and make trouble."

David shook his head in disbelief.

"We believe it is why some in the family were hesitant to meet you," continued Carlo. "But now, you have shown us you came to claim nothing, only to meet your Italian cousins and see the home of your grandfather. It will make everyone happy. No more problems, I think."

"What about Carilda?" asked David, looking at Bianca, wanting to include her more directly in the conversation. "What happened to your mother?"

Through Carlo, Bianca answered, "Mama lived to be almost one hundred years old. She was alert and productive till the very end, dying right here in this villa. We were all by her side when she died. I inherited this villa from her. My sisters and I inherited the vineyard and the olive orchard and eventually I bought my sisters' share of the vineyard.

"I thought your mother didn't receive an inheritance when Carmela died."

"My mother did not receive Egisto's share as he had wished, but Francesco did give her the vineyard."

"When was the last time you saw my grandfather?"

�֎

THE LAST TIME *I saw zio Egisto was in 1959, fifteen years before he died. He brought Violenza and her daughter, and Silverio's daughter with him. They stayed the entire summer that year. My Renzo and Lucia were the same ages as Egisto's grandchildren and the times we had together—swimming, hiking, eating, drinking wine—oh, it was wonderful. Danilo was still alive too. Truly, those were the days!*

In August, just a few days before he left, we found out that Egisto had gone to visit Marietta Tarabella. He didn't tell anyone beforehand. He just showed up at her door one afternoon and said, "May I come in?"

I know this—and all of Ripa knew it—because Marietta's daughter Vittoria was there at the house at the time. Marietta was a widow, so what did it matter? But to hear Vittoria tell it, her mother was ecstatic, which only made Vittoria all the more angry and upset. She said Egisto and Marietta spent the entire day talking and that at one point her mother asked her to go into town and do some errands for her. According to her, Egisto stayed for dinner and then left about 8:00 in the evening.

Believe me, it was the talk of the town. For my generation, it still is.

❧

After Carlo translated for Bianca, explaining the last time she had seen Egisto, David said, "Actually, my grandfather was quite an enigma, wasn't he?"

"What do you mean—enigma?" Carlo looked puzzled.

"Well," said David. "With all my grandfather had going for him, he never remarried. To our knowledge, he never dated again. That's why I was so shocked when you told me about Marietta Tarabella. We had no idea he had ever loved another woman. And as for him being an anarchist when he was young, we never knew that either. Before he died, he was very interested in religion. At least, he spent all his time in the library reading books about Jesus and the Church."

A hush fell over the cousins. Uncorking the last bottle of Bertozzi wine, Carlo suddenly stood up. "We have saved the best wine for last."

"Salute!" Carlo exclaimed, raising his glass in a toast. "To the Italian and the American Bertozzis!"

"Bravo!" shouted the cousins.

It was after midnight when everyone finally went to bed and although Bianca's house was as silent and warm as a mother's womb, no one slept.

Bianca was thinking about how happy Egisto would have been to know that his grandson had finally come to Italy. Armida would be pleased also. It was very significant. It was fate. Of course, she knew David couldn't be expected to understand just *how* significant it was. He had never known his grandmother. For him, Armida was simply a faceless mystery, someone who had wounded his grandfather, mother and uncle and never returned to make things right. Bianca, however, had great faith in people's ability to change. She had discerned the potential in Armida the last time she had seen her, even though no one else could see it.

Behind her closed, tired eyes, Bianca felt the memory of her father and mother, and Armida and Egisto. It was as though they were smiling down on her from the vineyard overlooking her villa, their arms linked in a sort of military posture, a stance of reconciliation, a show of victory. If she died tonight, she thought, she would die a happy woman.

In Carilda's old room, in what used to be Carilda's bed, David and his wife lay next to each other thinking about the profundity of their visit. What would David's mother Babe think after all these years when she found out that her father had loved another woman? When she found out the source of Armida's madness? Egisto, the quiet, gentle father and grandfather, had harbored a secret in his heart none of them would have ever guessed.

As their eyelids grew heavy and their limbs numb, the last thing the Americans heard before drifting off to sleep was the dulcet voice of a lone, male tenor singing a passionate aria to the stars, somewhere in the vicinity of Bianca's vineyard.

author's note

"*Bianca's Vineyard*" is a narrative biography based on a real family whose names have been accurately recorded. However, due to limited information during Armida Sigali's tenure in Lago d'Iseo, several characters in this book are fictional. The Carditi family of Forte dei Marmi is one such example.

The only information Violenza Bertozzi had of her mother's tragic death was from her father, Egisto, who recounted to her some of the results of the investigation. He had been told by the private detective he hired that a German SS officer had kept Armida captive, and that mysterious markings on her body indicated she was likely abused and then murdered. Egisto always maintained that Armida would never have drowned herself because of her overriding fear of water.

After nearly a decade of intensive research and, ironically, the very week this manuscript was completed, I received a document from Monte Isola shedding revelation on the last year of Armida Sigali's life. It revealed that Armida was actually the housekeeper of Prince Junio Borghese at his palatial villa on San Paolo Island in Lago d'Iseo. A German SS officer was garrisoned at Borghese's villa, lending credence to Egisto Bertozzi's assertion of foul play. *The Carditi family in this book in no way represents the person or character of this official or any of his family members, nor does the character of Werner Kolbe reflect the person of the German officer.*

The document from Italy simply states that on March 21, 1945, the family's female cook, Armida Sigali, threw herself into the lake and drowned. Her body was found near San Paolo (St. Paul) Island.

Most tragic was the unexpected death of Bianca Frediani Corrotti one year after this project was started. It is a great consolation for me to know how much she enjoyed reading transcripts of this manuscript before she died. She is heaven's gain and Earth's loss.

Salute, Bianca!

acknowledgements

THE PUBLICATION OF *Bianca's Vineyard* was a blend of divine encounters, the unflagging support of family and friends, and the extraordinary skills of a team of professional editors and photographers.

Thank you, thank you, thank you, Dave, Rachel, Luke, and Hannah for loving me through years of tedious research and writing, and indulging my obsession with nonno's story. Luke and Marika, there's no pricetag to match your great talent in filming and photography.

To my dad, my sisters, and to all my friends who encouraged me throughout the long process to not give up, I appreciate you more than you'll ever know. Mom, you always believed *"Bianca's Vineyard"* would be published. I know you're smiling in heaven.

None of this would have been possible without the miraculous intervention of Veronica Arrosti of Camaiore, Italy. To you, Veronica, I'm eternally grateful for reconnecting the Bertozzi families. You are beautiful, inside and out.

To the Sigali family, and Luigi Bertozzi's descendants and their spouses—especially the indefatigable Carlo Corrotti, whose research for me was priceless—*mille grazie* for your incredible generosity. You have made me, an in-law, feel as much a part of your family as if I had your blood flowing through my veins. Sharing our lives has been a delight and an honor.

Sandra Byrd, not only are you a prolific author and a brilliant editor, but your spirit of mentorship never ceases to amaze me. Because of you, I was able to take the story to another level. *Merci!*

A big "thank-you" goes to copyeditor Julie Talbot who went through my manuscript with a fine-toothed comb and made it perfect, and to Jennifer Omner of ALL Publications who formatted the book for print. Oregon women to the rescue!

Steve Shultz: I'm indebted to you for coaxing me into my destiny and relentlessly encouraging me to publish.

And I haven't forgotten you, Christine Potter. You're the one, who after first hearing me tell the story, said, "This story needs to be written. Write a book." As usual, you planted the seed.

To order a DVD featuring "Behind the Scenes of Bianca's Vineyard" and an interview with Violenza "Babe" Neumann, go to www.teresaneumann.com

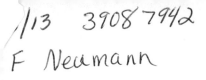

/13 3908 7942

F Neumann

CPSIA information can be obtained at www.ICGtesting.com
Printed in the USA
BVOW030412300712

296506BV00002B/1/P

9 780983 121008